Y0-BBD-491

Process Flow Scheduling:
A Scheduling Systems Framework
for Flow Manufacturing

Sam G. Taylor
University of Wyoming

Steven F. Bolander
Colorado State University

Contents

Preface

This book presents a scheduling framework for flow manufacturing plants. Widely accepted and well-documented frameworks for other manufacturing environments currently exist. PERT/CPM techniques are widely used for scheduling project environments; MRP for job shops; and JIT for simple continuous flow or repetitive manufacturing environments. But what about all the plants that have more complex flow environments? These plants are not MRP job shops with significant amounts of work in process nor do they fit the stockless, scheduleless environment of JIT. This book begins to address the scheduling system needs of these plants.

The material we present is based on our experiences as practitioners, researchers, educators, and occasional consultants over the past 25 years. Each of us has held full-time jobs where we directed the development and implementation of scheduling systems in different process industry companies. While holding these jobs, we independently discovered a major gap between process industry scheduling needs and the established scheduling paradigms. We were troubled, searched for solutions, and found none in the scheduling literature. Regrettably, we were not very quick in finding an answer.

The principal focus of our research during the past 15 years has been the search for a framework that links the diverse practices of many flow manufacturing companies into a coherent structure. We have conducted five research-oriented workshops for process industry practitioners to exchange ideas, visited many process industry plants, conducted three surveys, and reviewed commercial scheduling software targeted primarily for the process industries. Using this research, we finally hit pay dirt with the development of a concept that we call *process flow scheduling*.

This research resulted in a number of publications in *Production and Inventory Management Journal,* presentations at APICS conferences, and presentations at APICS Process Industry Symposia. These publications and presentations provide the foundation for this book. Chapters 2 and 3, as well as major parts of chapters 4 and 5, are based on material previously published in *Production and Inventory Management Journal.* However, chapters 6–10 consist of new research material that further develops process flow scheduling concepts.

This research has been funded by the University of Wyoming and Colorado State University. Since this is a research project, we have limited this book to presenting material not found elsewhere in the literature—except for the above-mentioned material from our previously published articles. While this book presents an integrative framework for scheduling flow manufacturing plants, it does not repeat material available elsewhere. A more comprehensive treatment would include chapters on forecasting, lot sizing, safety stocks, seasonal production planning, multiplant production planning, and many other topics that are available from other sources. While we recognize the need for a comprehensive book, it is beyond the scope and funding for this research project.

We are indebted to many others who have influenced us and assisted in our scheduling research. Some have attended workshops and shared information on their scheduling systems. Others have provided technical and editorial reviews. Still others have provided financial, administrative, and emotional support for our endeavors. Among those who share in the credit for this book are the nine companies that provided the cases for this book and the APICS Process Industry SIG Steering Committee, which supported its publication. Thanks are also due to the reviewers—Edmund Schuster of Welch's, Dr. Stuart Allen of Pennsylvania State University—Erie, and Dr. Tom McKaskill of Ross Systems.

We also wish to acknowledge the efforts of Nancy Green of the APICS editorial staff, who made our writing much more readable.

We hope that this book will provide practitioners and systems developers with new ways to view their scheduling problems and systems and, after reflection, will allow them to use the concepts to develop improved scheduling systems. We also hope that educators find the process flow scheduling paradigm a useful framework for integrating the diverse literature on planning and scheduling techniques into a coherent system for flow manufacturing. Finally, we hope that researchers are stimulated to investigate new approaches for scheduling flow manufacturing firms.

Although the primary emphasis of this book is on process industry scheduling problems, the concepts apply in other manufacturing environments. The scheduling needs for some repetitive manufacturing firms are similar to those for process industries. (See, for example, the Sylvania Lighting case in appendix A.) Thus process flow scheduling applies to any manufacturing environment where there is a directed flow through the process.

We have tried to present the material in a logical order; however, we recognize that some readers may want a "quick start." If you want a quick overview of the basics, first read chapter 3 and then look over the examples in chapter 4.

Chapter 1

Perspectives

Your inventory investment is too high, delivery performance is poor, and frantic expediting often disrupts production schedules. Communications among purchasing, operations scheduling, and marketing are filled with accusations, excuses, and enmity. You wonder if there is a better way to plan and schedule operations. Senior management is painfully aware of the problems and is beginning to ask questions.

You currently have an in-house planning and scheduling system that has evolved over the years. It works—but not very well. Moreover, it is quite difficult to maintain. You don't want to reinvent the wheel, so you attend seminars in an attempt to find an alternative. One seminar discusses the logic and benefits of manufacturing resource planning (MRP II). A second suggests that Just-in-Time (JIT) is the way of the future. A third seminar focuses on theory of constraints (TOC). Though each approach includes interesting ideas, you still feel uncomfortable with the scheduling logic used in these systems—they simply don't seem to fit your business.

You wonder if you should expand your search, so you reevaluate older mathematical tools such as linear programming, statistical safety stocks, and EOQs. How can these techniques fit into an integrated system? The search continues. Surely there must be a standard system that will fit. The answer comes slowly as the reality of the situation begins to sink in—*there is no generally accepted planning*

and scheduling paradigm for high-volume process industries.

We too have suffered frustrations similar to the situation described above. For many years, we have not felt comfortable in applying established planning and scheduling paradigms in high-volume process industry environments. While such approaches as MRP II were sound in other situations, the scheduling logic just did not seem to fit the high-volume process industry environment we knew. However, other than custom systems, we had no alternative to offer.

A survey conducted by Plant-Wide Research Corporation and summarized in *Datamation* (Foley 1988) confirms that we are not alone in rejecting basic MRP II logic. This survey reports MRP II penetration rates of 16.1 percent for the chemical industry, 82.9 percent for pharmaceuticals, 4.2 percent for food and beverage, and 0.1 percent for other process industries. Moreover, MRP II has been widely publicized by consultants, vendors, academicians, and APICS over the last 20 years. Thus, it doesn't seem likely that many firms have escaped an MRP II pitch. Given the low MRP II usage in all process industry groups except pharmaceuticals, it appears that many knowledgeable process industry managers have rejected the MRP II paradigm for their operations.

If high-volume process industries are not using MRP II, then just what are they doing? Are there any similarities in their scheduling approaches? We believe so. This book unifies the practices of many high-volume process industries and some repetitive manufacturers into a common framework we call *process flow scheduling.*

The Origins Of Process Flow Scheduling

We have been muddling around in production and inventory control for more than two decades as practitioners, academicians, and occasional consultants. We finally stumbled on an idea that links the planning and scheduling practices of many process industry firms. It's a simple concept—quite remarkable given that we are both college professors. We found that many scheduling systems use *the process structure to guide scheduling calculations.* We christened this concept *process flow scheduling,* which in turn spawned the inevitable three-letter acronym *PFS.*

Now before you MRP II or JIT diehards write PFS off as the crackpot idea of a couple of academicians who are clearly out of touch with the real world of manufacturing, we offer the following. Process flow scheduling is not new. We did not invent PFS. It is a generalization—or if you like, a conceptualization—of what many schedulers already do. The basic concepts of PFS are embodied in manual systems, electronic spreadsheets, custom systems, and several commercial scheduling packages.

The origins of PFS systems are obscured. While we cannot claim to have developed process flow scheduling, we may have discovered it. Our discovery evolved from years of observation, analysis, and discussions with more than 50 companies. Manual variations of PFS systems have existed for decades. Now computer-based scheduling systems have significantly improved PFS systems by speeding calculations, presenting graphical displays of schedules and inventories, and incorporating simulation, optimization, and expert system capabilities.

PFS provides an integrative structure for planning and scheduling systems in a wide variety of high-volume process industries. This paradigm (1) links the scheduling practices of different firms and different industries, (2) unifies planning and schedul-

ing techniques such as lot sizing methods and safety stock theory into an integrated framework, and (3) enhances communication between practitioners, software vendors, and researchers of process industry scheduling systems.

Where PFS Applies

Process flow scheduling is a malleable concept that can be shaped to meet the needs of many different manufacturing environments. However, we are not so bold as to claim that all manufacturing environments are the same or that PFS has universal applicability. We firmly believe that planning and scheduling techniques must be tailored to a firm's manufacturing environment and to its competitive strategies.

While exceptions exist, many PFS users have the following characteristics in at least part of their operations:

- All products produced in a facility have similar routings leading to a *flow of material through a series of process stages.*
- Production is often scheduled to meet *forecasted demands* rather than individual customer orders. In other words, the plant produces to stock in anticipation of future demand rather than waiting for specific customer orders before initiating production. Alternatively, some companies backlog customer orders and use this backlog to facilitate efficient scheduling of extremely expensive facilities.
- Production is *authorized by production schedules.* Work orders are not issued.

The first characteristic is the most important. If you work in a flow shop environment (where all materials follow a similar routing through process stages), PFS generally applies, and you should read on. On the other hand, if you work in a job shop environment (where each product or job has a unique routing), stop now! This book is not intended for you unless you are considering conversion to a flow manufacturing environment or are just plain curious. We humbly suggest that most job shop purists could better spend their time reading a good MRP II book.

The second characteristic is not as prevalent as the first. However, our experience indicates that PFS users tend to make finished goods or intermediate products for stock. In practice, many plants produce a combination of make-to-stock and make-to-order goods. Moreover, there are many variations that position a firm somewhere on a continuum between the extreme positions of make-to-stock and make-to-order. For example, a firm may produce components to stock and blend products to customer orders. A firm can produce bulk materials for stock and package to customer specifications. In addition, items made exclusively for a particular customer may have annual contracts or blanket orders. These items can also be produced for stock before receipt of a specific order release. Although exceptions exist, most PFS users produce intermediate or finished goods for stock.

Companies that accumulate sales orders as a backlog of production requirements are an alternative to the above make-to-stock environments. The sequencing of production and the resulting timing of the sales orders are predefined by the company to its customers. While each order may follow a fixed routing, the order sequencing allows the company to group similar orders. This takes advantage of process technologies, natural product sequences, and economic run lengths. The steel industry is an example of this type of flow manufacturing.

The last characteristic concerns the authorization of production. PFS users tend to issue production schedules to line operators, who then execute these schedules. In contrast, MRP II systems use work orders to authorize production, and JIT systems use a visible demand pull signal to authorize production. PFS schedules are required because the production processes are unable to react quickly enough to the pull signals of a JIT system. Again there are exceptions to this rule—especially where PFS is combined with MRP II and JIT.

A manufacturing environment exhibiting the above characteristics in all *or some* of its production stages will favor the use of PFS concepts. Also note, as mentioned above, that some firms have effectively combined ideas from MRP II and JIT with PFS. Examples of these combinations will be given in chapter 4 and appendix A.

What Follows

The first part of this book begins with a detailed comparison of manufacturing environments and expands the above discussion on where PFS applies. Next we present a simple numerical example of PFS scheduling and develop three basic principles for all PFS systems. This is followed by five brief cases that illustrate the use of process flow scheduling. Using this background, an integrated planning and scheduling PFS framework is developed. This framework shows how various techniques can be combined into a system for making long-, intermediate-, and short-range operating decisions.

The second part of the book describes alternative scheduling techniques. First we examine different ways in which a single stage or cluster may be scheduled. We then delve into alternative ways of scheduling multiple stages.

Finally, in the last chapter, we compare PFS to MRP II, JIT, and TOC systems and present recommendations for integrating these frameworks.

The purpose of this book is to introduce the basic concepts of process flow scheduling. The book is not intended to be a comprehensive treatment of process planning and scheduling systems. The authors recognize that many issues that the scheduler deals with on a daily basis remain unresolved. Among those are determining run lengths, structuring cycle strategies, sizing safety stocks and decoupling inventory, determining optimum product production sequences, resource trade-offs, demand and capacity strategies, etc. Many of these issues are discussed in current literature and will not be topics of this book.

Instead, we do hope to provide materials that develop a construct that gives a common structure for process industry planning and scheduling systems. We hope that this will produce a common base for improving communication between process industry firms, provide a base for future research and problem solving, provide a base for better understanding of differences and similarities among firms, and provide a base for educating employees. Much work remains for us, our academic colleagues, vendors, and users to further develop the concepts presented herein. This book is intended to stimulate the reader to break from established paradigms and develop more effective scheduling systems. We challenge our readers to take these ideas, adapt them to their environments, implement them in their organizations, and then share their experiences in APICS meetings and publications.

References

Foley, M J. 1988. Post-MRP II: What comes next? *Datamation*, 1 December, 24, 32, 36.

Chapter 2

Manufacturing Environments

There is a growing consensus that planning and scheduling systems should be tailored to specific manufacturing environments. In contrast, 15 years ago some consultants proclaimed that MRP II would fit the needs of all manufacturers. They were dead wrong! Despite all the proselytizing and hype associated with MRP II, only 13 percent of all manufacturing firms used MRP II systems in the late 1980s (Foley 1988). The 1980s brought the rise of JIT systems. While JIT systems have proven successful in some flow operations, they just don't work in classical job shops. Examination of today's manufacturing systems leads one to the unmistakable conclusion: *A manufacturing system should be tailored to its environment.*

This chapter compares two different manufacturing environments—flow manufacturing and job manufacturing. First we contrast the marketing and production environments of flow and job manufacturing. Then we discuss the impact of these environments on planning and scheduling systems.

Marketing Environment

One of the most important factors in developing a business strategy is differentiating a firm's products from those of its competitors. The amount of product differentiation can be viewed as a continuum. Custom products are at one end of the spectrum, and commodity products are at the other end. Industry groups and individual companies often have products at several different points along the product differentiation spectrum.

Flow manufacturers tend to have less product differentiation than job manufacturers. Accordingly, flow manufacturing is generally associated with products at the commodity end of the product differentiation spectrum, while job manufacturing is generally associated with more differentiated products. In order to compare the marketing environments of flow manufacturing and job manufacturing, we will contrast characteristics of commodity products with those of differentiated products.

Table 2.1 summarizes differences between marketing environments. Commodity marketing emphasizes product availability and price; differentiated product marketing emphasizes product features.

Commodities are often sold from stock, while differentiated products are frequently made to order. Commodity products generally have a limited number of products within a product family (product grades), while differentiated product families may have an unlimited number of products. Commodity products have few—if any—changes in product specifications, while differentiated products may be designed to customer specifications.

A commodity is generally sold in large volume to several customers. On the other hand, a differentiated product may be committed to a particular customer for a specific use. Commodities frequently have a relatively low value-to-weight ratio. Therefore, transportation costs often represent a higher portion of the cost of goods sold for commodities than for differentiated products.

Many differentiated products are sold in discrete units, and serial numbers or lot numbers are assigned to each unit. In contrast, commodity products are produced in nondiscrete units; production, sales, and inventory records are in pounds, gallons, tons, barrels, or similar units of measure.

Production Environment

Manufacturing facilities can be classified along a continuum, with job shops at one end and flow shops at the other end. A job shop is a manufacturing facility in which materials flow through the shop with routings dependent on each job. A flow shop is a manufacturing facility in which materials flow

through the plant with a fixed routing. Most manufacturing facilities fall somewhere between a pure job shop (random routings where jobs could start and finish in any work center) and a pure flow shop. The operations of flow manufacturers lean toward the flow shop end of the continuum, while the operations of job manufacturers are closer to the job shop end. We will contrast production environments of flow and job manufacturers by comparing job shops with flow shops.

Comparison of Job Shops and Flow Shops

Table 2.2 summarizes the differences between job shop and flow shop manufacturing environments. By definition, a flow shop has fixed routings and uses fixed-path material handling equipment, such as conveyors and pipes. In contrast, a job shop has variable routings and must use such variable-path material handling equipment as forklift trucks and tote bins.

Job shops and flow shops use different plant layouts. The layout of a job shop is by manufacturing process. For example, a job shop may have one work center where all grinding is done and another work center for all welding. If a job requires grinding, welding, and then grinding, it would first go to the grinding workstation, then to welding, and finally back to grinding. However, the layout of a flow shop is determined by the product. If a product requires grinding, welding, and then grinding, a production line would be designed with two grinding work-

Table 2.1 Comparison of Market Environments	
Differentiated Products	Commodity Products
• Marketing emphasis on product features	• Marketing emphasis on product availability and price
• Many products	• Few products
• Many product design changes	• Few product design changes
• Consumer demand	• Derived demand
• Low sales volume	• High sales volume
• High unit value	• Low unit value
• Low transportation costs	• High transportation costs
• Discrete units	• Nondiscrete units

stations separated by a welding workstation. The production line in a flow shop is therefore laid out according to the processing requirements of the product it is designed to produce.

Job shops and flow shops differ significantly in their capabilities. A job shop has flexible general-purpose equipment that produces a wide variety of products. In contrast, flow shops have specialized equipment that efficiently produces a group of closely related products. Job shops emphasize flexibility at the expense of efficiency. Flow shops emphasize efficiency, but require a certain amount of repeatability. This limits their flexibility.

Flow shops generally have longer lead times for increasing capacity than job shops. To efficiently use their relatively high capital investment in facilities, flow shops tend to operate more shifts per day and more days per week than job shops. Thus, flow shops have less flexibility to increase capacity by adding shifts or working overtime.

Since flow shops are production lines designed for a group of closely related products, the line capacity can be determined by examining the bottleneck process. In contrast, a job shop is designed to produce a wide variety of products. In a job shop, the load created by different products in each work center often varies widely. The capacity of each work center can be specified in staff hours and machine hours; however, the aggregate capacity of the plant depends on the mix of products being manufactured at a point in time. Since the product mix changes frequently in a job shop, the aggregate capacity is difficult, if not impossible, to define.

The work force requirements are significantly different for job shops and flow shops. Job shops are generally labor-intensive and use skilled workers to build the product. A strike in a job shop will shut down the plant. Some flow shops, such as assembly lines, are also labor-intensive and will also be shut down by strikes. However, in many other flow shops, such as oil refineries, the number of operators is so low that management personnel can run the plant during a strike.

Table 2.2 Comparison of Production Environments	
Job Shop	Flow Shop
• Variable routings	• Fixed routings
• Variable-path material handling equipment	• Fixed-path material handling equipment
• Process layout	• Product layout
• Flexible equipment	• Specialized equipment
• Low volume	• High volume
• Shorter lead time to increase capacity	• Longer lead time to increase capacity
• Capacity is difficult to define	• Capacity is well defined
• Labor-intensive	• Capital-intensive
• Strikes shut down plant	• Strikes have lower impact
• Skilled workers build the product	• Highly specialized, trained operators monitor and control process equipment
• Significant work-in-process inventories	• Low work-in-process inventories
• Often warehouse work-in-process inventories	• No warehousing of work-in-process inventories
• Jobs not overlapped between work centers	• Job overlapping
• Equipment failure shuts down a machine	• Equipment failure shuts down the plant
• Late receipt of a purchased part delays a customer order	• Raw material shortage for a basic raw material shuts down the plant

Job shops and flow shops differ in the relative amount of work-in-process inventory. In job shops, work in process buffers variations in work center loads that are caused by variations in product mix. This permits better use of work center capacities. In contrast, the processes in a flow shop production line are balanced for the limited group of products that can be produced by the line. Thus, work in process is not required to help smooth work loads. However, flow shops may need some work in process to buffer sequential operations from short-range variations in processing rates. In a flow shop, the amount of work-in-process inventory is relatively small compared to the throughputs. Accordingly, storage facilities for work-in-process inventories are provided in the process flow rather than a separate storage area.

The low work-in-process inventories in flow shops create a need for extremely reliable equipment. If a particular piece of equipment in a production line breaks down, the entire line must stop production after upstream work in process is consumed or downstream storage capacity is filled. Job shops have more work in process, variable routings, and more flexibility to increase capacity through extra shifts and overtime to speed recovery from an equipment failure. Job shops, therefore, are not as dependent on reliable equipment as flow shops.

The effect of late material is different in job shops and flow shops. In a job shop, the late receipt of a purchased part may delay a customer order and increase inventories of other parts used in making the item unless these parts are rescheduled. In contrast, a shortage of a basic raw material in a flow shop can shut down the entire plant.

Linking Marketing And Production Environments

A firm's manufacturing facilities need to fit its marketing environment. Figure 2.1 shows a product-process matrix. Horizontal positions on the matrix represent the degree of product differentiation discussed in the above section on marketing environments. Vertical positions on the matrix represent the process spectrum including job shops and flow shops. As shown in figure 2.1, most industries tend to fall along the principal diagonal of the product-process matrix. Notice that process industries tend to fall in the lower right portion of the matrix while fabrication and assembly industries tend to fall in the upper left. Exceptions certainly exist. For example, pharmaceutical and specialty chemical manufacturers are in the upper left quadrant while container manufacturers are in the lower right.

An individual firm's position on the product-process matrix relative to the position of its competitors can be an important factor in a firm's business strategy (Hayes and Wheelwright 1979a, 1979b). Many firms in the central portion of the matrix are attempting to improve their manufacturing efficiency by moving downward toward the flow shop end of the process spectrum. On the other hand, when a firm moves toward a flow shop, it may lose some of its flexibility to produce a wide variety of products or it may need to enforce scheduling sequences that could reduce its ability to respond to rush orders. Ideally, a firm will move off the diagonal and toward the lower left corner. This provides increased product variety along with the efficiencies of a flow shop.

Planning System Characteristics

Having examined the marketing and production environments of flow manufacturing and job manufacturing, we now examine the effect these environments have on the design of a planning and scheduling system. A firm's system should be consistent with its position on the product-process matrix. Firms producing commodities in a flow manufacturing environment require a significantly different planning system than firms producing differentiated products in a job manufacturing environment. Our discussion divides planning systems into long-range, intermediate-range, and short-range planning systems.

Long-Range Planning

Flow manufacturing industries develop extensive long-range requirements plans. Because flow manufacturing is more capital-intensive than job manufacturing, capital budgeting decisions have a much greater impact on financial performance in flow manufacturing firms. Accordingly, flow manufacturing firms must pay more attention to facilities decisions than job manufacturing firms do.

Two important long-range decisions are plant capacity and plant location. In flow manufacturing environments, plants are designed for a specified throughput, and all equipment is sized for this capacity. Since many flow manufacturing plants operate seven days a week and three shifts per day, it is impossible for these plants to significantly increase capacity with overtime or extra shifts. Thus, increases in manufacturing capacity require the design and construction of new facilities. Since flow manufacturers often need highly specialized, automated equipment, significant capacity increases may require construction lead times of three or more years.

Plant location is another important long-range planning area. Flow manufacturers often transport high volumes of materials that have low values compared with their weight. Thus, transportation costs represent a higher portion of the cost of goods sold for these industries. To minimize transportation costs, flow manufacturing firms may use multiple plant locations and break-bulk operations through distribution centers. Since the products of competing flow manufacturers are quite similar, price is an important factor in marketing these products. A poor plant location can increase transportation costs to the point where the plant cannot compete.

Long-range plans for materials, staffing, energy, and waste disposal are also important for many flow manufacturers. In order to assure a long-range supply of key raw materials, flow manufacturers

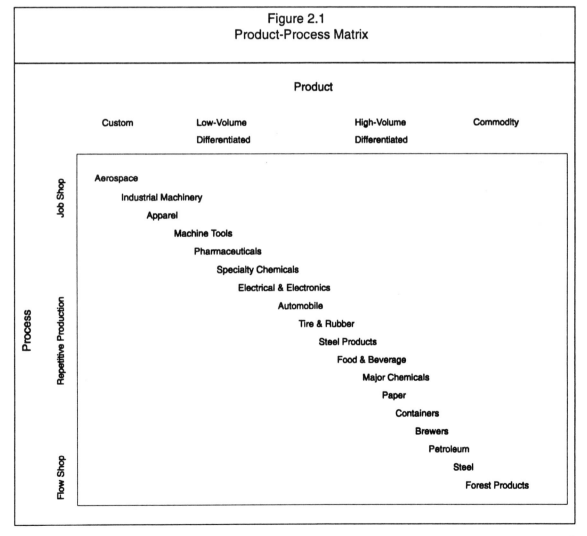

Figure 2.1
Product-Process Matrix

Product

Custom   Low-Volume   High-Volume   Commodity
              Differentiated   Differentiated

Process

Job Shop

Aerospace
    Industrial Machinery
        Apparel
            Machine Tools
                Pharmaceuticals
                    Specialty Chemicals
                        Electrical & Electronics
                            Automobile

Repetitive Production

                                Tire & Rubber
                                    Steel Products
                                        Food & Beverage
                                            Major Chemicals
                                                Paper
                                                    Containers
                                                        Brewers

Flow Shop

                                                            Petroleum
                                                                Steel
                                                                    Forest Products

frequently enter into long-range supply contracts. Many flow manufacturers need a highly specialized work force. Accordingly, long-range staffing plans must be developed to hire and train these workers. Many flow manufacturers are energy-intensive and consequently require long-range energy plans. Many flow manufacturing firms, particularly those in process industries, have waste products that must be disposed of in a manner consistent with environmental laws. Plans must be developed and permits obtained for emission and disposal of these waste substances.

Job manufacturers, which produce differentiated products in job shop environments, tend to place less emphasis on long-range resource planning and more emphasis on product design. In this portion of the product-process matrix, product features are a key factor in corporate strategies. A flexible manufacturing facility that can quickly produce new product designs is important for these firms. Although they must develop plans for equipment, personnel, materials, energy, and waste disposal, job manufacturers tend to use general-purpose resources that can be acquired in less time than the specialized resources used in flow manufacturing. Thus, job manufacturing firms put less emphasis on long-range process planning and more emphasis on product planning.

Intermediate-Range Planning

Intermediate-range production plans are concerned with the use of resources. These plans generally cover time horizons extending over the next three to eighteen months. A company may have

more than one production plan. For example, production plans by quarter may be developed during the annual budgeting period. Subsequently, monthly production plans may be generated during each quarter. Table 2.3 summarizes areas that are emphasized in flow manufacturing production plans.

Sourcing decisions are concerned with assigning customers to warehouses and, in turn, assigning warehouses to plants. Sourcing decisions are generally more important in flow manufacturing than in job manufacturing because flow manufacturers tend to have more plants and more warehouses and spend a higher percentage of their sales dollars on transportation. Flow manufacturers frequently use linear programming to help develop sourcing plans.

In many flow manufacturing plants, products are produced on a regular cycle. The sequence of products is often dictated by product or process technology. For example, products may be sequenced from light to dark, high viscosity to low viscosity, or wide to narrow. Determining the target sequences and cycle lengths is an important production planning problem for flow manufacturers.

Some process industry flow manufacturers produce blended products, such as gasoline or cattle feed. These firms try to develop a minimum-cost blend of ingredients that meets product specifications. Linear programming is frequently used, particularly in the petroleum industry, to develop minimum-cost blends.

Flow manufacturers tend to produce products to stock; as a result, a large percentage of their inventory investment is in finished goods inventory. One function of finished goods inventories is to buffer

---

Table 2.3
Areas Emphasized in Flow Manufacturing Production Plans

- Sourcing decisions
- Sequencing products through facilities
- Optimizing product blends
- Determining target safety stocks
- Coordinating production and maintenance plans
- Temporary shutdown of a plant or line to reduce inventory
- Exchange or swapping agreements
- Determining material requirements
- Developing aggregate production plans

the plant from variations in product demand. This is accomplished with a safety stock of finished product. Thus, the use of statistical techniques to size safety stocks is an important element of production plans for flow manufacturers.

Coordinating maintenance plans with production plans is more important in flow manufacturing. In flow manufacturing, production lines must be shut down periodically to perform maintenance. Because many flow manufacturers, particularly those in process industries, operate three shifts per day, seven days per week, it is impossible to perform maintenance during an off-shift or on weekends. In addition, flow manufacturers have less work-in-process inventory. Consequently, when one process unit shuts down, the preceding and succeeding processing units must also shut down. The net effect is that when major maintenance is scheduled, the line, or possibly the entire plant, is not producing. This interruption in production must be considered in plant production plans.

When forecasted demand is less than plant capacity, production must be reduced or inventories will build. Two strategies for reducing production are (1) to throttle the plant back to a rate equal to demand, or (2) to run the plant at full capacity and periodically shut down to reduce inventories. A major area of cost savings created by using periodic shutdowns is a reduction in energy costs. Since flow manufacturers in process industries tend to be energy-intensive, the shutdown strategy is used more in flow manufacturing than in job manufacturing. Repetitive manufacturers using assembly lines often use the shutdown strategy. Using line balancing techniques, their assembly lines are designed to operate at one rate. Thus, production is cut by reducing the operating hours rather than by cutting the production rate.

Flow manufacturers tend to produce products at the commodity end of the product differentiation spectrum. When a firm produces an undifferentiated product, it can enter exchange or swapping agreements with competitors to reduce transportation costs. Exchange or swapping agreements are a common practice in the petroleum, commodity chemical, and primary metal industries. These agreements are important in developing production plans for these flow manufacturing industries.

Some flow manufacturers develop material plans for key raw materials directly from their production plans. In these firms, the production plan sets the rate at which the plant will operate. In addition, these firms have a few key raw materials that are required for every product made on the line or in the plant. Therefore, after setting the aggregate production rate for the plant, a material plan can be developed for these key raw materials.

Flow manufacturers tend to develop aggregate production plans. It is generally easier to define aggregate capacity for flow manufacturers than for job manufacturers. Flow manufacturers have line flows, and the capacity of the bottleneck operation limits the capacity of the production line. In addition, flow shop production lines are designed to produce a relatively small group of closely related products. Thus, it is relatively easy to aggregate these product demands and plan production by product groups for a production line with relatively well-defined capacity. In contrast, job manufacturers have more difficulty in aggregating both processes and products. This leads to production plans that have more product and process detail.

Production plans for job manufacturing firms require greater coordination with labor plans than for flow manufacturers. Production plans for job manufacturing often adjust plant capacity by changing the labor hours. This is accomplished by changing the amount of overtime, the number of shifts scheduled, or the size of the work force. In contrast, labor is relatively independent of throughput in many flow manufacturers, which tend to be highly automated. Thus, labor tends to be relatively fixed, and labor plans are not closely coupled to production plans.

A review of the above differences in the production planning process shows that flow manufacturers must place more emphasis on production plans than do job manufacturers because the marketing and production environments require and allow more emphasis.

Short-Range Planning

Short-range plans are concerned with developing operating schedules. These schedules should be consistent with the intermediate-range production plans but have more product, process, and time detail. There is often more than one operating schedule. One schedule might cover a period of a month or more. Another schedule for the same plant might only cover a week but have hourly detail for each shift within the week.

Scheduling Methods

Flow manufacturing and job manufacturing differ markedly in their approaches to production scheduling. Flow manufacturers usually have a good estimate of line capacities. Moreover, because their products tend to have less differentiation, they tend to be more concerned about keeping unit costs low through high utilization of equipment. Consequently, flow manufacturing firms generally develop finite capacity schedules for production lines and then check inventories for intermediate and finished products. If there are problems with materials running out, the line schedule must be changed. We call this processor-dominated scheduling because the process equipment (production line) is scheduled before materials.

In contrast, job manufacturers tend to use a material-dominated scheduling approach. The capacity of a job shop depends on the order mix, which changes frequently. This causes bottlenecks that float among work centers depending on the load generated by a particular product mix. These floating bottlenecks create a far more challenging scheduling environment than in the flow manufacturing environment described above. In job manufacturing environments, an initial material schedule is often developed using the estimated lead times and backward scheduling approach of MRP II. After developing this material plan, capacities of the work centers are checked. If some work centers are overloaded, the material plan is revised to obtain a feasible plan. The differences in scheduling logic (processor-dominated versus material-dominated) will be treated in some detail in later chapters.

In a scheduling system, both materials and capacity must be planned. The question to be answered is which to do first. A material-dominated procedure, such as a closed-loop MRP II system, can minimize material investment. A processor-dominated technique can use equipment most efficiently. For a job manufacturer producing custom products, a material-dominated scheduling method is appropriate. For a flow manufacturer producing commodity products, a processor-dominated scheduling method is appropriate. However, as shown by the product-process matrix given in figure 2.1, many flow manufacturing industries and job manufacturing industries are somewhere between these two extremes. Nevertheless, firms in these industries must choose either a material-dominated or a processor-dominated scheduling method.

It must also be recognized that many variations exist in flow manufacturers. The reader will observe these variations in the case examples presented in chapter 4 and in the appendix. Furthermore, not only are there variations between different companies, but in many situations the variations occur within the same company. These may occur between different divisions or even within the same process train in the same division. A process train is here defined as a sequence of process stages, decoupled by inventory, that are required to produce a product or a family of products. Therefore, both material- and processor-dominated systems can exist in parallel or in series within the same company.

Scheduling System Characteristics

Table 2.4 lists characteristics of flow manufacturing scheduling systems. The first of these, which has just been discussed, is a greater use of processor-dominated master production scheduling methods. Since flow manufacturers have more plants and warehouses, they place a greater emphasis on distribution requirements planning and interplant transfer planning. The production schedule in flow manufacturing industries tends to be driven more by production plans, short-range demand forecasts, and distribution requirements plans than by customer orders. Because the production schedule in flow manufacturing is often buffered from customer orders by a finished goods inventory, there is often less customer interference in the production schedule.

Lot sizes in some process flow industries are dictated by facilities design or by manufacturing practices for ensuring product quality. For example, a lot size may depend on the capacity of a batch reactor or storage tank. In other cases, such as in canning meat products, manufacturing practices require a daily washout to maintain product quality. These washouts provide logical lot sizes. Nevertheless, there are many other situations in flow manufacturing operations where lot sizes are not constrained. In these plants, lot sizing techniques are an important tool in developing production plans and schedules.

Fewer items, well-defined capacity, and fixed routings make scheduling generally easier in flow manufacturing. In many firms the schedule is the authority to produce, and manufacturing work orders are not issued. Furthermore, since sequencing is generally accomplished in the production plan or the production schedule, daily dispatch lists are not needed. However, since there is no dispatch list, schedules often have time intervals of days, shifts, or hours.

Fitting Frameworks To Environments

The manufacturing environments we described in a previous section become the first clue in determining the types of industries in which process flow scheduling should be applied. Even the name we used in describing the environments—i.e., *flow manufacturing*—sets the stage. But there is a more important issue that needs to be discussed: Namely, can any planning/scheduling approach be universally applied in all manufacturing environments with the same level of success? Our position—no!

Each planning/scheduling approach is founded upon basic assumptions and logic. Each of those assumptions and logic has related strengths and weaknesses. If these strengths and weaknesses match up well with a particular company's environment and operating characteristics, the planning/scheduling approach has strong potential for success. Without such a match, the approach probably will not be successful. For example, companies often jump on the bandwagon of a new technique only to find themselves adapting the way they have

done business in the past to this new approach. Years later the company continues to adapt its business to the new approach even though the approach has never produced the expected results. Finally the company discards the technique and either goes back to its old ways of doing business or jumps on the bandwagon of another new approach to repeat the cycle. Who or what is at fault here?

Is the technique or the company at fault? Probably neither. The technique and its related logic are still valid and are probably working well at other companies. Is it the company's fault for not being able to adjust and make the technique work? The answer in some cases is no! The company made a valid effort to adjust to the new approach but failed because the new technique forced the company to operate in way that did not match well with its manufacturing environment.

A paper company's experience illustrates this point. The company's information systems group was considering using an order-driven MRP II system to schedule its pulp mill and paper machine as well as its cutting and packing operations. The MRP II system would drive material requirements based upon order due dates defined by the customer.

The company concluded that the order due dates from an MRP II system did not fit well with the sequencing constraints imposed by the process technology. The critical process stage in a paper mill is papermaking, which is performed by a paper machine. Paper machines can cost more than $100 million, can operate around the clock, and must be efficiently utilized for a profitable mill. To achieve

---

Table 2.4 Scheduling System Characteristics for Flow Manufacturers
• Greater use of processor-dominated scheduling
• More emphasis on distribution requirements planning and interplant transfer planning
• Closer coupling of production schedules with forecasts, production plans, and distribution requirements plans
• Less customer interference with production schedules
• Lot sizes may be dictated by facilities design or by manufacturing practices for ensuring product quality
• Schedule is the authority to produce
• Sequencing is generally accomplished in the production plan or production schedule
• Schedule generally has smaller time intervals

high efficiencies on a paper machine, paper grades are traditionally scheduled in efficient sequences based on color and the paper's basis weight. The normal time to complete a production cycle through all colors and basis weights is generally several weeks. While an MRP II system could be adapted to this environment, its emphasis on due dates and subordination of production sequences was judged a poor fit. The firm wisely chose not to implement an MRP II system.

Other companies have not been so fortunate. The mismatch between scheduling logic and manufacturing environment is not always as striking as in the paper company. How many times have companies adopted a new planning technique and failed to achieve the expected results? These companies are dismayed—others have achieved exceptional results; why can't they? Some would attribute these failures to lack of management support, poor training, poor records accuracy, and a lack of discipline. While these can cause failure, one often-overlooked factor is fit. We strongly believe that there are many ways to configure a planning and scheduling system. We maintain that the fit between system logic and manufacturing environment is an important factor in the success of planning and scheduling systems.

Flow manufacturers operate in a different environment from job manufacturers. Different demands are placed on the planning and scheduling system. Each system framework is founded upon certain basic assumptions and logic. Each framework has its own strengths and weaknesses. If a framework's strengths match a particular manufacturing environment, the chances of success are greatly improved.

So where does process flow scheduling fit? The product-process matrix provides a useful view. Figure 2.2 shows a rough estimate of the range of applicability of PFS and MRP II systems. PFS and JIT are most applicable in the lower right corner, while MRP II fits best in the upper left. In the central portion of the matrix, no technique dominates. If process technology allows the use of JIT scheduling concepts, JIT should be used in the flow manufacturing regions. However, if sequencing and minimum run lengths (lot sizes) are important scheduling considerations for flow manufacturers, PFS should be considered.

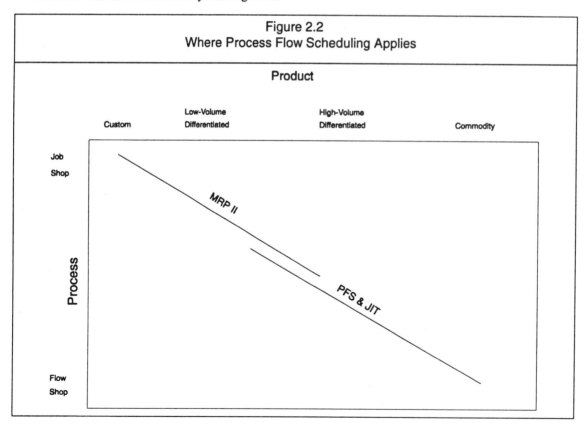

Figure 2.2
Where Process Flow Scheduling Applies

While some firms operate exclusively in one part of the matrix, other firms operate in both regions. For example, a repetitive manufacturing firm might use a parts fabrication job shop to feed a final assembly line flow shop or a process industry manufacturer may produce a limited number of products in a flow manufacturing environment and convert these intermediate products into many finished products in a job manufacturing environment. These firms, which have a mixture of job and flow manufacturing operations, require *different scheduling systems for different stages of their manufacturing process.* MRP II would be appropriate for the job manufacturing portion of the operation, and JIT or PFS would be appropriate for the flow manufacturing operations.

It is important to understand that process flow scheduling can be used effectively by many manufacturers; however, it is not for everyone. PFS is primarily for flow manufacturers who cannot fully implement JIT scheduling practices. It is also important to understand that if your operation has a combination of job and flow manufacturing, you can probably benefit from using more than one type of scheduling logic.

Process flow scheduling is a system with wide-reaching applications. PFS can be structured as an independent system. PFS can be used within an MRP II system, or MRP II can be used as a stage scheduler within the PFS structure. PFS can even be looked at as a structure for a company's supply chain system. Process flow scheduling can be many things to many companies, but it cannot be all things to all companies. If you are in a flow manufacturing environment and have had difficulty applying MRP II and JIT logic—read on. PFS may help. The next chapter will examine a simple example of PFS and develop three basic principles that apply to all PFS systems.

References

Foley, M. J. 1988. Post-MRP II: What comes next? *Datamation*, 1 December, 24, 32, 36.

Hayes, Robert H., and Steven C. Wheelwright. 1979a. Link manufacturing process and product life cycles. *Harvard Business Review,* January-February.

Hayes, Robert H., and Steven C. Wheelwright. 1979b. The dynamics of process-product life cycles. *Harvard Business Review,* March-April.

Chapter 3

Process Flow Scheduling Concepts

It is now time to focus on PFS and look at what it really is and what it can do. Process flow scheduling is a type of scheduling system that uses the process structure to guide scheduling calculations. As we indicated in chapter 1, PFS has been used by process and repetitive manufacturing companies for many years. These firms often develop custom computer systems that incorporate the PFS logic. However, the similarities among these systems have only recently been recognized and documented.

In this chapter we introduce the reader to basic PFS calculations and present three major principles of PFS. This provides an essential foundation upon which an understanding of PFS can be built.

Basic Calculations

The purpose of this section is to illustrate PFS calculations with a simple example. We will begin by describing a hypothetical company's process flow. We then present a flowchart for the scheduling procedures and give a numerical example of each scheduling step. We conclude with a discussion of the limitations of this example.

Polygoo Manufacturing

The United Chemical Company manufactures three grades—A, B, and C—of a viscous liquid called Polygoo. These grades are each sold in one-gallon cans and five-gallon pails. The products are designated by grade and package; thus, A1 is grade A in a one-gallon can, and A5 is grade A in a five-gallon pail. Similarly B1, B5, C1, and C5 designate the other finished products.

The products are shipped daily from a plant warehouse in truckload and carload quantities. The demand has no seasonality and does not vary by day of week. The forecasted daily demand is shown in table 3.1.

Figure 3.1 gives the process structure for the Polygoo process train. The triangles represent inventories, and the rectangles represent operations. Production begins when the feed stock, F, is withdrawn from inventory and processed in the stage 1 reactor. The reactor operates twenty-four hours a day, seven days a week. The reactor production rate for all grades is 100,000 gallons per day. Bulk Polygoo is stored in large tanks that buffer stage 1 reactor operations from packaging operations.

Product quality considerations determine the minimum production run lengths. Grade switches are

Table 3.1 Demand			
Product	Volume, Units	Volume, Gallons	Percent of Total
A1	30,000 cans	30,000	30
B1	20,000 cans	20,000	20
C1	10,000 cans	10,000	10
A5	4,000 pails	20,000	20
B5	2,000 pails	10,000	10
C5	2,000 pails	10,000	10
			100%

made by changing the reactor temperature and pressure, which in turn affect the molecular weight of the Polygoo. These grade switches, which are made without shutting down the reactor, generate off-specification transition material. If the process operated as a batching operation, each switch would require a shutdown of the reactor, and setup time would be necessary. The transition material may be

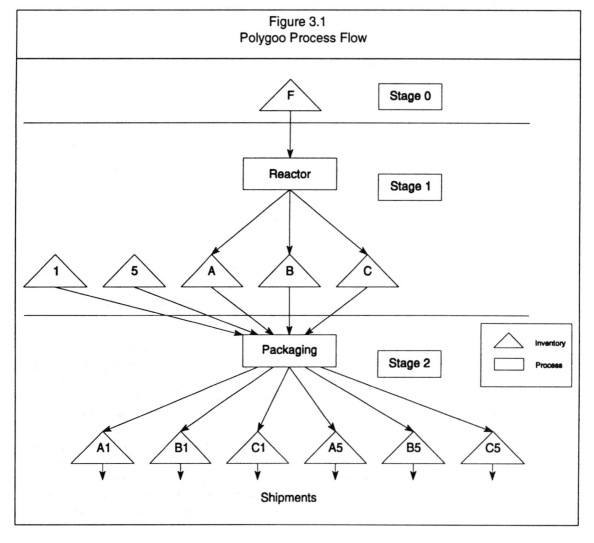

Figure 3.1
Polygoo Process Flow

upgraded to meet product specifications by blending it with a sufficient quantity of prime (high-quality, on-specification) material. Consequently, to achieve a constant blending ratio, each grade requires a minimum run length of one day to blend off the transition material.

The second-stage operation is packaging. Here bulk products are withdrawn from the storage tanks and packaged in one-gallon cans or five-gallon pails. Thus, in figure 3.1, product A1 is produced by combining inventory A with inventory 1 (one-gallon cans) in the packaging operation. The other products are produced in a similar manner.

The packaging line, which is much less expensive to operate than the reactor, is only operated one shift per day, seven days per week. The packaging line operates at a rate of 100,000 gallons per shift. It can therefore fill 100,000 one-gallon cans or 20,000 five-gallon pails in one shift. Grade changes can be accomplished without washing out or shutting down the packaging equipment. However, when the container size is changed, the line must be shut down for a four-hour setup. This setup is performed after the normal eight-hour shift and does not affect the line capacity.

The bulk inventories between stage 1 and stage 2 are needed for several reasons. First, a surge capacity is needed because the reactor produces twenty-four hours a day while packaging only consumes eight hours a day. The surge capacity provides a temporary storage of bulk material (A, B, and C) between the reactor and packaging processes. Second, a buffer protects the reactor against unscheduled downtime on the packaging lines. Without a buffer between the reactor and the packaging lines, the reactor would have to shut down when the packaging line breaks down. Because of limited reactor capacity and large capital investment in the reactor,

such a shutdown would be unwise. Finally, the bulk inventories can be used to decouple the reactor and packaging schedules. This allows the flexibility to schedule each stage with different lot sizes and in different sequences.

Target Inventories

We will assume that management has established target minimum and maximum levels for each plant inventory. The feed stock is received in 1,000,000-gallon quantities and stored in three 500,000-gallon dedicated tanks. Accordingly, the feed stock inventory has a maximum level of 1.5 million gallons. A planned minimum two-day feed stock requirement (200,000 gallons) is used to buffer the plant against supply variations.

The bulk products are stored in 320,000-gallon tanks, with one tank for each grade. In order to leave an operating cushion, the planned maximum inventory for each grade is 300,000 gallons. A planned minimum of one day's average requirements is used for bulk inventories. This translates to 50,000 gallons for grade A, 30,000 gallons for grade B, and 20,000 gallons for grade C.

The finished goods inventories are stored in packaged goods warehouses. Safety stock levels have been established for each product using a statistical analysis of demand variations, target customer service levels, and production frequencies. These safety stocks, as shown in table 3.2, establish planned minimum inventories.

There is excess package goods warehouse space, and no maximum levels are placed on finished goods inventories. However, the benefits of minimizing inventory are recognized, and finished goods inventory minimization is a scheduling objective.

Table 3.2 Safety Stocks	
Product	Minimum Inventory
A1	100,000 gallons
B1	70,000 gallons
C1	40,000 gallons
A5	15,000 pails
B5	12,000 pails
C5	12,000 pails

Production Campaign Cycles

A production campaign cycle is a sequence of production runs in which all major products for a process unit are produced. A Polygoo reactor campaign cycle involves the production of grades A, B, and C. The campaign cycle length is the period of time needed to cycle through all grades. Some companies visualize a campaign cycle as a schedule wheel. Figure 3.2 shows sample schedule wheels. The campaign cycle length is the time required for one revolution of the schedule, where the faster the schedule wheel is turned, the shorter the campaign cycle length and the lower the inventories. The wheel is turned to the right; thus, the production sequence for the Polygoo reactor schedule is A, B, C; and the Polygoo packaging schedule is A1,

B1, C1, A5, B5, C5. All products are produced in each cycle.

The minimum campaign cycle length for the reactor is controlled by the minimum production run length for the lowest volume grade. Grade C constitutes 20 percent of total demand, and since the minimum grade run length is one day, grade C can be produced no more frequently than once every five days, which in turns sets the minimum campaign cycle length. This calculation may be formalized by

$$T_{RMIN} = \frac{T_{CMIN}}{F_C} = \frac{1}{0.2} = 5 \text{ days},$$

where T_{RMIN} is the minimum campaign cycle length, T_{CMIN} is the minimum run length for grade C, and F_C is the fraction of production time devoted to grade C. Since the production rates are the same for

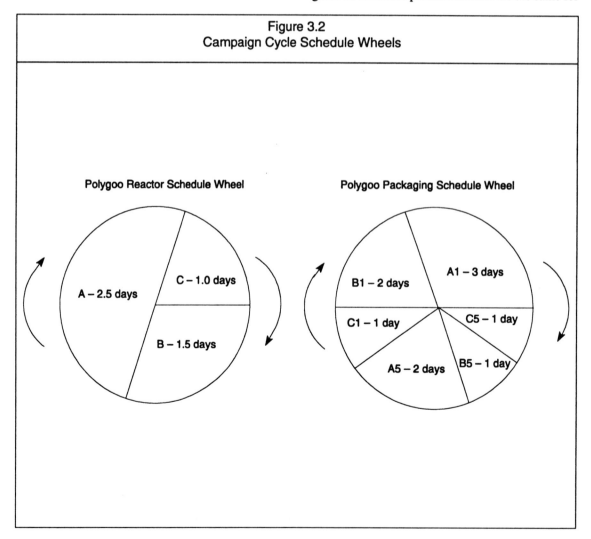

Figure 3.2
Campaign Cycle Schedule Wheels

Polygoo Reactor Schedule Wheel

A – 2.5 days
C – 1.0 days
B – 1.5 days

Polygoo Packaging Schedule Wheel

B1 – 2 days
A1 – 3 days
C1 – 1 day
C5 – 1 day
A5 – 2 days
B5 – 1 day

all grades, F_C is calculated from C's percent of total demand. The target run lengths for grades A and B are found by

$$T_{AMIN} = F_A T_{RMIN} = (0.5)\, 5 = 2.5 \text{ days}$$
$$T_{BMIN} = F_B T_{RMIN} = (0.3)\, 5 = 1.5 \text{ days.}$$

The reactor schedule wheel in figure 3.2 illustrates the target run lengths and production sequence for the reactor.

A campaign cycle for the packaging line produces all six products. Manufacturing practices require a minimum packaging run of one shift for each product. Accordingly the minimum campaign cycle length for packaging, T_{PMIN}, is found from the product with the minimum packaging run length. Products C1, B5, and C5 are tied for the lowest volume product. Any of these could be used to calculate the minimum campaign cycle length. Product C1 will be used:

$$T_{PMIN} = \frac{T_{C1MIN}}{F_{C1}} = \frac{1}{0.1} = 10 \text{ days,}$$

where T_{C1MIN} is the minimum production run length for Product C1 and F_{C1} is the fraction of packaging time devoted to C1.

Using the minimum packaging campaign cycle length, target production run lengths for each product may be calculated from where T_i is the target run length for product i and F_i is the fraction of packaging time devoted to product i

$$T_i = F_i T_{PMIN}.$$

This calculation results in the following target production run lengths: $T_{A1} = 3$ days; $T_{B1} = 2$ days; $T_{A5} = 2$ days; $T_{C1} = 1$ day; $T_{B5} = 1$ day; and $T_{C5} = 1$ day.

The production sequence is also important in packaging. Setups may be minimized by grouping package sizes together. Consequently all one-gallon products will be scheduled in one group and all five-gallon products in a second group. Thus, a typical packaging campaign sequence would be A1, B1, C1, setup, A5, B5, C5, setup. The target run lengths and sequence are illustrated in the packaging schedule wheel shown in figure 3.2.

Scheduling

A flowchart for scheduling tasks is given in figure 3.3. The scheduling procedure begins by developing a forecast, which is used to reverse flow schedule the processes; i.e., schedule in the direction opposite

from the process flow needed to produce the product. This forecast is used to help set target run lengths as described above. Next a trial schedule for the packaging line is proposed, as shown in the Gantt chart at the top of figure 3.4. The production run lengths for the Gantt chart use the target run lengths depicted in the schedule wheel of figure 3.2.

Using the trial production plan and the demand forecast, finished product inventory projections are shown in figure 3.4 using the production-demand-inventory (PDI) record. Table 3.3: Polygoo Packaging Schedule provides numerical data. Note that the quantities in this record are expressed in thousands. Beginning inventories are shown in period 0.

The period row in each record gives the day associated with each column. The production row entries are obtained from the Gantt chart and the packaging rate of 100,000 gallons per day for all products. The demand row entries are obtained from the forecasts of daily demand.

The last row in a PDI record is inventory. The beginning inventory is shown in period 0. The inventories in subsequent periods are calculated by adding the current period's production to the prior period's ending inventory and subtracting the current period's demand. Rather than display the PDI records, it is often easier to work with inventory line graphs as shown in figure 3.4.

The projected finished product inventories can now be checked against their target minimums and maximums. In this example the projected inventories are above their minimums and there is no maximum, so we can proceed with scheduling the next stage. If projected inventory levels were unacceptable, the trial packaging schedule or the forecast would need to be revised. This is shown in the scheduling flowchart (figure 3.3) by the check of product inventories and the first "No" "Revise Schedules" branch.

Next, a trial schedule for the reactor is proposed, and bulk inventories for A, B, and C are checked. This procedure is similar to that just presented for the packaging stage. The Gantt chart at the top of figure 3.5 shows the trial reactor schedule. The corresponding PDI records are presented in table 3.4 and the related inventory line graph is given in figure 3.5. Note that the demand for bulk Polygoo depends on the packaging schedule. Thus, the number of gallons of A demanded in day 1 is calculated by $1 \times$ (A1 production in day 1) + ($5 \times$ A5 production in day 1) = $(1 \times 100) + (5 \times 0)$ = 100,000 gallons.

The inventories in the PDI records are now checked against their maximums and minimums. Alternatively, the plots of the PDI inventory rows shown in figure 3.5 may be used. If the bulk inventories are not within their prescribed bounds, it will be necessary to revise the reactor schedule, the packaging schedule, or the forecast. This is shown in the scheduling flowchart (figure 3.3) by the check of A, B, and C inventories and the second "No" "Revise schedules" branch. Since all inventories for the example are within their limits, scheduling can proceed to the final step.

Scheduling the feed stock in stage 0 is the last step. The demand for feed stock is calculated from the production schedules for A, B, and C. Thus, the demand for F in period 1 is calculated from $1 \times$ (A production in period 1) + $1 \times$ (B production in period 1) + $1 \times$ (C production in period 1) = (1×100) + (1×0) + (1×0) = 100,000 gallons.

When projected feed stock inventories fall below the planned minimum, receipts of feed stock are scheduled. A receipts-demand-inventory (RDI) record for feed stock is given in table 3.5 and shown as a graph in figure 3.6. The calculations begin by projecting the inventory in period 1. The demand of 100 is subtracted from the 200 in inventory at the end of period 0. This gives a trial inventory of 100, which is below the minimum inventory level of 200. A receipt of 1,000 is scheduled in period 1. This brings the inventory in period 1 to 1,100. Similar

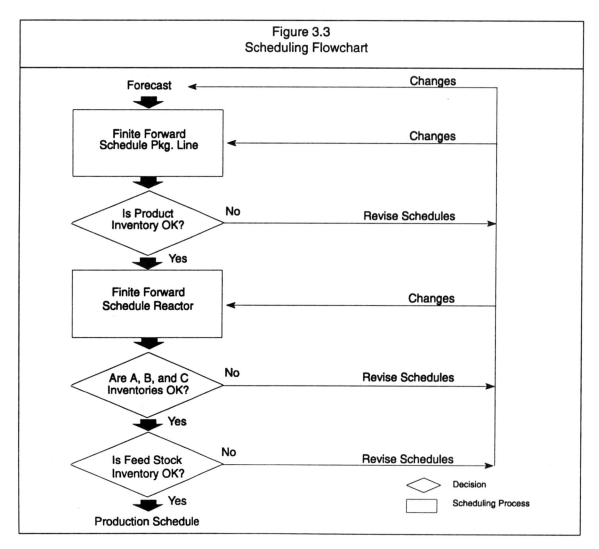

Figure 3.3
Scheduling Flowchart

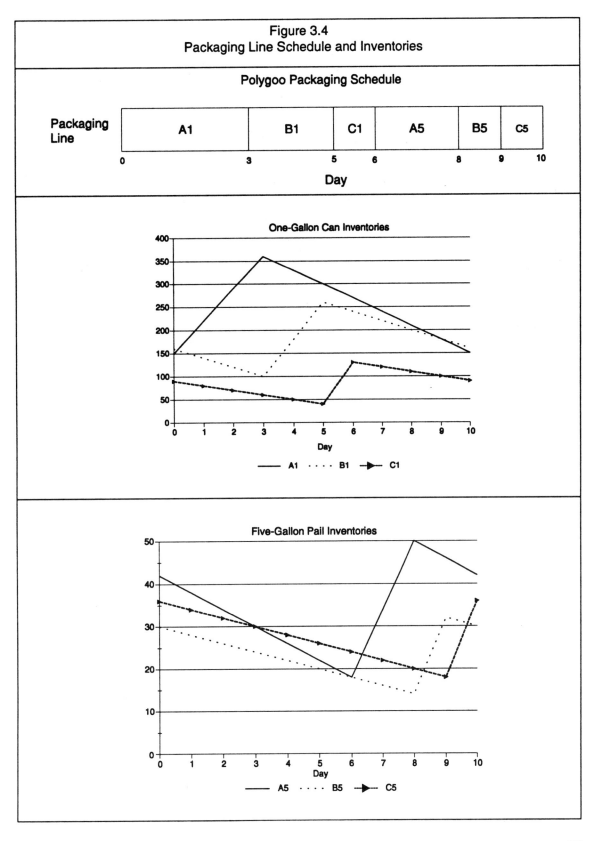

Figure 3.4
Packaging Line Schedule and Inventories

calculations are performed for subsequent periods, and the resulting inventory is plotted.

Note that the above calculation for the feed stock supplier is based solely on material. The feed stock supplier must check to verify that there is adequate inventory or capacity to meet the raw material requirements of Polygoo. If the requirements can be met, the schedule is complete. If not, earlier schedules will need to be revised as shown by the flowchart in figure 3.3. Since stage 0 schedules material before capacity, a material-dominated scheduling approach, which will be discussed in the next section, is used.

This material-dominated scheduling contrasts with the processor-dominated scheduling exhibited by the scheduling of stage 1 and stage 2. In these stages, the processor and its related capacity were scheduled first by scheduling the production campaign cycles. Following this processor schedule, material inventories were checked to ensure feasibility of the schedule. Both material and capacity are needed to produce the product. However, determining the scheduling sequence identifies the relative importance of materials versus capacity and, therefore, where the company places its emphasis. These issues will be discussed at some length in chapter 6.

Table 3.3 Polygoo Packaging Schedule (PDI Record)											
Product A1											
Period	0	1	2	3	4	5	6	7	8	9	10
Production		100	100	100							
Demand		30	30	30	30	30	30	30	30	30	30
Inventory	150	220	290	360	330	300	270	240	210	180	150
Product B1											
Period	0	1	2	3	4	5	6	7	8	9	10
Production					100	100					
Demand		20	20	20	20	20	20	20	20	20	20
Inventory	160	140	120	100	180	260	240	220	200	180	160
Product C1											
Period	0	1	2	3	4	5	6	7	8	9	10
Production							100				
Demand		10	10	10	10	10	10	10	10	10	10
Inventory	90	80	70	60	50	40	130	120	110	100	90
Product A5											
Period	0	1	2	3	4	5	6	7	8	9	10
Production								20	20		
Demand		4	4	4	4	4	4	4	4	4	4
Inventory	42	38	34	30	26	22	18	34	50	46	42
Product B5											
Period	0	1	2	3	4	5	6	7	8	9	10
Production										20	
Demand		2	2	2	2	2	2	2	2	2	2
Inventory	30	28	26	24	22	20	18	16	14	32	30
Product C5											
Period	0	1	2	3	4	5	6	7	8	9	10
Production											20
Demand		2	2	2	2	2	2	2	2	2	2
Inventory	36	34	32	30	28	26	24	22	20	18	36

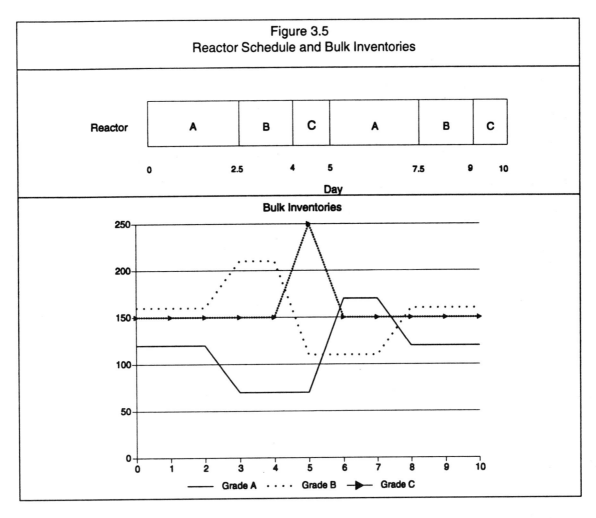

Figure 3.5
Reactor Schedule and Bulk Inventories

Scheduling the Alternatives

The scheduling example provided above generated a nice neat result with few, if any, problems. Unfortunately, that is not reality. So let us deviate slightly to interject a problem and discuss how that problem might be solved.

As the reader may recall from figure 3.5 and table 3.4, grade A's production was based upon the assumption that 120,000 gallons of grade A already existed in inventory. However, suppose that the reactor foreman just informed you of an error. Instead of 120,000 gallons, only 20,000 gallons of grade A are in inventory. Human error placed a 1 in front of the 20,000 gallons. Something that would never occur in your firm—right? Anyway, what impact will this error have? A review of table 3.6, which summarizes the new PDI record, shows a shortage of material occurring from period 3 through

period 5. Our production system is short 30,000 gallons of grade A material.

So how do we solve the situation? Initially, we might look for a solution by adjusting the production schedule of the Polygoo reactor. A longer production run of grade A that produced an additional 30,000 gallons would be needed. Or, more practically, let us just run grade A for three full days, producing an additional 50,000 gallons. This solves the shortage of grade A material, but does it create any other problems? Two issues need to be investigated: Do we have feed stock available to support the increased production, and does the extension of the reactor schedule create any shortages of grade B or C because their starting dates are pushed out into the future by one-half day?

A review of figure 3.6 and table 3.5 shows that there is ample feed stock available for any reactor schedule change in period 3. No problem here. A

Table 3.4
Reactor Production-Demand-Inventory Record

Grade A											
Period	0	1	2	3	4	5	6	7	8	9	10
Production		100	100	50			100	100	50		
Demand		100	100	100	0	0	0	100	100	0	0
Inventory	120	120	120	70	70	70	170	170	120	120	120
Grade B											
Period	0	1	2	3	4	5	6	7	8	9	10
Production				50	100				50	100	
Demand		0	0	0	100	100	0	0	0	100	0
Inventory	160	160	160	210	210	110	110	110	160	160	160
Grade C											
Period	0	1	2	3	4	5	6	7	8	9	10
Production						100					100
Demand		0	0	0	0	0	100	0	0	0	100
Inventory	150	150	150	150	150	250	150	150	150	150	150

review of table 3.4 shows that starting the reactor schedule for grade B or grade C one-half day later will create no availability problems for either of these products. For example, grade B's production would start in period 4. This would reduce the inventory level of grade B in period 3 and period 4 to 160,000 gallons. More than enough inventory. A similar result occurs for grade C, and no problem is created. We have solved the problem at this stage without any iterative changes needed in the other schedules; i.e., the packaging schedule or the feed stock schedule.

It might be appropriate to take this example one step further. Suppose that the above adjustment in the reactor schedule did create later problems for the availability of grade B or grade C material. If so, we might need to look at the downstream packaging schedule for a solution. A review of the PDI schedule of product A1 (as presented in figure 3.4 or in table 3.3) indicates that there is an adequate supply of finished product to meet immediate demands for the product. The amount is ample to allow for a reduction in the packaging schedule for product A1, thereby reducing the amount of grade A material needed. Product A5's packaging schedule, which does not take place until period 7, is not affected by the shortage of grade A material in periods 3 and 4. Therefore, an adjustment in the packaging schedule

has resolved the problem created in the reactor schedule.

Similar methods of interactive stage-by-stage problem solving are common and sometimes everyday occurrences. In our above example, the problem was solved easily. It will not always be this easy, and at times it may be impossible to find a feasible solution that avoids all negative circumstances. However, as will be discussed in more detail in later chapters, the stage-by-stage reconciliation of materials and capacity along with the interactive problem solving provides a useful approach to a sometimes very complex planning and scheduling problem.

Summary of Polygoo

Polygoo illustrates simple process flow scheduling calculations. While this example is representative of the logic and calculations used in PFS systems, it should be recognized that many variations exist. Since stages were scheduled from last to first, Polygoo illustrates reverse flow scheduling in a make-to-stock environment. Moreover, processor-dominated scheduling with finite forward scheduling was used in stages 1 and 2 for the reactor and packaging operations while material-dominated scheduling was used in stage 0 for the feed stock.

Feed Stock	0	1	2	3	4	5	6	7	8	9	10
Period											
Receipts		1,000									
Demand		100	100	100	100	100	100	100	100	100	100
Inventory	200	1,100	1,000	900	800	700	600	500	400	300	200

Table 3.5
Feed Stock Requirements Schedule

The example illustrates a scheduling logic much different from MRP logic. PFS scheduling logic uses the *process structure* to guide scheduling calculations while MRP uses the *product structure* to guide scheduling calculations. Also note that both material and capacity were reconciled in each stage before proceeding to schedule the next stage.

Many process industry firms and some repetitive manufacturers use PFS logic for scheduling all or part of their operations. While some firms use custom software, other firms use commercial finite scheduling software. Many of these PFS implementations use logic similar to that illustrated above for Polygoo.

Process Flow Scheduling Principles

Our research for the past 15 years has focused on planning and scheduling systems in process

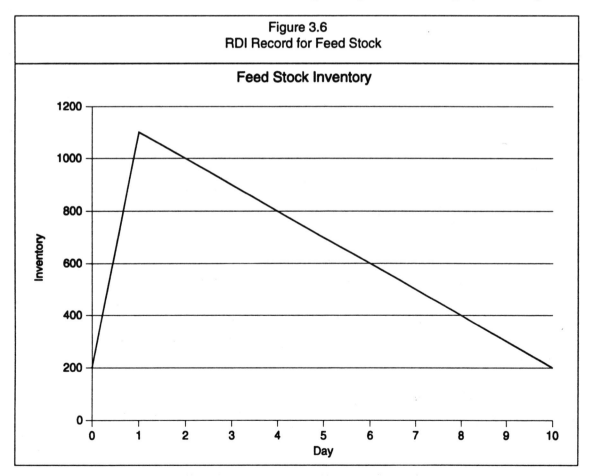

Figure 3.6
RDI Record for Feed Stock

Grade A											
Period	0	1	2	3	4	5	6	7	8	9	10
Production		100	100	50			100	100	50		
Demand		100	100	100	0	0	0	100	100	0	0
Inventory	20	20	20	−30	−30	−30	70	70	20	0	0

Table 3.6
PDI Record

industries. This research has included many discussions with scheduling practitioners in the process industries. Our study of scheduling systems has culminated in three principles for process flow scheduling systems. We now explain these principles.

Process Structure Guides Calculations

The first process flow scheduling principle is *Scheduling calculations are guided by the process structure.*

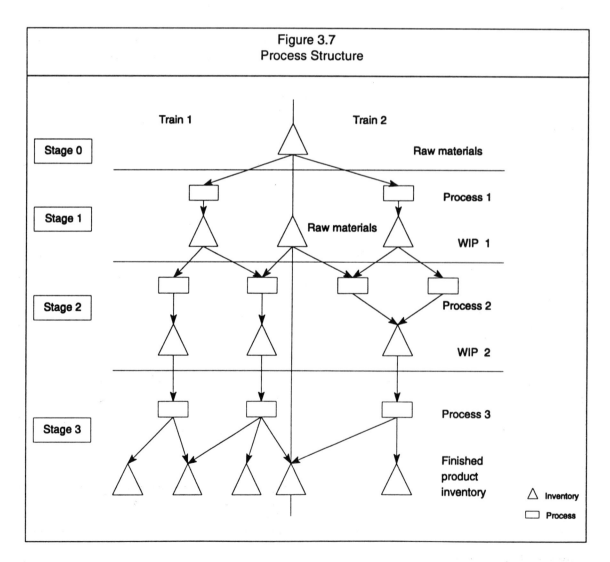

Figure 3.7
Process Structure

This principle is the dominant concept underlying all PFS systems.

A classification procedure and terminology are needed to define process structures. Figure 3.7 illustrates our proposed classification and terminology. A process structure consists of process units, clusters, stages, and trains. A process unit performs a basic manufacturing step, such as polymerization, mixing, or packaging. Process units are combined into single-unit clusters or multiple-unit clusters at each stage, with stages separated by inventories. Processes that are not separated by inventories are best combined in a cluster allowing that cluster to be managed as a single entity. Separating different stages/clusters with inventory allows these stages/clusters to be scheduled somewhat independently.

Finally, stages are organized into process trains. A process train is a fixed, sequential series of process stages in which a family of products is produced. No material is usually transferred from one process train to another, although process trains may use common raw materials and produce common products. We

emphasize *usually* here, because a few exceptions to this nontransfer of material exist.

Stage/Cluster Scheduling Alternatives

The second PFS principle specifies alternatives for scheduling single stages:

Stages/clusters are scheduled using processor-dominated scheduling (PDS) or material-dominated scheduling (MDS) approaches.

In order to operate a process stage/cluster, schedules are required for both the processing unit and the materials. If the processing units are scheduled before the materials, processor-dominated scheduling (PDS) has been used. Conversely, if materials are scheduled before the processor, material-dominated scheduling (MDS) has been used.

Any process cluster in a PFS system is scheduled using either PDS or MDS. Because of the importance of PDS and MDS in stage/cluster scheduling, we will briefly illustrate them for the system shown in figure 3.8. This system has a single train with a

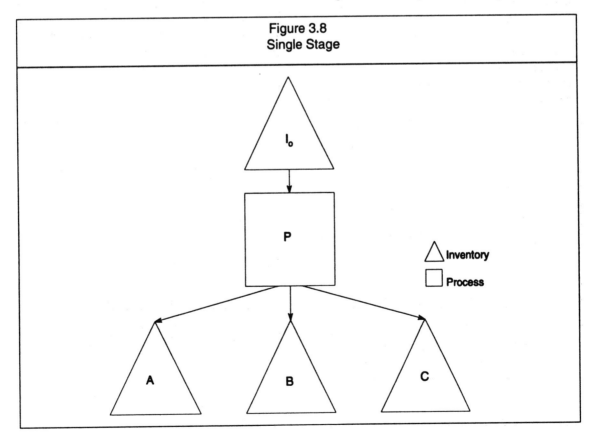

Figure 3.8
Single Stage

I_o

P

△ Inventory
☐ Process

A   B   C

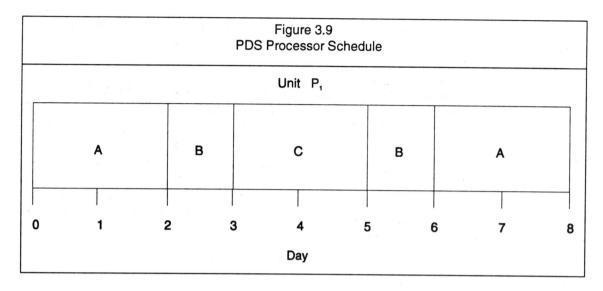

Figure 3.9
PDS Processor Schedule

Unit P_1

single stage, a single process cluster, and a single unit. The system produces three products: A, B, and C.

Processor-Dominated Scheduling

Processor-dominated scheduling first develops a finite capacity schedule for the processor and then schedules materials. Figure 3.9 shows a Gantt chart for the processor in our example system. Gantt charts are commonly used to display the production sequence and run lengths while observing finite capacity limits. They are created by starting at time zero and forward scheduling through time. When

Gantt charts are used in this manner, they are a finite forward scheduling technique.

After the processor has been scheduled, the finished product inventory is checked. Figure 3.10 shows a time-phased material record for product A of our example. The requirements are at a uniform rate of 100 units per day and are shown in the first full row. These finished product requirements may be determined from a forecasting system. Production of A is only scheduled for days 1 and 2, as specified by the Gantt chart in figure 3.9. Since we assume a production rate for A of 400 units per day,

Figure 3.10
PDS Material Schedule

Product: A

		Day					
		1	2	3	4	5	6
Requirements		100	100	100	100	100	100
Production		400	400				
Inventory	200	500	800	700	600	500	400

the production row in figure 3.10 shows 400 for days 1 and 2.

The last row in the material record shows projected inventories. Currently, 200 units are in inventory. The inventory in each remaining period is obtained by adding production to the prior period's inventory and subtracting the requirements. For example, the inventory in period 1 is obtained by adding the current production of 400 to the prior period's inventory of 200 and then subtracting the requirements of 100. This gives an inventory of 500 for period 1.

An alternate way of displaying the information in the material record is with an inventory line graph, as shown in figure 3.11. Desired target minimum and maximum inventories can also be displayed. We have only shown and discussed material plans for product A. Material plans for products B and C would also need to be developed.

If the inventories for products A, B, or C violate their target minimums or maximums, the schedule for stage 1 must be revised. This can be done by revising the production schedule (figure 3.9) or possibly by changing the forecast or the response to the forecast. After satisfactory processor and material schedules are obtained for stage 1, a raw material schedule can be developed. If supply problems are encountered, the stage 1 schedules will need to be revised.

This procedure is essentially the same as that illustrated earlier for Polygoo. Let us now examine MDS for the same single-stage system shown in figure 3.8.

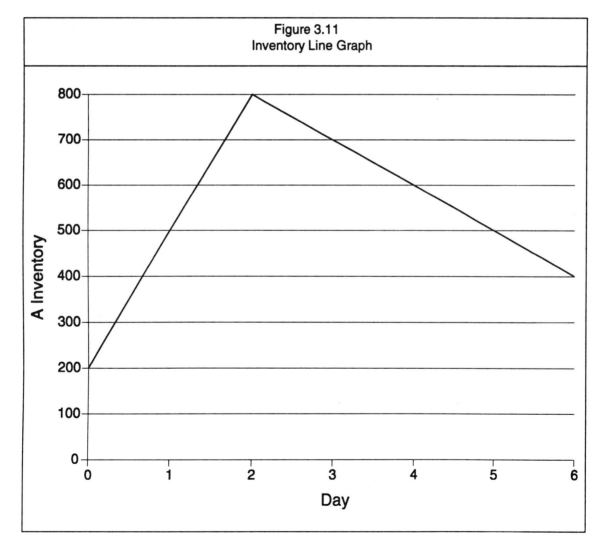

Figure 3.11
Inventory Line Graph

Figure 3.12
MDS Material Scheduling

Product: A

Min: 100

Production Lot Size: 800

Daily Production Rate: 400

Day

		1	2	3	4	5	6
Requirements		100	100	100	100	100	100
Production			400	400			
Inventory	200	100	400	700	600	500	400

Material-Dominated Scheduling

As shown in figure 3.12, material-dominated scheduling begins with a time-phased material balance record. The data for product A indicate that the minimum planned inventory is 100; the production lot size is 800; and the daily production rate is 400. The numbers in the time-phased record are derived in a manner quite similar to MRP. When the projected inventory drops below the planned minimum of 100, a production run of 800 is scheduled at a rate

of 400 per day. MDS requires that similar schedules be developed for products B and C.

Having completed the material schedules for the stage, we now develop a schedule for the processing unit. Figure 3.13 gives a load profile for the processing unit. Note that the product A production of 400 in both day 2 and day 3 shown in figure 3.12 is reflected in the load shown in figure 3.13. This example has a load in period two that exceeds the capacity of 400. A scheduler must now intervene

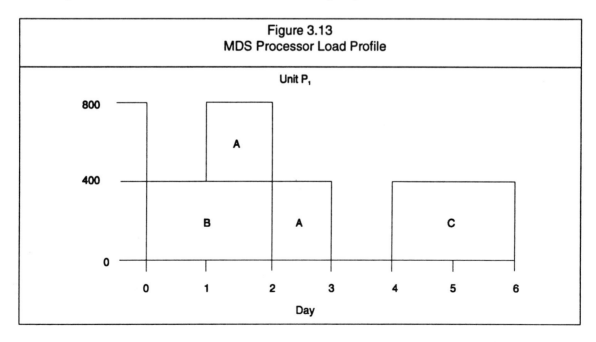

Figure 3.13
MDS Processor Load Profile

and adjust (1) production run lengths, (2) minimum planned inventories, (3) production rates, or (4) other variables in order to achieve a feasible schedule. Finally, raw material schedules are developed. However, if these prove infeasible, adjustments must be made to the previous schedules to achieve system feasibility.

These simple examples illustrate single-stage or single-cluster scheduling, which is the basic building block of PFS. An important feature is the use of scheduler intervention to resolve infeasibilities at each stage as the schedule is being constructed. Either PDS or MDS approaches are used.

Note that MDS scheduling logic is similar to, but not identical with, MRP logic. A closed-loop MRP system develops material plans for *all* materials before developing processor capacity plans. In contrast, our MDS example first scheduled finished products, then the processor for the single stage, and finally the raw materials.

Our simple MDS example does not use order releases or lead time offsets, which are fundamental concepts in an MRP system. Instead, the example illustrates the use of a rate-based scheduling system with no lead time offsets. However, if a particular scheduling environment requires either order releases or lead time offsets, they could be included and the stage scheduled using MRP scheduling concepts. PFS is flexible enough to operate either way.

What's Best

The selection of PDS or MDS for a given stage depends on the particular scheduling environment. In general, PDS should be used when (1) capacity is relatively expensive, (2) the cluster is a bottleneck, or (3) setups are expensive. Conversely, MDS should be used when (1) materials are relatively expensive, (2) there is excess capacity, (3) setup costs are negligible, or (4) the cluster consists of a set of processing units that operates like a job shop. Both PDS and MDS approaches are illustrated in the various case examples presented in chapter 4. Additional detail and examples for single cluster scheduling are given in chapter 7.

Process Train Scheduling Alternatives

The third PFS principle specifies alternatives for scheduling process trains:

Process trains are scheduled using reverse flow scheduling, forward flow scheduling, or mixed-flow scheduling.

The first principle of PFS requires that the process structure be used to guide scheduling calculations. However, process stage schedules can be linked together in many ways to form a process train schedule. Figure 3.14 shows an example process structure for a simple three-stage system. Let's look at the three alternatives.

Reverse Flow Scheduling

Reverse flow scheduling builds a schedule by proceeding backwards through the process structure, scheduling one stage at a time. In figure 3.15, reverse flow scheduling begins with the last stage—stage 3. Either PDS or MDS can be used for stage scheduling. We will use PDS in this example. A Gantt chart (similar to figure 3.9) is used to create a trial schedule for processor P_3.

Downstream finished-product inventories are then checked. The inventories may be displayed as a line graph of inventory versus time. A separate plot is needed for each finished product; however, several inventory plots can be displayed on one graph by using symbols or by color coding different products.

If the trial schedule yields unacceptable inventory levels for one or more products, a new schedule must be proposed and inventories checked. When a satisfactory schedule has been obtained for stage 3, the scheduling computations move to stage 2.

A similar processor-dominated scheduling procedure is used for stage 2. First, a Gantt chart is used to schedule P_2, and inventories are then checked with line graphs. If a problem (such as an inventory level below its target minimum level) surfaces, the schedule of P_2 is adjusted. Alternatively, the downstream schedule for P_3 or the forecast for the finished products may be revised.

When a satisfactory schedule is obtained for stages 2 and 3, stage 1 is scheduled. The procedure used in stages 2 and 3 is repeated for stage 1. Finally, the raw material inventories, I_0, are checked. If supply problems surface, the previously developed schedules and inventory projections must be revised.

Since the schedule was constructed by proceeding against the material flow from finished products to raw material, it is called reverse flow scheduling. This example also illustrates the use of processor-dominated scheduling at each stage. It should be noted that reverse flow scheduling can use MDS, PDS, or a combination of the two. Reverse flow scheduling is used by Scott Paper, Exxon Chemical, Sylvania Lighting, and Eastman Kodak/Kodak Park. Brief discussions of these cases are presented in chapter 4 and appendix A.

Forward Flow Scheduling

An alternative procedure, forward flow scheduling, begins with the initial processing step and forward schedules through the process structure. Therefore, it schedules in the same forward movement as material moves through each process step to becoming a final unit.

Initial observation suggests that forward flow scheduling is the least likely alternative to occur. However, firms that are severely limited in some way in the availability of key material are likely candidates for using this approach. Companies that process by-products produced by another company

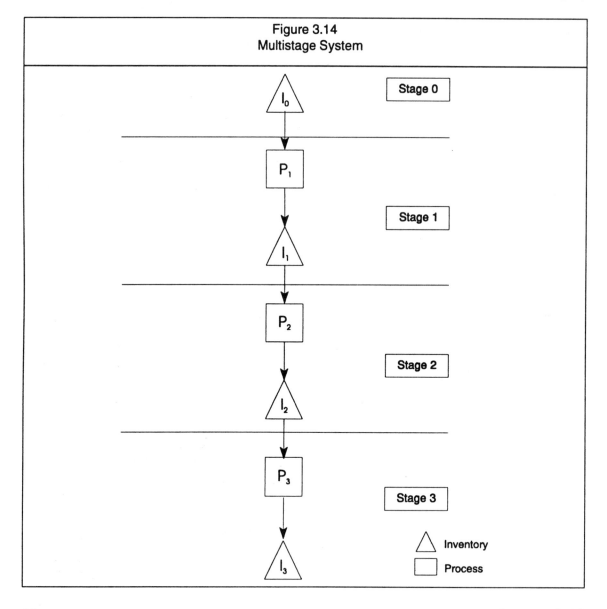

Figure 3.14
Multistage System

or food companies that are dependent upon a short harvest cycle are examples where forward scheduling makes sense. The EG & G case presented in chapter 4 illustrates forward flow scheduling. As with reverse flow scheduling, the forward flow schedule can be created using PDS, MDS, or a combination of approaches.

Mixed-Flow Scheduling

Mixed-flow scheduling combines forward and reverse flow scheduling concepts. Consider again the simple three-stage example process structure shown in figure 3.14. However, suppose that in this case process P_2 requires an expensive piece of equipment that is also a bottleneck. Efficient operation of the plant requires efficient utilization of this bottleneck process.

In order to efficiently use the bottleneck, P_2, it is scheduled first (see figure 3.16) using a Gantt chart. This PDS schedule pushes production into the buffer inventory represented by I_2. Stage 3 can now be scheduled using either PDS or MDS. We have chosen to illustrate MDS, which first develops a material plan for I_3 and then schedules the processor P_3.

The inventory I_2 is a reconciliation point. The PDS schedule for P_2 pushes production into I_2, while the

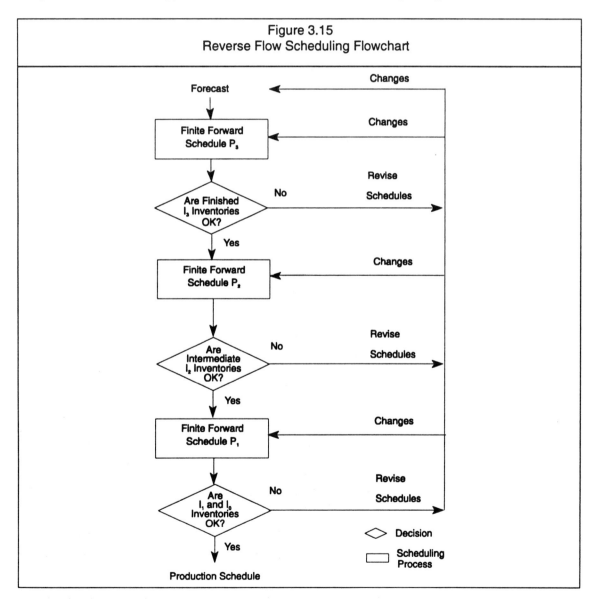

Figure 3.15
Reverse Flow Scheduling Flowchart

schedule for P_3 pulls material requirements from I_2. If the resulting inventory for any item in I_2 is below its minimum or above its maximum, adjustments will be required in the schedules for P_2 or P_3. Alternatively, the forecasted demand for the finished product, I_3, may be modified. Stage 1 and the raw materials in I_0 may be reverse flow scheduled after achieving an acceptable schedule for stages 2 and 3.

Since mixed-flow scheduling combines forward and reverse flow scheduling, forward scheduled production from an upstream stage must be reconciled with downstream material requirements at some time in the process structure. This reconciliation point is where *push* meets *pull*.

Armstrong, Coors Brewing, Eastman Kodak/Colorado, and Inland Steel use mixed-flow scheduling. These cases, which are discussed in chapter 4 and appendix A, illustrate many variations in mixed-flow scheduling. Additional detail on train scheduling procedures is given in chapter 9.

The three principles presented here form the foundation for all process flow scheduling systems. It should be noted that PFS is a general approach to scheduling, not a rigidly defined technique. Accord-

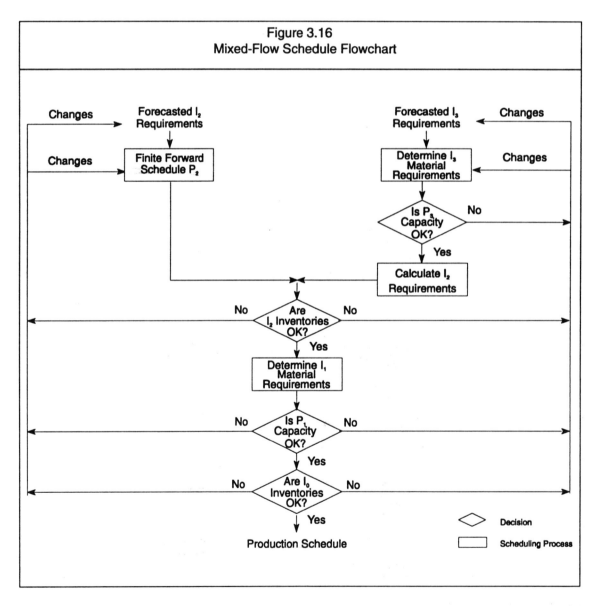

Figure 3.16
Mixed-Flow Schedule Flowchart

ingly, these principles can be implemented in many ways.

Summary

What has the reader been exposed to in this chapter? We began by presenting a short example to demonstrate the typical scheduling calculations used in a PFS environment. This simplistic example probably left the reader with many questions; e.g., what if this happened, or how do you react to this type of problem? At that point, we were attempting to provide a rough understanding rather than all-inclusive answers and approaches. We then summarized and discussed the basic principles upon which PFS is based, along with explanations of these ideas.

An understanding should be forming in your mind regarding the basic thrust and logic of PFS. Does it make sense? Does the structure of PFS fit into your manufacturing environment? If it does not, you may wish to turn your attention to reading material on MRP II or perhaps JIT. If PFS looks like it might fit but you are still not convinced, the next chapter provides specific case examples from companies you probably recognize. We hope that some of you have found that PFS makes sense and that someone is finally addressing your problems and speaking your language.

References

Bolander, S.F., and S.G. Taylor. 1990. Process flow scheduling: Mixed-flow cases. *Production and Inventory Management Journal* 31, no. 4:1–5.

Hubbard, D.T., S.G. Taylor, and S.F. Bolander. 1992. Process flow scheduling in a high-volume repetitive manufacturing environment. *Production and Inventory Management Journal* 33, no. 4: 21–26.

Taylor, S.G., and S.F. Bolander. 1990. Process flow scheduling: Basic cases. *Production and Inventory Management Journal* 31, no. 3:1–4.

Taylor, S.G., and S.F. Bolander. 1991. Process flow scheduling principles. *Production and Inventory Management Journal* 32, no. 1:67–71.

Chapter 4

Cases

This chapter presents brief overviews of the use of process flow scheduling in five companies. These cases illustrate similarities and differences in process flow scheduling applications and demonstrate the use of PFS in a wide range of process industries.

Another key point is the interactive nature of the scheduling calculations. Flowcharts of each plant's scheduling procedures show that PFS scheduling involves a trial-and-error simulation of alternative schedules until a satisfactory schedule is obtained. PFS systems are primarily concerned with obtaining a feasible schedule. In most PFS systems, optimization is a secondary objective.

These cases illustrate the full range of strategies for scheduling multiple stages. Exxon Chemical uses reverse flow scheduling, EG & G uses forward flow scheduling, and Kodak and Coors use mixed-flow scheduling. The last case, Simplot, illustrates single stage scheduling. After reading these cases and studying the associated process structures and scheduling flowcharts, you should understand these broad strategies for scheduling process trains. The details of process unit and process cluster scheduling, which will be covered in subsequent chapters, are omitted in these cases.

As you read these cases, note that we use the terms *stage* and *cluster* interchangeably. The usage fits, since there is only one cluster per stage in these cases. However, in later chapters the terms are not interchangeable.

Exxon Chemical

Exxon Chemical Company produces higher olefins, oxo alcohols, and plasticizers in its Baton Rouge, Louisiana, chemical plant. Figure 4.1 shows a simplified process flow for Exxon Chemical's intermediates plant. The process begins with the production and recovery of olefins from feed stocks obtained from Exxon's adjacent oil refinery. The olefins are converted to alcohols in stage 2, and the alcohols are converted to plasticizers in stage 3. Each stage is separated by inventories, which are stored in large tanks.

Process technology places some restrictions on plant scheduling. Products must be produced in a prescribed sequence based on molecular weights. Minimum run lengths (lot sizes) must be observed to meet quality specifications. Moreover, maximum run lengths also must be observed, or tanks will overflow. Other factors complicating scheduling are (1) availability of feed stock from the Exxon oil refinery, (2) the arrival of some feed stock in large marine (ship and barge) parcels, and (3) the need for occasional maintenance shutdowns for periods of more than two weeks.

Cases

Exxon Chemical uses a hierarchical planning and scheduling system with production plans driving production schedules. Figure 4.2 is a flowchart for the scheduling process. An interactive, reverse flow scheduling procedure develops rolling schedules over a four-month horizon.

A commercial finite scheduling package aids in preparing schedules. The software allows the scheduler to input a trial schedule in the form of a Gantt chart. The resulting impact on inventories is calculated and displayed on a line graph of inventory versus time. This graph can be used to determine whether inventories are above target minimums and below target maximums. The scheduling procedure is conceptually similar to the Polygoo example in chapter 3.

As shown in figure 4.2, the plasticizer stage is finite forward scheduled based upon product demands and available plasticizer production capacity. The scheduler ensures that adequate inventory is available to meet all product demands while fully utilizing plasticizer production capacity—i.e., the scheduler reconciles both the use of capacity and the availability of inventory. The finite schedule of the plasticizer stage then defines material requirements for the upstream alcohol stage. Once again, the scheduler finite schedules the alcohol stage, ensuring that alcohol inventories are adequate to meet downstream requirements of the plasticizer while not overloading storage capacities of the alcohol inventories. If problems occur at the alcohol stage, schedules may need to be adjusted at the plasticizer

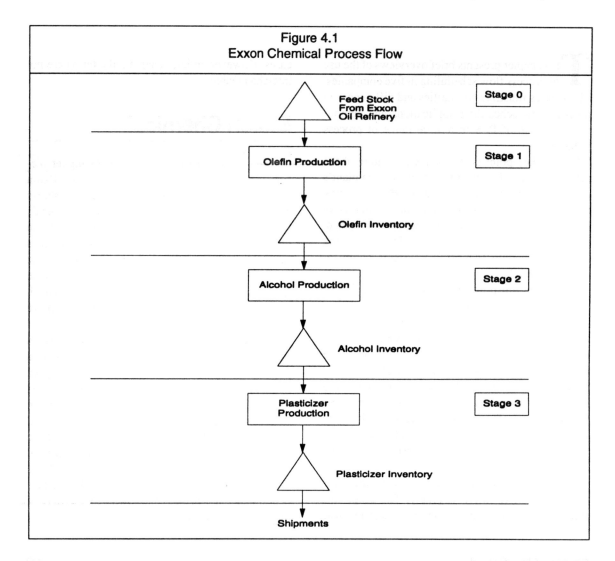

Figure 4.1
Exxon Chemical Process Flow

stage. This interactive stage-by-stage scheduling continues through all upstream stages.

Schedule infeasibilities may occur at any stage during the scheduling process. For example, suppose that a shortage of feed stock from the oil refinery occurs because of an unscheduled shutdown at the refinery. Adjustments will be necessary at the olefin production stage and may be required in all stages. In the worst case, a shortage of feed stock could impair the ability to meet finished product demand.

Points of interest regarding Exxon Chemical's scheduling practices are

- Gantt charts are used for finite forward scheduling each process stage with a processor-dominated scheduling procedure.
- A reverse flow scheduling procedure is used.

- Material and capacity are both planned at a stage before the next (upstream) stage is scheduled.
- The schedules are the authority to produce. Work orders and dispatch lists are not used.

This case illustrates reverse flow scheduling. The appendix gives three additional examples of reverse flow scheduling. The Scott Paper case is very similar to Exxon Chemical. Eastman Kodak/Kodak Park, illustrates reverse flow scheduling where two stages are scheduled using MRP. The Sylvania Lighting case shows how a repetitive manufacturer is using process flow scheduling. Another example of the use of PFS in repetitive manufacturing is given in Taylor and Bolander 1990. Let's now look at an example of forward flow scheduling.

EG & G: Rocky Flats Division

EG & G is an operating contractor managing the Department of Energy's Rocky Flats Plant in Colorado. The plant operates as an integral part of the weapons complex for the United States government. The process described in this case study recovers plutonium from by-product materials produced by other plant processes. These by-products vary in chemical makeup and concentrations; these variations affect processing and scheduling. Figure 4.3 provides an overview of the process flow, and figure 4.4 gives an overview of the scheduling system.

This process can be best characterized as a chemical recovery operation. In this process a key material in varying chemical states is recovered into a pure form that can be reused. However, available feed material, rather than demand for the finished product, drives the recovery process. Even when demand exists, the process does not operate if feed material is not available.

The scheduling process is a finite-capacity plan that schedules material availability for downstream process stages. Based on available input material, process rates are defined for the dissolution stage—stage 1 in figure 4.3. The dissolution stage is finitely scheduled. This schedule projects the amount of dissolved material that moves into downstream storage tanks and the amount of recycled material that

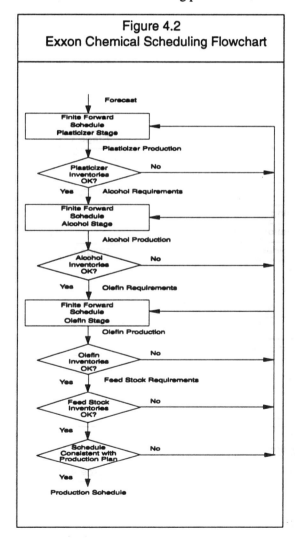

Figure 4.2
Exxon Chemical Scheduling Flowchart

is used again as input material. Since yield and chemical makeup vary, the material in the storage tanks is chemically analyzed. A blend of materials from the storage tanks is moved into the blending tanks, maintaining the plutonium concentration within an acceptable range. Because storage and blending tanks have limited capacity, downstream stages must be run. If the tanks reach their capacity limits, the dissolution stage is shut down.

After the material availability has been defined and the blend tanks have been scheduled, the precipitation process is finitely forward scheduled. This identifies the material flow to the calcination process. Since the precipitation and calcination processes are not decoupled, both processes must be operating in order to run either. They are therefore treated as a single stage for scheduling purposes.

Following the calcination process, the calcined material (now in a solid form) is stored in inventory, decoupling the calcination stage from the fluorination stage. Because of operational problems, the fluorination stage is never run at the same time as the calcination stage. These stages are normally run during alternate weeks. Using available inventories, the fluorination stage is finitely forward scheduled based upon the flow rates for this process. A time-phased plan of projected fluorinated material inventory is created from this schedule. If the strict limits on storage quantities are exceeded, the preceding stage(s) must be shut down.

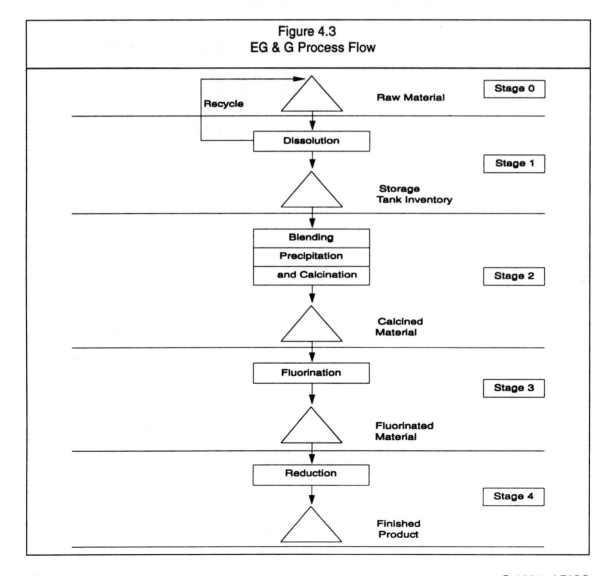

Figure 4.3
EG & G Process Flow

The final stage, reduction, is scheduled in the same manner as the earlier stages. Available fluorinated material is finitely scheduled against reduction's capacity, and output of finished product is projected.

Once the schedules have been completed for each stage, they can be used to generate requirements for support materials needed at each process stage. In addition, employee assignments must be made to support the schedules. If employee limits are vio-

lated, the production schedules must be revised to live within these constraints.

EG & G's scheduling system illustrates several key process flow scheduling concepts:

- The process structure guides the scheduling calculations.
- The stages are finitely scheduled using processor-dominated scheduling. Material and capacity are reconciled for each stage before the next stage is scheduled.
- A forward flow procedure is used to schedule the process train. Scheduling begins with the initial stage; successive stages in the process train are then scheduled until the final stage has been scheduled.
- Secondary resource requirements (support material and labor) are calculated after the equipment and primary material schedules have been developed.

Forward flow scheduling *pushes* material through a process train. An example of forward flow scheduling for an agricultural chemical manufacturer is given in Bolander and Taylor 1983. Some food processors also use forward flow scheduling to schedule the processing of agricultural products that must be processed in conjunction with the harvest season. In all these cases, the production schedules are decoupled from short-range demands for finished products. In these operations production schedules are driven by (1) availability of a raw material that must be processed quickly and/or (2) a production plan that requires a large buildup of finished product before a highly seasonal demand.

The previous two examples illustrated reverse flow and forward flow scheduling. The next two cases, which use a mixed-flow strategy, illustrate another common approach used by many companies. Because of differences in manufacturing and marketing environments, different mixed-flow strategies exist.

Eastman Kodak: Colorado Division

Eastman Kodak's Colorado Division manufactures high-volume photographic films using a process illustrated in figure 4.5. Raw materials include purchases from vendors as well as stock transfers

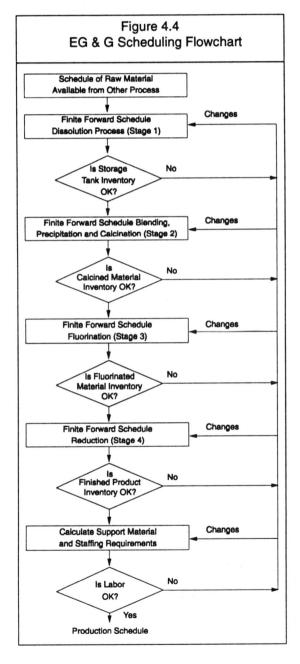

Figure 4.4
EG & G Scheduling Flowchart

from other Kodak plants. The first stage is the preparation of chemicals, emulsions, and support. The second stage is the film-coating operation. The final stage is the finishing operation, where full-width coated rolls are processed to customer configurations and then packaged.

Figure 4.6 describes the scheduling procedures. Scheduling begins in stage 2 by creating a finite capacity schedule for the film coater. Plant schedules and operations center on efficient utilization of the coater. Products are sequenced in product families through the coater in economic production lot sizes. The production sequence depends on process technology. The coater schedule pulls material from chemical, emulsion, and support inventories and pushes material to full-width coated roll inventories.

The second scheduling step develops material and capacity schedules for the finishing area, which is stage 3. The item-level forecast for finished products pulls material out of finished-goods inventory. The need to replenish finished-goods inventories drives the production schedule for finishing operations. In a manner similar to MRP, materials are scheduled first, and capacity requirements are then reviewed.

Next, the material schedule developed in stage 3 is checked against the availability of product in full-width coated roll inventory. The finishing schedule pulls material from the full-width coated roll inventory while the coater schedule pushes material into the full-width coated roll inventory. Conceptually, this is where push meets pull. If the inventory is above target maximums or below target minimums,

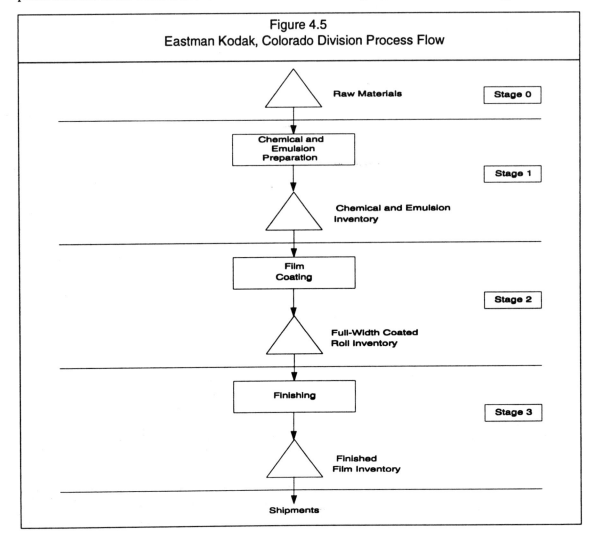

Figure 4.5
Eastman Kodak, Colorado Division Process Flow

the trial finishing or coating schedules must be revised. In some situations, the forecast must also be revised.

After feasible material and capacity schedules for stages 2 and 3 are developed, schedules are developed for stage 1, the chemical and emulsion preparation area. The material requirements needed to execute the coater schedule drive these schedules. Commercial MRP software is used in developing material and capacity schedules for this stage, which operates as a specialty chemical job shop. Upstream raw material inventories and downstream chemical and emulsion inventories are checked against target minimums and maximums. If problems are found, schedules are revised until a satisfactory schedule is obtained.

Kodak's scheduling system illustrates several points:

- Process flow guides scheduling calculations.
- The film coater stage (stage 2) is scheduled before upstream and downstream stages. This results in a mixed-flow scheduling approach.
- Material and capacity are planned for each stage before proceeding to plan another stage.
- The film-coating stage schedules capacity before material to use capital-intensive equipment efficiently. Since the processor (film coater) is scheduled before materials, this is another example of processor-dominated scheduling.

The Armstrong World Industries case (in appendix A) illustrates a similar mixed-flow scheduling

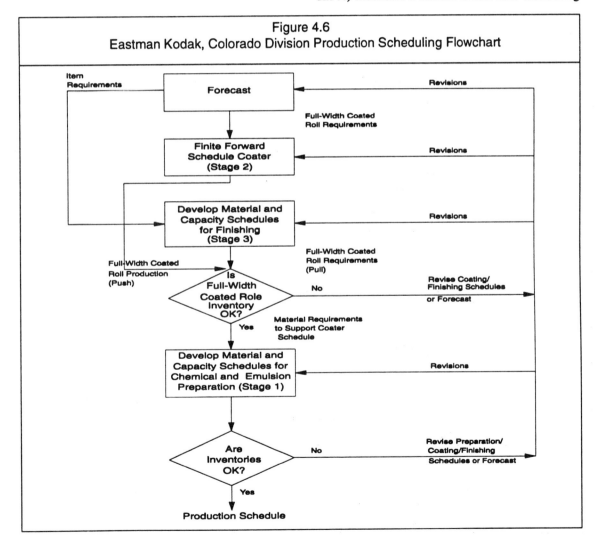

Figure 4.6
Eastman Kodak, Colorado Division Production Scheduling Flowchart

approach. The Armstrong and Kodak Colorado plants both have a capital-intensive process stage at an internal position in the process flow. Efficient scheduling of this internal stage is critical for efficient plant operations. Thus, the critical internal stages are scheduled first. The Inland Steel case, also presented in appendix A, illustrates a similar mixed-flow scheduling approach, but in a make-to-order environment.

Kodak (Colorado Division), Armstrong, and Inland Steel all use a mixed-flow scheduling logic that begins by scheduling an internal stage and then moves outward to schedule the initial and final stages. We call this an *inside-out* mixed-flow scheduling procedure. Let's now look at a different mixed-flow strategy.

Coors Brewing Company

Coors Brewing Company brews and packages seven brands of beer, distributing them worldwide in about 400 packaged products. Figure 4.7 presents the flow of materials in Coors' brewing and packaging facility in Golden, Colorado. Raw materials are combined in a malting and brewing process to produce wort, which is fermented in tanks. When fermentation is complete, the product is transferred to aging tanks. From the aging tanks, the product is blended to achieve desired alcohol content, filtered, and moved to a finishing facility. The beer is then packaged in cans, bottles, or kegs and distributed.

The planning and scheduling focus of the stages (shown in figure 4.8) varies in content and approach.

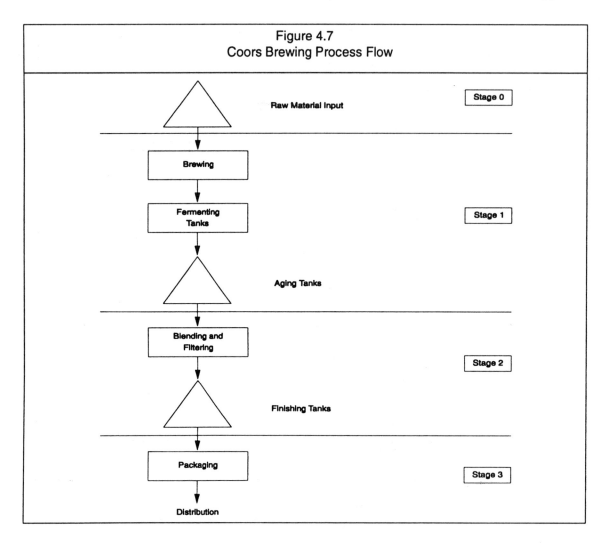

Figure 4.7
Coors Brewing Process Flow

Stage 1, the brewing stage, is scheduled as a make-to-stock operation using a custom-built, internally programmed scheduling package. Brand forecasts are used to create schedules for the brewing stage. Brewing requirements, which include seasonal buildups of product, are finitely loaded on the seven brew lines. Particular attention is paid to inventory distribution among the brands to ensure an acceptable product mix. Completion of each brew forward schedules the needs of fermentation tanks. Completion of fermentation, likewise, forward schedules the need for aging tanks. Therefore, the brewing schedule defines the downstream tank requirements for fermentation and aging. Inventory mixes are continuously evaluated, and brewing schedules are changed when inventories are too small or too large.

Packaging, a make-to-order schedule, drives the other stages. Although exceptions do exist, most package types are scheduled for production every week. Orders accumulated during the previous week are finitely loaded against the available packaging lines. Particular attention is paid to product sequences (which can result in major or minor setups) and line rates while trying to load truck and railcars directly from the packaging lines. This packaging schedule defines the brands and the volumes of each that must be blended. If the blending stage can support the packaging schedule, the packaging schedule is finalized, packaging crews are assigned, transportation to distribute the product is arranged, and packaging material schedules are finalized. If any of the above material or capacity requirements cannot be met, the schedules are reworked until a

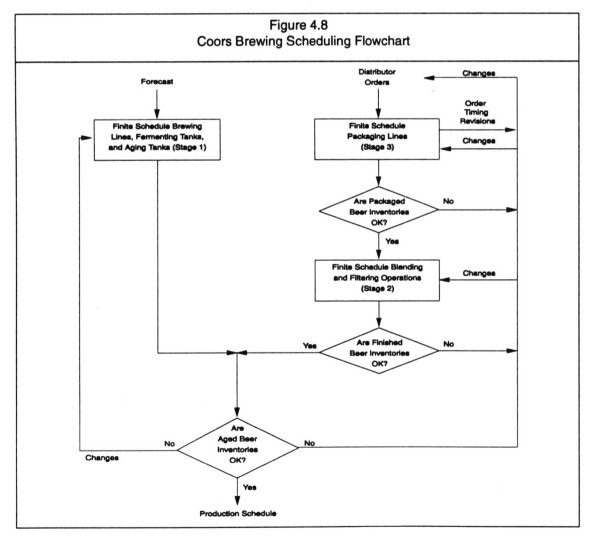

Figure 4.8
Coors Brewing Scheduling Flowchart

feasible plan is developed. As a last resort, customer orders are placed on allocation.

The Coors scheduling process is also interactive. In the short run, scheduling conflicts between brewing and packaging result in scheduling changes on the packaging lines. Lead times in brewing prevent short-run changes in the brewing schedule.

Coors Brewing illustrates an *outside-in* mixed-flow scheduling logic. At Coors Brewing, scheduling begins at each end of the process structure and converges at the aged beer inventories. Here the *push* from brewing meets the *pull* from customer orders. The outside-in scheduling procedure allows decoupling of the long-lead-time brewing operations from the short-lead-time, order-driven blending and packaging operations. Note also that the decoupling occurs at a point in the process flow where there is a significant increase in the number of items—relatively few brands are produced; however, several hundred products are sold because of variations in packaging.

The Coors scheduling system illustrates several process flow scheduling concepts:

- The process structure guides schedules.
- Processor-dominated scheduling is used in all stages.
- An outside-in, mixed-flow procedure is used.
- A combination of forward flow and reverse flow scheduling is used to schedule the process trains. The upstream schedules *push* material into aged beer inventories using a forward flow scheduling procedure that is driven by the production plan. The downstream schedules use reverse flow scheduling to *pull*

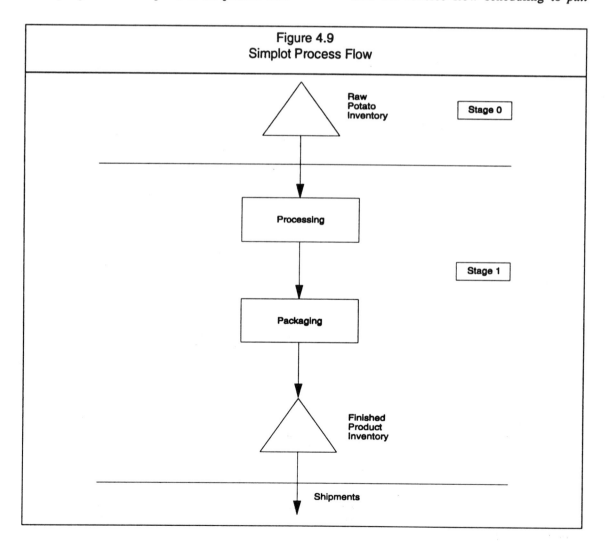

Figure 4.9
Simplot Process Flow

through the final production stages based on customer orders.

Our final case illustrates still another variation of process flow scheduling. The J.R. Simplot Company has a single stage, but still uses process flow scheduling principles.

Simplot

The J.R. Simplot Company processes raw potatoes into a variety of frozen potato products. The Northwest (Idaho and Oregon) potato processing operations have four plants with a total of 24 production lines. Figure 4.9 shows the process flow for a typical line. Raw potatoes are first processed through a sequence of operations including skin removal, cutting, blanching, frying, and freezing. The processed potatoes are immediately packaged without being stored in a bulk processed form. This results in a single-stage process train, which can be scheduled as a single unit.

A production plan, developed with the aid of a mathematical programming model, guides Simplot's production schedules. The production plan covers a seven-month planning horizon. The plan specifies the amount of each product family that will be produced on each production line for each month.

The production schedules use the product assignments and volumes from the production plan to develop detailed schedules for each line. Figure 4.10 gives an overview of the production scheduling process.

Scheduling begins with a quick check to determine if any finished products are out of stock. A custom finite forward scheduling program is used to schedule all production lines for a three-week scheduling horizon. The schedule shows the cases of each item to be produced and the sequence of production. A Gantt chart, which shows the four-hour interval in which an item is scheduled to be produced, provides schedule visualization.

The scheduled production quantities are then used to simulate inventories over the next three weeks. The weeks-of-sales coverage for each item is calculated and used to determine if inventories are balanced. When inventory problems are identified, the line schedules are changed. This iterative process continues until the schedule is satisfactory.

Several features of Simplot's system are worth mentioning:

- PFS principles apply to single-stage systems.
- Finite forward scheduling is used to schedule the single processing stage. In this processor-dominated scheduling technique, the processor is scheduled before materials. Note, however, that a quick check for stockouts is made before scheduling the production lines.
- Because some products are produced on more than one production line, trial production schedules are developed for *all* lines before inventories are checked.
- Reverse flow scheduling is used. Stage 1 is scheduled first, and then raw potato requirements are calculated for stage 0.

Analysis

The five cases presented above, the five additional cases in appendix A, our experience, and discussions

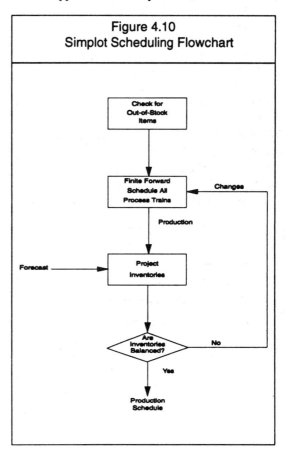

Figure 4.10
Simplot Scheduling Flowchart

Cases

with many others in the process industries have helped us form some tentative conclusions regarding the nature of PFS applications. These conclusions are listed in table 4.1.

Our first conclusion is that PFS applies in a wide variety of industries. The five plants discussed above and the five plants discussed in appendix A produce a variety of products, ranging from paper, light bulbs, food, and film to industrial chemicals, steel, building products, and plutonium. However, note that all 10 plants use flow manufacturing concepts, and their operations can be described with a process flow diagram.

Finite forward scheduling is used frequently in PFS systems. All 10 plants use finite forward scheduling in one or more process stages. Finite forward scheduling is effective for scheduling flow shop production in least-cost sequences and within finite capacity limits.

We also note that PFS may use different scheduling techniques in different stages. For example, the Kodak (Colorado Division) plant uses MRP for two stages and finite forward scheduling for the bottleneck stage. Again, PFS provides the logic that links the stage schedules together.

Another conclusion is that PFS may be used with MRP or as a stand-alone system. Sylvania and Armstrong, both of which are included in appendix A, use MRP as a raw material planning system and PFS for plant scheduling. Both Kodak plants use MRP for scheduling those stages in a PFS system that are job shops. Thus, PFS is a multistage scheduling philosophy at Kodak, while MRP is a single-stage scheduling technique. In contrast, Scott Paper, Exxon Chemical, EG & G, Coors Brewing, Inland Steel, and Simplot use PFS concepts without MRP

for the operations described in this chapter and the appendix.

It is interesting to note that all 10 plants reconcile material and capacity within a stage before beginning to schedule the next stage. Decoupling inventories between stages provides natural points for decomposing the train scheduling problem into a set of simpler single-stage problems. Since this stage-by-stage reconciliation appears to be quite common, we have been tempted to suggest it as a fourth PFS principle. However, we believe that some multistage scheduling techniques may be in use. Moreover, we believe that future developments will lead to the implementation of multistage scheduling systems.

Finally, we observe that PFS principles apply to single-stage systems as well as multistage systems. A single-stage system, such as that shown for Simplot in figure 4.9, has only two inventories and one processor. We use the term *single stage* in this type of situation because there is only one complete stage—stage 1. Note, however, that there is also an inventory in stage 0, but no processor.

Single-stage systems can be scheduled with reverse flow or forward flow procedures. Reverse flow scheduling schedules stage 1 before checking the stage 0 inventories. Forward flow scheduling first schedules the arrival of stage 0 materials and then schedules their processing in stage 1. Accordingly, PFS principles apply to single-stage systems: The process structure guides scheduling calculations, the stage may be scheduled using material-dominated or processor-dominated scheduling approaches, and forward or reverse flow scheduling may be used.

In analyzing the 10 plants, we have developed several reasons for using PFS. We expect this list,

Table 4.1 General Conclusions
• PFS principles apply in a wide variety of process industries.
• Finite forward scheduling is frequently used in PFS systems.
• Different process stages may use different scheduling techniques.
• PFS may be used with MRP or as an independent system.
• Material and capacity are generally reconciled within a stage before the next stage is scheduled.
• Although single-stage systems are relatively simple, PFS principles still apply.

Table 4.2
Reasons for Using PFS

- Use stage capacity efficiently
- Schedule in a natural production sequence
- Decompose a large scheduling problem into several smaller problems
- Eliminate work orders
- Adjust for mix-dependent production rates in sequential stages
- Resequence jobs through sequential stages

given in table 4.2, to grow as the concept of PFS is developed further.

One reason for using PFS is to use stage capacities efficiently. All 10 companies use finite forward scheduling (a processor-dominated scheduling approach) to help obtain high-capacity utilization of the processors in a particular stage. In addition, Kodak Colorado's and Armstrong's scheduling systems use mixed-flow scheduling procedures to place the highest priority on efficient utilization of the bottleneck stage.

A second reason for using PFS is to facilitate the development of schedules in natural sequences. These sequences may be based on molecular weights (Exxon Chemical), color (Scott Paper), widths (Inland Steel), or other factors. Sequences are easily scheduled using finite forward scheduling, which, as noted in the general conclusions, is often used in a PFS system.

Another reason for using PFS is to simplify scheduling calculations. PFS breaks a large train scheduling problem into a set of smaller stage scheduling problems. Kodak's plants illustrate this by decoupling the emulsion, coating, and finishing stages. A single MRP system could be used to schedule all stages simultaneously, but this would create difficulties in scheduling coater capacity.

Another way PFS simplifies scheduling is by reducing the *hidden factory* of computers and paperwork that processes transactions. If PFS is used without MRP, work orders can be eliminated. As noted before, six of the ten plants did not use MRP, and the schedules were the authority to produce.

In some situations PFS is used to help adjust for mix-dependent production rates in sequential stages.

This situation was noted for Inland, where inventories were used to buffer the stages from each other in order to facilitate high equipment utilization.

One last situation where PFS proves useful is when jobs must be scheduled in different orders through two sequential stages. Inland also illustrates this use of PFS to accommodate different sequences in the steel-making stage and the subsequent rolling stages.

Summary

PFS principles are being used by flow manufacturing firms. Only recently have these principles been recognized and documented. The cases in this chapter indicate that PFS is a useful and flexible paradigm that explains how many flow manufacturing firms approach scheduling. Several tentative conclusions have been reached on the applicability, nature, use, and rationale for PFS systems.

References

Bolander, S.F., and S.G. Taylor. 1983. Time-phased forward scheduling: A capacity dominated scheduling technique. *Production and Inventory Management* 24, no. 1:83–97.

Taylor, S.G., and S.F. Bolander. 1990. Process flow scheduling: Practice and concepts. *American Production and Inventory Control Society 33rd International Conference Proceedings.* 390–392.

Chapter 5

System Framework for Process Flow Industries

Our previous discussions of PFS have focused on the detailed issues surrounding the concepts. However, it is also important that the reader recognize that PFS typically exists in an overall structure that differs from more traditional MRP II structures. In other words, the overall planning and scheduling framework is different. While it might be argued that the basic decisions made by any business are similar, the specific focus of the decisions and location of where those decisions are made does change. As we worked with many of the companies documented in this book, it was our experience that their planning and scheduling frameworks differed from the MRP II systems previously documented. Therefore, in order to provide the reader with an understanding of the structure within which PFS typically operates, it is important to document this framework.

Manufacturing literature abounds with systems frameworks. These integrated systems are often called *manufacturing resource planning* or *MRP II* systems. A traditional example of an MRP II framework is given in Wight 1981. A process industry variation of an MRP II framework was developed in an APICS Process Industry SIG-sponsored workshop. This framework was documented in 1981 by Taylor, Seward, Bolander, and Heard (1981a and 1981b).

While these MRP II frameworks have been adopted by many companies, it appears that many firms are using other methods. In previous chapters we referred to a study compiled by Plant-Wide Research Corporation indicating that only 13 percent of U.S. process manufacturers use MRP II systems (Foley 1988). While this data does not include custom MRP II systems or extensively customized MRP II packages, one is definitely left with the impression that many firms use something other than MRP II. The objective of this chapter is to present a framework that better fits many high-volume flow manufacturing firms.

The previous chapters have documented the planning and scheduling practices of some high-volume flow manufacturers. Chapters 1, 2, and 3 provided generalized results, and chapter 4 gave specific examples. This chapter extends the work on process flow scheduling and proposes a framework for high-volume flow manufacturers. We begin by presenting the process flow framework and then summarize the results of a survey that was used to validate the proposed framework.

Process Flow Systems Framework

Figure 5.1 describes a systems framework for process flow industries. This framework includes elements that are similar to the MRP II framework presented by Taylor, Seward, Bolander, and Heard (1981b). The MRP II framework provided for both hierarchical and operational integration of production and inventory plans. Hierarchical integration of the plans is concerned with integrating long-, intermediate-, and short-range plans. In contrast, operational integration is concerned with integrating plans through the entire material flow—from raw materials through all intermediate stages of in-process inventories, ending with finished product delivery.

Within this MRP II structure, the highest level of aggregation was in the resource requirements plan

that developed strategic plans for acquiring the resources necessary for future operations. Intermediate-range plans were concerned with planning the use of resources over an annual or quarterly budget period. And short-range, detailed planning specified what was required, when it should be produced, and where it should be produced. Throughout this MRP II framework, the hierarchical structure was based upon the product structure: production planning, master scheduling, material planning, capacity planning, material control, and capacity control.

The PFS framework (figure 5.1) retains the basic hierarchical structure of the prior framework, except the new hierarchy is based on the process structure instead of the product structure. Long-range forecasts are used in developing strategic resource requirements plans, intermediate-range forecasts are used to develop tactical production plans, and short-range forecasts and customer orders are used to develop detailed operating schedules. In designing

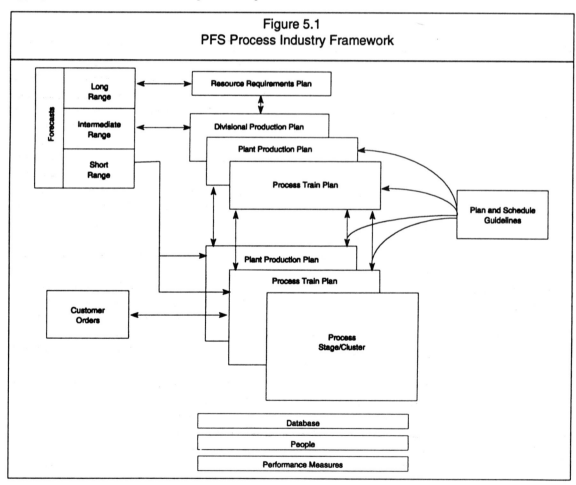

Figure 5.1
PFS Process Industry Framework

the forecasting system, many issues need to be resolved. Among these are such issues as the required level of product and geographic detail, the time horizon, the time intervals, and the frequency of forecast updates. Alternative forecasting techniques can be used; these should be selected based upon the technique's accuracy and cost. Further consideration should be given to the ability to integrate managerial judgment and market intelligence with the quantitative approach used by the forecasting technique. And finally, the organizational structure must motivate sales and marketing personnel to provide detailed and accurate judgments and to clearly define who is responsible for maintaining a valid and responsive forecasting system.

Data and people are the foundation on which the system is built and the performance of all activities is measured. The foundation of a planning and scheduling system is an educated, trained work force whose members are responsible for developing, operating, and maintaining an effective and efficient planning/scheduling and control system. Because inventories typically represent more than 20 percent of a company's assets and the schedule's development and execution are critical linkages to customers, it becomes imperative that professional personnel have the proper training and tools to perform their jobs.

Furthermore, the performance of each module and of the overall system should be monitored and controlled. Data must therefore be collected for measurable attributes, and that actual performance must be compared to standards. Deviations may be corrected by education, training, improved techniques, and more accurate and timely planning data. These modules are similar in both the MRP II framework and the PFS framework. But here is where the similarities stop. Let's now look at the planning and scheduling modules in detail.

Process Structure Guides Plans and Schedules

The PFS framework uses the process structure to guide planning and scheduling tasks. This structure, discussed to some extent in earlier chapters, consists of divisions, plants, process trains, stages, clusters,

and units, as figures 5.2 and 5.3 show. A corporate or company division consists of plants and process trains. Divisions are parts of a company that produce a group of related products. Below the divisions are plants, which compete with each other for their share of the division's products and production. Each plant may be further divided into process trains. These process trains, often called production lines, may produce finished product or intermediate products that are used by another plant or process train.

As figure 5.3 indicates, a process train is a sequential series of processing equipment that produces a family of related products. These products are produced along a routing defined by the process train. Different process trains may produce common products and consume common raw materials during production. While material is normally not transferred between process trains, exceptions to this rule exist in some companies.

Each process train can be further divided into process stages. Process trains may have one stage or multiple stages. If multiple stages exist, each stage must be decoupled from other stages in the process train. This decoupling is accomplished with inventory, which allows each process to be scheduled as a separate entity with different lot sizes and production sequences. In contrast, if materials flowing between two stages are only separated by small surge stocks, the processes should probably be scheduled as a single entity and viewed as a process cluster within a single stage. Therefore, a process cluster is the entity that is actually scheduled; it represents one or more process steps within a stage.

A process train would ideally have only one stage. This would allow materials to flow continuously through the process train—thus conforming to JIT principles. However, many firms have "rocks" that are simply not economical to remove. Consider, for example, the Inland Steel case. The first stage, steel making, bases sequences on alloy chemistry and produces slabs for intermediate stock. The second stage, hot rolling, sequences operations based on coil widths. We would like to eliminate the inventory of slabs that decouples steel making from hot rolling. However, most steel mills are unable to run the same production order sequence in steel making and hot rolling. Thus, decoupling intermediate inventory allows each process to be run independently and more efficiently.

In some situations, this decoupling inventory is similar to the buffering approach suggested by the theory of constraints (TOC) (Goldratt and Cox 1986) and synchronous manufacturing philosophies (Umble and Srikanth 1990). These philosophies suggest placing buffers in front of the constraining operation to ensure that the constraint is fully utilized. In addition, schedules for nonconstraints are then subordinated to the constraint schedule to synchronize operations.

Finally, process clusters are at the lowest level of the process structure. Internal to a process stage are one or more process clusters. The process cluster represents the scheduling entity. This entity may be a single unit, multiple units in parallel, or even multiple units in series. Units within the cluster are typically not separated by inventory, and the cluster is therefore scheduled as a single entity. Processes within the cluster may have similar or dissimilar processing capabilities, but they are coupled by shar-

ing common input or output materials. Material is not transferred between parallel process units within the same cluster. A process unit is typically a single piece of equipment or a series of closely coupled pieces of equipment; i.e., a process cluster. Parallel units within a stage may perform similar tasks—for example, parallel packaging lines. However, process units may also perform different operations. For example, a process stage may consist of a plastic molding operation and an ingredient blending operation that are combined in the next stage, a filling operation. Chapters 6, 7, and 8 include more detailed discussions of various types of clusters and how they can be scheduled.

Furthermore, each process cluster/unit may be operated in one or more ways. Each different way of operating is called an activity. Activities may differ by outputs, by inputs, or by operating rates. For example, a reactor may produce different molecular weights of a polymer from the same monomer, a

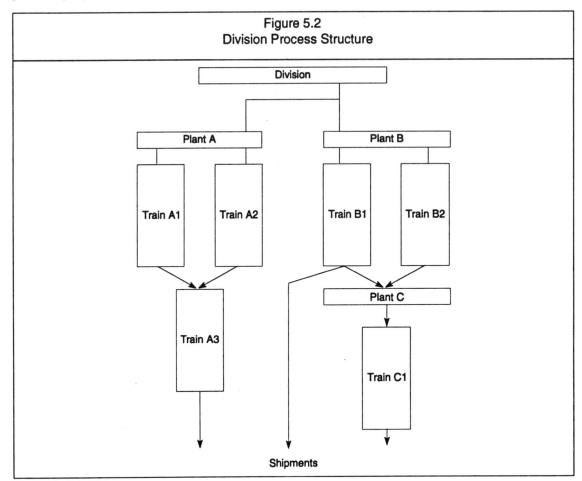

Figure 5.2
Division Process Structure

blender may produce gasoline using different blends of input components, and the time required to cook ingredients may vary with the raw material's physical or chemical characteristics, thereby affecting cooker capacity and energy consumption.

Production Planning

Production planning uses a hierarchical decision-making approach that is guided by the structure of divisions, plants, and trains. As figure 5.1 shows, production planning begins with developing division plans. In a multiplant environment, these divisional plans are developed at the corporate level with possible plant consultations.

Table 5.1 lists typical division planning decisions. These include aggregate plans for material, equipment, labor, energy, and any other critical resources.

The plans, linked to annual business plans, generally have monthly or quarterly time intervals and cover a range of one to two years. Resource levels are set to match demand expectations, and products are assigned to plants based upon costs, quality, customer service, and labor considerations.

In some commodity industries, products may be exchanged (chemical industry terminology) or swapped (primary metals terminology). Exchange or swapping agreements between two producers provide for exchanging product at different locations or at different times. Location exchanges provide mutually advantageous savings in transportation costs, and time exchanges allow for coverage during major maintenance downtimes without building large inventories. Also, long-term supply contracts for critical raw materials are negotiated and strategies formulated.

Finally, capacity shortage or excess strategies are formulated to handle different demand conditions.

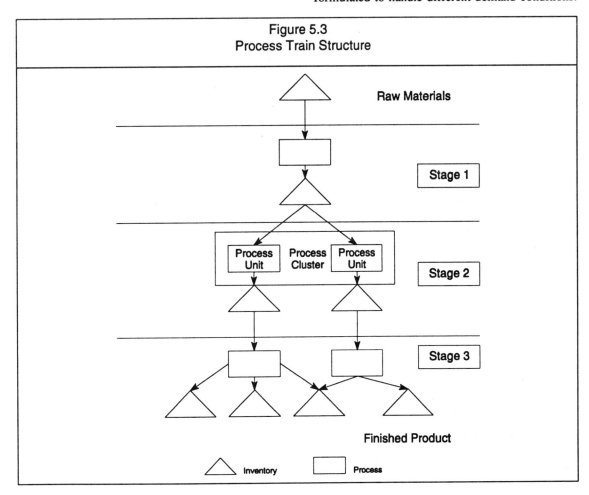

Figure 5.3
Process Train Structure

Raw Materials

Stage 1

Process Unit — Process Cluster — Process Unit

Stage 2

Stage 3

Finished Product

△ Inventory   ☐ Process

Table 5.1
Division Production Plans

- Product assignment between plants
- Division seasonality and resource plans
- Product mix and demand allocations among plants
- Product exchange agreements
- Raw materials contracts
- Capacity excess or shortage strategies

If demand exceeds capacity, for example, companies may select any of several actions, including subcontracting, placing customers on product allocation, or increasing overtime. If capacity exceeds demand, the company may choose from such alternatives as shutting down a line, temporarily closing a plant, or throttling output rates.

Following the formulation of division production plans, more details are added in the plant and process train plans. Decisions for plant plans and process train plans may be centralized at the divisional level or decentralized and made at the plant level. Selection of a centralized or decentralized approach is typically based upon management philosophies of control that exist in the corporate offices or is based upon the sophistication of the analytical tools used at the corporate offices. More sophisticated analytical tools, such as linear programming or simulation, may allow for a rapid evaluation of an integrated environment. This integrated evaluation would be more difficult if alternative strategies were evaluated from the plant level.

Also, a set of planning and scheduling guidelines is developed in collaboration between the plants and division headquarters. These guidelines provide targets for inventories, run lengths, sequences, and other areas that will be discussed later. Figure 5.1 shows that the plant production plan, the process train plan, and the planning and scheduling guidelines could be developed at either the division or the plant level.

Plant and process train plans disaggregate division plans into smaller time intervals and more process detail. The plant planning issues are summarized in table 5.2. The fundamental decision in multitrain plants is the assignment of products and demand to individual process trains based on operating costs, throughput, and quality issues.

Division plans, such as seasonal strategies, are integrated into plant production plans. Maintenance plans also become important in the plant plan since plants typically operate 24 hours a day, 7 days a week, and can perform maintenance only when the operations are shut down. Finally, plans may also be required for labor, energy, waste materials, or by-product production that are needed to support production plans or may alter them.

Process train plans can now be formulated. Table 5.3 summarizes goals of these plans. Product routing assignments and scheduling strategies to ensure quality product for each train are defined. Process trains may be scheduled independently if product demand is dedicated, or they may be scheduled concurrently if product demand is allocated to

---

Table 5.2
Plant Production Plans

- Assign product and demand to process trains
- Implement division strategies for seasonal production
- Integrate maintenance plans
- Integrate labor, energy, waste and by-product production

Table 5.3
Process Train Plans

- Define product routings and quality requirements
- Establish specific scheduling strategies for the process train
- Identify crew assignments
- Identify material requirements
- Match demand to output within defined inventory limits

---

multiple trains. Specific scheduling strategies must be formulated for how the train is to be scheduled; i.e., reverse flow scheduling, forward flow scheduling, or mixed-flow scheduling approaches. This will involve identifying constraints, make-to-order versus make-to-stock issues, and such other operating characteristics as run length and product switching requirements. Crew assignments are made, and line shutdowns or other throttling strategies that reduce product output are implemented. Material requirements are planned as required by the process train plans. Finally, specific demand patterns are matched to process train output plans to maintain inventory balances within defined target minimum and maximum guidelines.

After developing division plans and process train plans (or perhaps while developing these plans), guidelines are developed for detailed production scheduling. Table 5.4 describes these guidelines. Lot-sizing models, sequencing algorithms, statistical safety stock models, and simulation models are used to set these guidelines. These guidelines provide a foundation that schedulers will use on a daily basis as they develop operating schedules.

Production Scheduling

Production scheduling disaggregates the plant and process train plans into schedules with sufficient time, process, and product detail for execution by the direct labor work force. The schedules are issued to the operators and become the authority to produce. Work orders are typically not used or needed. As figure 5.1 shows, scheduling inputs are short-range forecasts and customer orders, plant and process train plans, and scheduling guidelines. These inputs form the basis for developing process stage schedules and process cluster schedules.

Process stage/cluster schedules translate product demands, process characteristics, and scheduling guidelines into specific schedules. If multiple process clusters exist at a process stage, each individual cluster must also be scheduled. If only one process unit exists, process stage scheduling and process cluster scheduling become the same thing.

Process stage/cluster schedules specify run times or run quantities for each product produced in a stage over the scheduling horizon. Scheduling wheels, which are discussed in chapter 3, represent a common approach used in developing these stage/cluster

---

Table 5.4
Scheduling Guidelines

- Target campaign cycle lengths
- Target run lengths by process and product produced
- Target sequences by process
- Target minimum and maximum inventories
- Target customer service levels
- Product switching strategies

---

schedules. Many times, scheduling begins at the critical resource stage. Upstream and downstream stages are scheduled after scheduling the critical resource unit using reverse flow, forward flow, or mixed-flow scheduling. In addition, production sequences are defined, production run lengths are set, and switching strategies are incorporated in a time-phased processor schedule for each stage/cluster. Time-phased schedules for input material, output production, by-product production, crew assignments, and waste output can be developed using these stage/cluster schedules. As explained and discussed in earlier chapters, this process stage/cluster schedule may use either processor-dominated scheduling (PDS) or material-dominated scheduling (MDS) approaches.

Production scheduling creates several outputs. The primary output is a schedule for each process stage/cluster. Different systems display these schedules in many different formats. One such format is the Gantt chart, which is used in most commercial finite scheduling software. Other types of manual schedules or related spreadsheet outputs may also be used. Another output is an inventory projection for each product, which typically is in the format of a line graph of inventory versus time.

Complementing the proposed schedules are graphic displays or exception reports that highlight schedule violations. Since production scheduling is concerned primarily with finding an acceptable and feasible schedule, violations may be either unacceptable or acceptable. Examples of unacceptable violations would include a schedule that produced too much and overflowed a tank. An acceptable violation might be producing product out of the normal sequence, resulting in higher operating costs but meeting customer demands. Other violations might include orders shipped late, inventories above target maximums or below target minimums, run lengths not consistent with guidelines, and materials not available to support production.

Scheduling is done much more frequently and in greater detail than production planning. Schedulers live in a world of rush orders, canceled orders, forecast errors, late supplier deliveries, equipment breakdowns, off-specification product, power outages, and other events that require operations to be rescheduled frequently.

Contrasting the Frameworks

Some significant differences set the PFS framework apart from MRP II frameworks. First, the PFS framework disaggregates by process structure: divisions, plants, trains, stages, clusters, and units. In contrast, MRP II frameworks disaggregate by product structure: product families, final assemblies, subassemblies, and parts.

Second, divisional production planning for PFS companies takes on a different dimension than for MRP II companies. Because many companies operate in a multiplant/multiwarehouse environment, division plans require that allocations be made among the multiple facilities. Therefore, there must be a greater level of analysis of costs, quality capabilities, throughput rates, and capacities of each facility. Specific material and capacity issues are resolved at a higher level and in more detail than in most MRP II environments. This detail is achieved because of the greater competitive emphasis on costs and because there are fewer end items, which makes the detailed analysis feasible.

Planning and scheduling at the plant level incorporate a different perspective by using the process structure to guide calculations instead of the product structure used in MRP II systems. Process train plans and stage/cluster schedules replace master scheduling, material planning, capacity planning, material control, and capacity control. Scheduling in a PFS environment is quite different:

- Processor (capacity) may be scheduled before materials; materials before the processor; or both scheduled simultaneously.
- Material and capacity are generally reconciled at each state before scheduling the next stage.
- Scheduling may begin at any point in the process structure.
- Little if any slack time exists in the schedules.
- Lead times are based on processing time and do not include queue time.
- Work orders are not required. The schedule is the authority to produce.
- Customer orders are frequently scheduled on a specific process.

Verifying the Framework

A questionnaire and appropriate documentation were mailed to 39 high-volume flow manufacturers. As shown in table 5.5, the results of the survey clearly provide support for the new PFS framework. All 17 responding companies indicated that the PFS framework described some part of their operations. Furthermore, 15 companies felt that the PFS framework best described their operations. And finally, the companies indicated that a high percentage (76 percent) of their operation was described by the PFS framework, versus 15 percent for the MRP II process industry framework and 9 percent for some other specified structure. From this sample of high-volume flow manufacturers, the results clearly indicate strong support for the PFS framework.

While the survey results indicate strong support for the PFS framework, comments from some of the companies add additional insights. Though the structure may need to be refined, strong support was indicated by such comments as the following:

> PFS documents the process and scheduling characteristics at *** Co. much more accurately than the MRP II framework. The comprehensive framework described clarifies the relationship of capacity-based planning with PFS and materials-based planning with MRP II.

> Excellent concept. We're using the PFS model in some of our training programs to help our planners understand the logic of what they are doing. However, we still must live within the confines of a traditional MRP II system at many of our locations.

> This work is important so that people have a framework to assist with planning and scheduling; otherwise, many numbers are pulled out of the sky.

> The PFS framework is the best description of the planning and scheduling methodology I have seen within the process type industries.

An additional verification was accomplished at a research workshop held in Denver, Colorado, in 1990. At the workshop, several companies were asked to define the hierarchical steps that they followed in their planning/scheduling system. Each company drew a hierarchical pyramid identifying the planning process and planning levels within the company. From these definitions, each company's process was checked against the general framework being proposed. Even though the companies differed markedly, the process flow scheduling framework provided a good fit for each company. It provided a unifying structure. But don't take our word for it; let us take a look at two of the companies already discussed in chapter 4. We will look at Simplot and Exxon Chemical.

Simplot

Simplot provides the simplest example. Simplot represents a single-cluster system composed of skin removal, cutting, blanching, frying, and freezing. Therefore, even though there are 4 plants and 24 production lines, the hierarchical integration of the planning/scheduling system is shallow; i.e., only

Table 5.5 Survey Results		
PFS describes some part of operation		
Yes – 17	No – 0	
Which framework (MRP II or PFS) best describes your operation?		
MRP II – 2	PFS – 15	
What percent of your operation is described by (average)?		
PFS	–	76%
MRP II	–	15%
Other	–	9%

three levels. Figure 5.4, which shows the hierarchical pyramid drawn by the Simplot representative, demonstrates the three levels.

The top-level planning defined by Simplot is business unit plans. These plans correspond to the divisional production plans identified in the PFS framework. At the business planning level, marketing forecasts are developed to satisfy financial goals. However, since these forecasts do not necessarily reflect market activity, a midyear correction adjusts the planned production. At the business planning unit, raw potato material requirements are planned and reviewed, long-term contracts with growers are developed, and cooking oils are planned and purchased. In addition, long-term capital and human resources are planned.

The second level of planning is concerned with developing plant production plans. However, several factors complicate the process. First, since potatoes are harvested in the fall, specialized storage facilities were developed to store the product during the winter, spring, and summer. Before this mechanical long-term storage was available, the crop was processed in about six months; but since storage has improved, there is an excess of processing capacity. Second, the quality of the potato is sensitive to growing conditions and storage management. Third, weather influences the production plans. For example, when it is too hot in late summer, the refrigeration cannot handle the additional load, and lines must be slowed. When it is too cold in the winter, potatoes can freeze on the trucks and cannot be processed. Finally, sales vary, and age-dated inventories make it difficult to minimize stockouts yet not carry inventory.

The plant production plans are developed with the aid of a mathematical programming model. The plan, which covers a seven-month planning horizon, specifies the amount of each product family to be produced on each of the 24 production lines. The

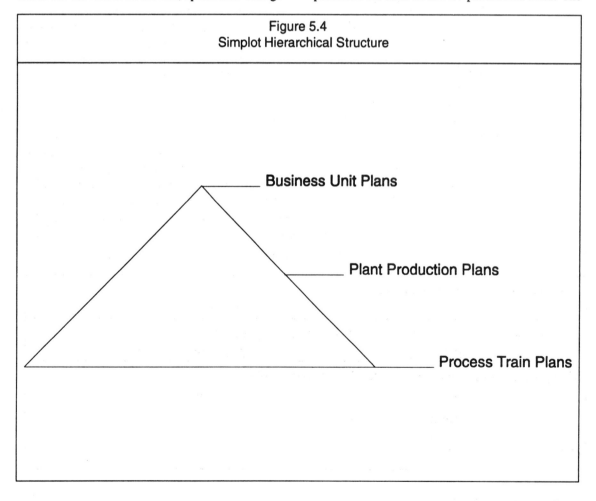

Figure 5.4
Simplot Hierarchical Structure

Business Unit Plans

Plant Production Plans

Process Train Plans

model's optimization logic considers inventory and its condition, production line capacity, conflicting demands for capacity, the production calendar, transportation costs, and plant economics. This develops planned production on each of the production lines and provides material requirement guidance for other purchased supplies. These plant production plans correspond to the plant production plan identified in the PFS framework. It is also important to note that the plans were developed at a centralized level. This allowed Simplot to evaluate economic and marketing trade-offs among the plants and their respective production lines.

The third and final level of the planning/scheduling process was the development of production schedules and the weekly purchasing of boxes, bags, and other supplies. The scheduling process uses a custom finite forward scheduling program in creating a three-week schedule. The schedule evaluates out-of-stock conditions and weeks of sales coverage in order to keep inventories in balance. In addition, production efficiency cuts are scheduled, normally to dedicated lines, to minimize cut changes. This third level of planning corresponds to a combination of the process train plan and the process stage/cluster schedules identified in the PFS framework. For Simplot, these framework elements are combined because of the simplicity of the one-stage/cluster process.

Exxon Chemical

Our second example comes from Exxon Chemical, also discussed in chapter 4. The hierarchical pyramid developed by Exxon Chemical is shown in Figure 5.5. Exxon Chemical represents a multiple-stage process with three distinct stages in its operations and five hierarchical levels in its planning/scheduling system. As such, Exxon Chemical presents a more complex environment

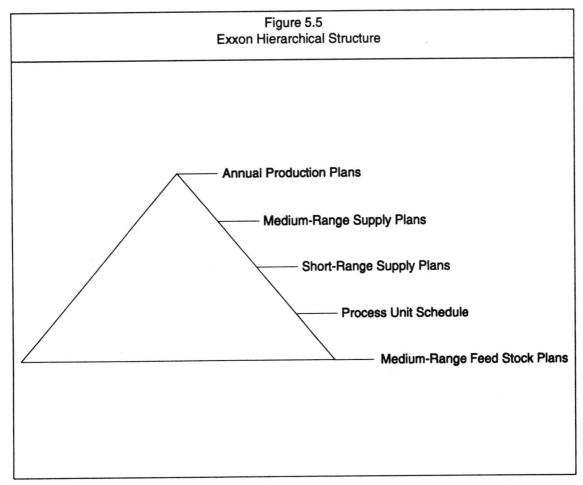

Figure 5.5
Exxon Hierarchical Structure

Annual Production Plans

Medium-Range Supply Plans

Short-Range Supply Plans

Process Unit Schedule

Medium-Range Feed Stock Plans

than that portrayed by Simplot. One might also add a sixth level to the Exxon hierarchy by including a strategic planning process at the top of its pyramid. However, the strategic planning process is accomplished at the corporate level and provides an overall financial and capital foundation for this specific chemical plant. And since we made no attempt to evaluate the entire corporation, we will focus just on this plant.

The planning/scheduling process begins with the development of annual production plans. These plans are developed in quarterly time buckets and present forecasted product demands, planned production at the plant, long-term supply commitments from the nearby Exxon oil refinery, and any additional raw material feed stock requirements. These annual plans correspond to the plant production plans identified in the PFS framework.

The second level of planning/scheduling at Exxon Chemical represents the development of medium-range supply plans. These medium-range plans are in monthly time buckets with a four-month focus. They pay specific attention to demand issues and related trends, supply issues and any known disruptions, and projected storage levels and their respective limits. These plans, referred to as the *joint plan optimization,* attempt to balance the relationship between planned production and supply requirements. The medium-range supply plans provide an additional level of detail to the above annual production plans. As such, the medium-range supply plans represent an extension of the plant production plans identified in the PFS framework. However, as they provide a two-level hierarchy to the production planning process, they also represent a variation.

The third level of planning/scheduling at Exxon Chemical is the development of short-range supply plans. This level of planning utilizes a commercial software package to finitely evaluate scheduling trade-offs between cycle optimization, product sequencing, minimum and maximum inventory positions, product quality, and meeting customer demand. The software package allows the scheduler to input trial schedules in the form of Gantt charts. The resulting impact on inventories is calculated and displayed with a line graph of inventory, allowing the scheduler to check whether demand is being met while keeping inventories at acceptable levels.

This third level of planning/scheduling proceeds by developing the schedule using a reverse flow

procedure. The last stage/cluster in the process train is finitely forward scheduled first. Once all issues are resolved at this stage/cluster, the schedule proceeds to the next upstream stage/cluster. The software allows the scheduler to interactively resolve issues level by level and between levels in the process train. Exxon refers to this process as the development of *process unit schedules.* These schedules represent the fourth level in Exxon's hierarchical planning/scheduling structure. The combination of Exxon's third and fourth levels of planning corresponds to the development of process train plans and process stage/cluster schedules, as identified in the PFS framework.

Finally, the last step in Exxon's planning/scheduling hierarchy is the development of *medium-range feed stock plans.* These feed stock plans identify the material requirements needed to support the above plans and schedules. If projected material supplies do not support the production plans and schedules, additional feed stock is sought, plans and schedules are changed, outside sources of finished product are sought, and/or customers might be placed on product allocations. Medium-range feed stock plans are similar to the process described in the process stage/cluster schedules in the PFS framework structure.

Summary

Simplot and Exxon Chemical, which are similar to other process companies, provide a good illustration of both the similarities and the dissimilarities. For example, both firms used the process structure and the overall framework of division, plants, and process trains as a guide. However, we also saw that the two companies illustrate different levels of hierarchical detail. Simplot, with a much simpler planning/scheduling system, did not require as many levels in planning and scheduling. Exxon illustrated a more complex environment, requiring many more levels in its planning and scheduling system. But the basic PFS framework structure was still there.

Framework Summary

A systems framework has been proposed for process flow firms. The planning and scheduling modules of this framework use the division and process train structures as a guide. While current MRP-based frameworks apply to many manufacturing environments, they do not apply in all situations. This framework presents an alternative that better fits many high-volume flow manufacturers.

This framework should not be considered a standard against which specific company systems should be measured. The intent of this chapter is to suggest a different planning and scheduling philosophy than is found in current literature. Readers can evaluate the applicability of the philosophy in specific manufacturing environments and adapt the framework as required.

Let's take a moment to reflect to see where we have been and where we are going. In chapter 3, you were introduced to process flow scheduling with a simple example and brief explanations of three basic principles. In chapter 4, you read overviews that broadly described the use of process flow scheduling in different plants. These cases validated the basic concept, but left many details of PFS unexplained. You have just finished investigating a broad framework that links scheduling to other modules in an integrated manufacturing planning and control system.

Now let's turn our attention to the details of process flow scheduling. First, we examine information flows for process clusters. This is followed by an analysis of scheduling alternatives for single-unit and then single-cluster stages. We conclude our examination of PFS scheduling by exploring multi-stage scheduling issues.

References

Bolander, S.F., R.C. Heard, S.M. Seward, and S.G. Taylor. 1981a. *Manufacturing Planning and Control in Process Industries.* Falls Church, Va.: APICS.

Foley, M.J. 1988. Post-MRP II: What comes next? *Datamation,* 1 December 1988, 24, 32, 36.

Goldratt, Elijah M., and Jeff Cox. 1986. *The Goal: A Process of Ongoing Improvement.* North River Press.

Taylor, S.G., S.M. Seward, S.F. Bolander, and R.C. Heard. 1981b. Process industry production and inventory planning framework: A summary. *Production Inventory Management* 22, no. 1:15–33.

Umble, Michael M., and M.L. Srikanth. 1990. *Synchronous Manufacturing.* South-Western Publishing Co.

Wight, O.W. 1981. *MRP II: Unlocking America's Productivity Potential.* Williston, Vt.

Chapter 6

Process Cluster Information Flows

Since PFS schedules are built by linking cluster schedules, process clusters are the building blocks of PFS systems. Whether designing a custom PFS system or evaluating commercial software, designers and schedulers should carefully evaluate the availability and quality of cluster scheduling inputs. In addition, they should also closely review output information and its presentation format. Figure 6.1 gives an overview of cluster scheduling inputs and outputs.

Data Requirements

Cluster scheduling inputs are divided into two categories—data and scheduling guidelines. Data can be further classified as material requirements, inventory status, resource availability, and production activity data. The material requirements for a process cluster come from customer requirements (independent demand) or from the input requirements of a downstream stage (dependent demand). Requirements are either orders or demand rates spread over time.

Cluster scheduling also requires data on the current inventory status of all input and output materi-

als. This data must include on-hand balances by stockkeeping unit. Additional stock status data may include age, shelf life, lot tracking information, allocated quantities, and any scheduled receipts.

The next data category is resource availability. All resources that can constrain the production schedule need monitoring. These resources may include process unit (or machine) hours, labor hours, and energy requirements. In certain circumstances, less conventional resources must be considered, such as emission, effluent, and exposure limits on waste and toxic substances.

The last category of data requirements is production activities. A production activity quantifies the amount of input materials and resources required to produce the output material. Consider, for example, the single unit packaging cluster shown at the top of figure 6.2. The feed, bulk X, is packaged in 8-, 16-, and 32-ounce bottles to produce small (S), Medium (M), and large (L) bottled products.

As shown in the table of production activity data in the lower portion of figure 6.2, each package size requires a different production activity. The first column (small) shows the materials and resources needed to make one small bottle of X. Negative column values show consumption of materials or resources, while positive values indicate production.

The first two column entries show that the small packaging activity consumes eight ounces (0.125 gallons) of X and one 8-ounce bottle. The third entry shows that one small bottle of X also requires 0.001 packaging hours. (This example assumes that small bottles are filled at a rate of 1,000 bottles per hour.) The last entry (row small X) indicates that the production activity produces one small bottle of X. The other columns of figure 6.2 show similar production activity data for the medium and large products.

If you are familiar with material requirements planning systems, you will note that the production activity data has parent-child relationship information. However, production activity data differs from a bill of material. Note that unlike a bill of material for an MRP system, production activities include resource requirements. Thus, production activities combine data that an MRP system separates into the bill of material and routing files.

Another difference between production activity data and a bill of material is the extent of information in a record. A bill of material contains information on all the materials necessary to produce an end item. Production activity data, on the other hand, shows only the material and capacity requirements for a single process unit or process cluster. The production activity data for several stages must be linked together to obtain a complete picture of the resources required to make a finished product.

If you are familiar with linear programming models and their associated matrix generators, production activities should seem familiar. Production activities are similar to activities (also called columns or vectors) in linear programming models.

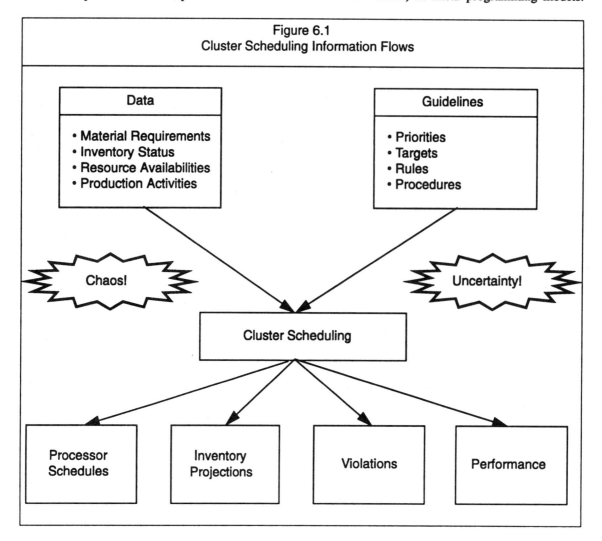

Figure 6.1
Cluster Scheduling Information Flows

This is not surprising, since the data structures used in matrix generators for linear programming models provided the basis for some commercial process flow scheduling packages. Thus, the data structures for many PFS systems are more like those for linear programming systems than for material requirements planning systems.

Scheduling Guidelines

The second type of information needed for cluster scheduling is guidelines. As shown in figure 6.1, scheduling guidelines consist of priorities, targets, rules, and procedures.

Priorities

Priorities evolve from business strategies and specify the relative importance of service, cost, inventory, and quality objectives. These priorities help resolve scheduling conflicts. For example, a scheduler may need to decide whether to accept a rush order. However, the scheduler has a dilemma. Producing the rush order will disrupt the least-cost production sequence and increase manufacturing costs. Priorities give the answer. If the business strategy emphasizes fast delivery, the scheduler should accept the order. On the other hand, if the business strategy emphasizes low costs, the scheduler should defer or decline the order. Performance measurement systems must reflect these competitive

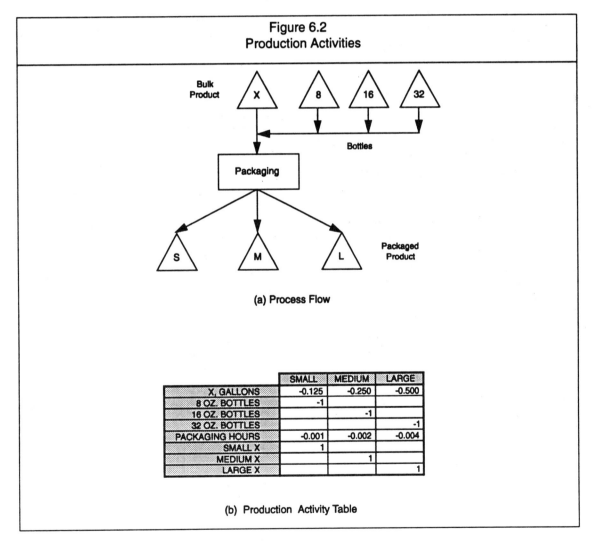

Figure 6.2
Production Activities

(a) Process Flow

	SMALL	MEDIUM	LARGE
X, GALLONS	-0.125	-0.250	-0.500
8 OZ. BOTTLES	-1		
16 OZ. BOTTLES		-1	
32 OZ. BOTTLES			-1
PACKAGING HOURS	-0.001	-0.002	-0.004
SMALL X	1		
MEDIUM X		1	
LARGE X			1

(b) Production Activity Table

priorities, and schedulers must be aware of these priorities.

Targets

Targets guide schedule development. They typically originate as part of the production planning process. Targets may include (1) minimum and maximum inventory levels, (2) production run lengths, (3) campaign cycle lengths, and (4) production sequences. Since several texts present techniques for establishing these targets (see references given at the end of this chapter), we will not provide the details of establishing these guidelines. We will, however, briefly discuss issues related to each of these targets.

Two common targets in make-to-stock environments are planned minimum and maximum values for each finished, intermediate (work-in-process), and raw material inventory. The minimum inventory values are safety stocks. These provide a buffer against supply disruptions (e.g., machine downtime) and requirements variations (e.g., forecast error or variations in downstream requirements).

The maximum inventory values may be *hard* or *soft* constraints. Hard constraints are based on equipment constraints, such as tank capacity, or on product constraints, such as shelf life. Alternatively, the maximum inventory may be a soft constraint. For example, an item's peak planned inventory generally occurs at the end of a production run. This peak inventory is the sum of the item's safety stock and its peak cycle stock. Since exceeding the planned peak does not create major problems, the resulting maximum inventory is a soft constraint.

Another target concerns run lengths or, equivalently, lot sizes. Lot sizes can also be classified as *hard* or *soft*. A hard lot size may evolve from such equipment constraints as the size of a batch reactor. In other situations, quality considerations may determine a hard lot size. For example, the Exxon Chemical case in chapter 4 has quality-based minimum run lengths. Product changeovers at Exxon Chemical create transition material that does not meet product quality specifications. However, blending transition material with prime material upgrades the transition material into salable product. The production run lengths, in turn, must be long enough to generate a sufficient quantity of prime product to blend off the transition material. The resulting minimum lot size is a hard constraint.

Soft lot size or run length targets are more flexible than the hard constraints. Classical lot sizing models yield soft lot sizes. When setup (changeover) costs are significant, a trade-off exists between setup costs and inventory carrying costs. Short run lengths result in frequent setups and correspondingly high setup costs. Conversely, long run lengths result in high inventories and high carrying costs. Classical lot sizing models calculate target lot sizes that minimize the sum of setup costs and inventory carrying costs. Dividing the resulting lot sizes by item production rates gives the corresponding "optimal" target run lengths. However, the resulting target run lengths can readily be shortened or lengthened, thus creating a soft constraint.

A third scheduling target is production frequency. Cyclic schedules are often used when a single machine produces several products. These production cycles have different names in different organizations. We use the term *campaign cycle*; however, others use the terms *schedule wheel, product wheel, rotation schedule,* or simply *campaign.* Guidelines help the scheduler decide (1) the approximate length of the campaign cycle and (2) whether to produce a product every cycle or to skip some cycles. This scheduling problem is commonly known as the multiproduct lot cycling problem or the *economic lot scheduling problem.* It is discussed in such books as Brown 1967, Hax and Candea 1984, Magee and Boodman 1967, and Silver and Peterson 1985, as well as numerous research articles, including Elmaghraby 1978.

The fourth target concerns production sequences. Natural production sequences often exist. Examples are light to dark colors, wide to narrow widths, thick to thin, and low to high molecular weight. If production schedules use these natural orders, setup costs can be minimized and product quality improved. In other situations, production sequences affect setup costs, but process technology may not establish a readily identifiable optimum production sequence. Here a sequencing algorithm that minimizes the setup costs should prove helpful. Several texts—including Baker 1974, Hax and Candea 1984, and Morton and Pentico 1993—give sequencing algorithms for a variety of scheduling environments.

Rules

Rules are another type of scheduling guideline shown in figure 6.1. While scheduling rules may be broken, they are somewhat firmer than the previously discussed targets. There is no clear distinction between targets and rules; however, targets tend to be developed by production planners and schedulers, and rules tend to be set by management and involve considerations with a significant impact on other functional areas. Examples of scheduling rules are (1) overtime must be less than eight hours per week, (2) schedules are frozen for a three-day horizon, (3) no changeovers on Sunday, and (4) the switch from product X to product Y should be made on day shift.

Procedures

The last category of scheduling guidelines shown in figure 6.1 is procedures. Scheduling procedures define how schedules will be developed and communicated to line workers and operating management. Generating schedules requires a blend of scheduler and computer tasks. Commercial PFS systems have commands to help schedulers build or modify processor schedules. Examples of commands are adding, deleting, extending, and replacing scheduled activities. Some vendor systems provide special algorithms to help generate and modify schedules. For example, algorithms might balance inventories of items within a product family or run a product family until an item in another family reaches its minimum planned inventory. Some vendors provide expert systems capability to assist in building schedules.

All scheduling systems must include procedures to convey the authority to produce to line operators. In many PFS systems, the authority to produce is the production schedule; however, some PFS systems use work orders. Some plants use both schedules and work orders. These plants have some clusters that are flow shops and other clusters that are job shops. The flow shop clusters control production with schedules, and the job shop clusters use work orders.

In addition to the above, scheduling procedures are needed for (1) scheduling frequency, (2) schedule time intervals ("buckets"), (3) schedule horizons, (4) responsibilities for various scheduling tasks, (5) sources and updating of scheduling data, and (6) techniques for linking the production plan with the production schedules.

Cluster Scheduling

Cluster scheduling involves the use of guidelines and data to generate schedules for each process unit in a cluster. In addition, inventory levels are projected for all input and output materials. The development of a schedule often begins with a computer-generated schedule that is developed using a spreadsheet or commercial PFS program. However, most situations require a scheduler to modify the computer-generated schedule. This usually involves a trial-and-error simulation of alternative schedules until a satisfactory schedule is obtained. Scheduling software assists the scheduler in this process by both simulating and evaluating alternative schedules.

Production scheduling is primarily concerned with creating a feasible schedule. However, schedule optimization is not ignored. The production plan makes many key decisions regarding aggregate production rates, aggregate inventory levels, and the above-mentioned targets for minimum inventories (safety stocks), run lengths, campaign cycle lengths, and production sequences. Here is where optimization occurs and the results are then passed as targets to the detailed scheduling process.

Production schedules include more product, process, and time detail than production plans. Schedules also consider additional rules that may have been ignored in developing production plans. The end result of scheduling is a detailed plan that unit operators can execute.

Exception messages report violations of scheduling rules and targets. Problems are resolved by referring to the competitive priorities, which specify the relative importance of service, cost, and quality objectives. Schedule performance may also be measured in terms of changeover costs, inventory carrying costs, and projected customer service levels. The following sections discuss these scheduling outputs in more detail. The next three chapters provide additional detail on scheduling techniques.

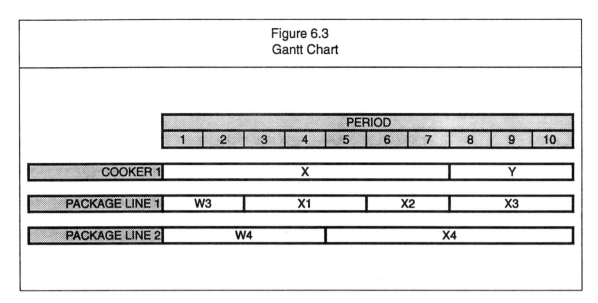

Figure 6.3
Gantt Chart

Processor Schedule Formats

Processor schedules use a variety of formats. In this section we present a sample of these formats.

These are but a few of the many ways to display processor schedules. Commercial software commonly uses electronic Gantt charts. These Gantt charts, as shown in figure 6.3, are usually horizontal bar charts that show scheduled activities over time. However, vertical Gantt charts are also commercially available and are used in some custom systems. While all commercial PFS systems use Gantt

Figure 6.4
Spreadsheet Vertical Gantt Chart

DAY	HOUR	LINE 1	LINE 2
26-Sep	8:00 AM	A	M
	9:00 AM	A	M
	10:00 AM	A	M
	11:00 AM	A	M
	12:00 PM	SETUP	M
	1:00 PM	B	M
	2:00 PM	B	M
	3:00 PM	B	SETUP
27-Sep	8:00 AM	SETUP	N
	9:00 AM	C	N
	10:00 AM	SETUP	N
	11:00 AM	SETUP	N
	12:00 PM	D	N
	1:00 PM	D	N
	2:00 PM	D	N
	3:00 PM	D	SETUP

charts, there are many variations in the use of colors and special symbols to display various activities and events on the chart. These differences are more than cosmetic. For example, a special format may be used to show that a process unit is shut down because of insufficient storage capacity for its output. These display variations and their information content are factors that differentiate competing scheduling packages.

Spreadsheets are probably the most common tool used for custom process flow scheduling systems. Informal surveys conducted by the authors indicate that these in-house spreadsheet systems far outnumber commercial installations. Figure 6.4 is a spreadsheet-based, vertical Gantt chart. Processor schedules are displayed by placing an appropriate activity code in each cell. Figure 6.4 shows what is commonly called a *bucketed format*. A *bucket* is a time interval such as one hour. A bucketed format divides the scheduling horizon into a set of time periods. Scheduling procedures normally allow only one product in each time bucket.

A second spreadsheet processor scheduling format is the processor load format illustrated in figure 6.5. The spreadsheet columns are for days, and the rows show products. Cell entries give the scheduled number of hours for each product on each day. The lower portion of figure 6.5 shows a corresponding bar chart. Vertical bars in this chart show the time allocated to each product. Both the spreadsheet and the vertical bar chart permit scheduling products for any period desired. Thus, product M1 in figure 6.5 could be scheduled for 19 hours and 23 minutes by simply displaying this information in the appropriate

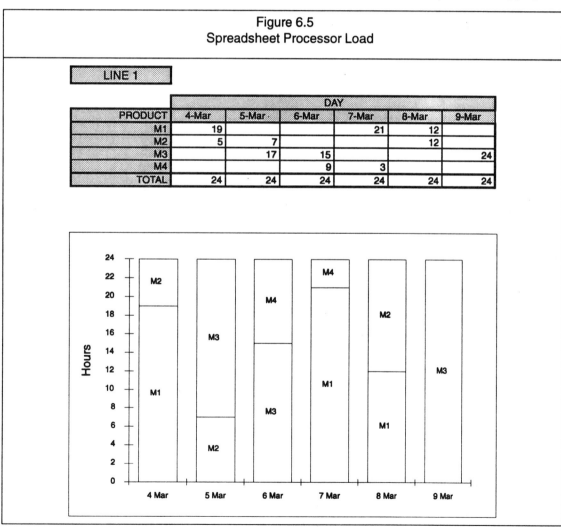

Figure 6.5
Spreadsheet Processor Load

LINE 1

PRODUCT	DAY					
	4-Mar	5-Mar	6-Mar	7-Mar	8-Mar	9-Mar
M1	19			21	12	
M2	5	7			12	
M3		17	15			24
M4			9	3		
TOTAL	24	24	24	24	24	24

| | | | Figure 6.6 | |
| | | | Event Schedule | |

| | QUANTITY (THOUSAND POUNDS) | RUN LENGTH (HOURS) | START TIME | |
GRADE			DAY	HR:MIN
A	5250	52.5	01 Jun	0:00
B	3300	33.0	03 Jun	4:30
C	1100	11.0	04 Jun	13:30
D	700	7.0	05 Jun	0:30
A	5250	52.5	05 Jun	7:30
B	3300	33.0	07 Jun	12:00
C	1100	11.0	08 Jun	21:00
D	700	7.0	09 Jun	8:00

spreadsheet cell. This format, which uses a time duration to specify the length of a production run, is called an *unbucketed format.*

The lack of information on the sequencing of products within each day is a weakness of the spreadsheet given in figure 6.5. Consider, for example, the sequencing of M1 and M4 on March 7. The spreadsheet does not indicate which product to schedule first. On the other hand, the bar chart can easily show the sequence by putting the first product at the bottom of a bar. Using this convention, we see that product M1 is scheduled before product M4 on March 7. But what if we wanted to schedule M4 first? Unfortunately, the spreadsheet software always plots M1 before M4. This may result in improperly displaying the production sequence.

An event schedule format, as shown in figure 6.6, uses an unbucketed format and provides detailed sequences. The grade column gives the production sequence. The next column specifies the run quantity. Dividing the run quantity by the production rate

(100,000 pounds per hour) gives the corresponding run length.

The run lengths and the initial start time provide information for calculating the start times for each production run. The finish time for the first run of product A is determined by adding the run length (52.5 hours) to its start time in the first column. The start time for product B is the finish time for its predecessor (product A) plus any setup time. In this example we assume that the unit is not shut down for changeovers. Thus, the setup time is zero, and the start time for B is the finish time for A. Additional production runs are scheduled in a similar manner through the schedule horizon.

One last sample format for processor schedules is a dispatch list. Figure 6.7 gives an example of a dispatch list. A dispatch list is a prioritized list of jobs for a process unit. Dispatch lists are commonly used in the production activity control modules of MRP systems. They specify the processing order for jobs in a work center. Sometimes, as shown in figure 6.7, a dispatch list may also contain data on

| | Figure 6.7 | |
| | Dispatch List | |

PART	QUANTITY
A-100	210
M-300	105
Q-270	400
D-730	320
F-520	250

the number of parts to be processed. In other cases, dispatch lists contain additional information, such as order due dates or input material availabilities.

Inventory Projection Formats

Inventory projections are a principal output from cluster scheduling calculations. Inventories are easily projected using simple material balance calculations. The upper part of figure 6.8 gives a spreadsheet format for these calculations. The inventory on March 7 is obtained by adding the day's production (100) to the prior inventory (500) and

subtracting the day's demand (50), to give 550 pounds at the end of the day. Although inventory projections use this type of calculation, most systems just display the projected inventories with line graphs, as shown at the bottom of figure 6.8.

When a cluster schedule has more than about 20 items, it becomes difficult to work with the inventory line graphs. This has been a major difficulty for several companies using commercial PFS software. One solution is to create reports with summary data for a specified period. For example, a report could show the projected maximum and minimum inventory levels for each item in a large group of items over the next month. Alternatively, the minimum inventory, expressed as days of sales, could be projected for each item over the next month. Exception

Figure 6.8
Inventory Projection Spreadsheet

DAY		7 Mar	8 Mar	9 Mar	10 Mar	11 Mar	12 Mar	13 Mar
PRODUCTION		100	100				100	100
DEMAND		50	50	50	50	50	50	50
INVENTORY	500	550	600	550	500	450	500	550

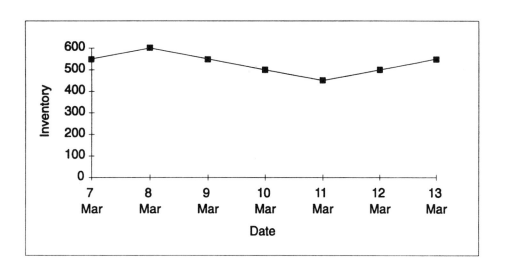

reports that summarize projected late orders, out-of-stock periods, and periods below target minimum inventories are also alternatives to inventory line graphs.

Another format for displaying inventories is a cumulative plot of production and demand. Figure 6.9 gives an example. At the end of day 0, the inventory is 350 pounds. This also represents the cumulative production carried forward from previous periods. The cumulative production remains at 350 pounds through day 1, which implies that no production took place on day 1. The cumulative demand plot shows that 50 pounds were required in day 1. The inventory at the end of day 1 (300) is the difference between cumulative production (350) and cumulative demand (50). Examination of the plot also reveals that the inventory of 350 will last until the end of day 5. Thus, at the end of day 1, there is a time

coverage of four days of demand. As this example shows, the cumulative production-demand plot is an effective tool for displaying both the inventory and its time coverage over the scheduling horizon.

One important aspect of developing inventory projections is the modeling of production and demand quantities. Production can be either continuous or batch. Continuous production both consumes and produces material throughout a scheduled run. The graph in figure 6.8 shows a typical inventory pattern for continuous production and consumption.

Batch production, on the other hand, consumes input materials at the beginning of a batch run and produces output materials at the end. The graphs in figure 6.10 show sample inventory patterns for batch production with a three-day processing time. The top graph gives the impact of an 800-gallon withdrawal of feed stock at the beginning of a batch

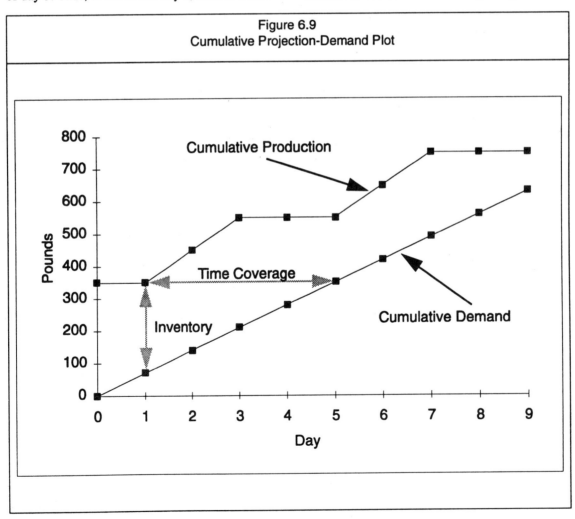

**Figure 6.9
Cumulative Projection-Demand Plot**

run. The bottom graph shows a corresponding 800-gallon addition to product inventory after the three days for processing have elapsed. As this example illustrates, batch production has large periodic impacts on inventory levels.

In a make-to-order environment, tracking finished goods inventories is different than in a make-to-stock environment. In a make-to-order environment, orders produced before their ship dates result in inventory. Conversely, orders produced after their ship dates result in late orders. In make-to-order environments, reports may give the anticipated late orders for a proposed schedule. Sometimes reports will also be developed for the early orders. These reports might show how early orders are, the per-centage of orders that are early, or the amount of inventory resulting from early orders.

Violations

Violations occur when a trial schedule breaks a scheduling rule or target. Exception messages warn schedulers of the violation. These messages may be conveyed by text, reports, or visual cues. For example, a text message might warn a scheduler that a proposed sequence violates quality guidelines. A report might identify items that are likely to exceed shelf-life specifications. A visual cue might be a bold, red line on an inventory line graph that shows

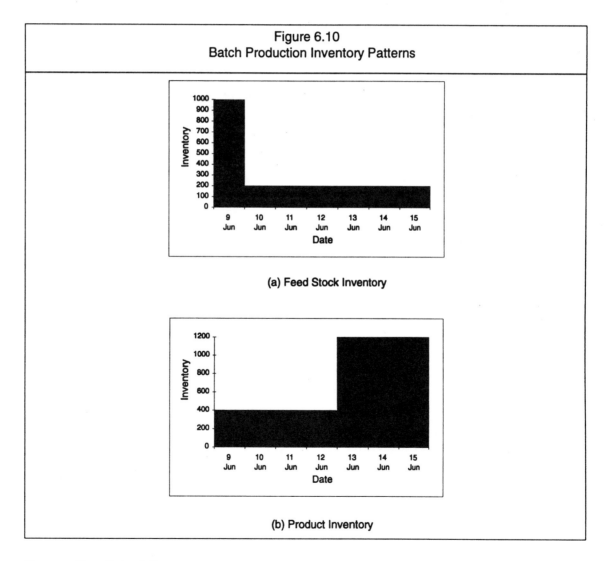

Figure 6.10
Batch Production Inventory Patterns

(a) Feed Stock Inventory

(b) Product Inventory

when an item's projected inventory drops below zero.

Performance

The last output depicted in figure 6.1 is performance. Performance can be measured in a variety of ways and against diverse objectives. Selection of performance measures deserves careful consideration. A state-of-the art planning and scheduling system can be a powerful competitive weapon. Unless it is pointed at the right target, however, the results will be disappointing. Management should define the competitive priorities and translate these priorities into performance indicators. An outdated weapon pointed at the right target is far more effective than the latest weapons aimed at the wrong target.

Several commercial systems use costs to measure schedule performance. Costs considered may include changeover costs, inventory carrying costs, stockout costs, overstock costs, fixed and variable operating costs, and idle time costs. In many implementations, these costs are pseudo costs in which the cost numbers drive the schedule toward a particular objective. For example, rather than attempt to measure the cost of stockouts or late shipments, the scheduling model might use very high penalty costs to drive schedules toward high service objectives at the expense of operating costs.

Another approach, used in both commercial and custom systems, is to offer a set of performance indicators. These indicators may be the number of stockouts or delayed orders, average inventory, number and type of changeovers, amount of overtime required, and amount of outside storage needed.

The number of changeovers is a difficult indicator to interpret. Operating costs increase—and in some cases quality decreases—with more frequent changeovers. On the other hand, frequent changeovers will lower inventories and increase the flexibility to respond to changing demands. Setting and interpreting performance indicators require a knowledge of the business environment, the firm's competitive strategy, and the trade-offs between different performance indicators.

Conclusion

After reading this chapter, you should know the data a PFS system requires and the information a PFS system supplies. You should also begin to realize that PFS is primarily concerned with obtaining feasible production schedules by simulating alternatives. However, there is still a major gap. How do you or your PFS software generate single cluster schedules? There are many ways, and we will explain a few in the next two chapters. Chapter 7 discusses alternate methods for scheduling single units within a process cluster. Chapter 8 discusses methods of linking the schedules for units within a cluster.

References

Baker, K.R. 1974. *Introduction to Sequencing and Scheduling.* New York: John Wiley & Sons.

Brown, R.G. 1967. *Decision Rules for Inventory Management.* New York: Holt, Rinehart and Winston.

Elmaghraby, S.E. 1978. The economic lot scheduling problem (ESLP): Review and extensions. *Management Science* 24, no. 6:587–98.

Hax, A.C., and D. Candea. 1984. *Production and Inventory Management.* Englewood Cliffs, N.J.: Prentice Hall.

Magee, J.F., and D.M. Boodman. 1967. *Production Planning and Inventory Control.,* 2d ed. New York: McGraw-Hill.

Morton, T.E., and D.W. Pentico. 1993. *Heuristic Scheduling Systems.* New York: John Wiley & Sons.

Salomon, M. 1991. *Deterministic Lot Sizing Models for Production Planning.* New York: Springer Verlag.

Silver, E.A., and R. Peterson. 1985. *Decision Systems for Inventory Management and Production Planning.* 2d ed. New York: John Wiley & Sons.

Chapter 7

Single-Unit Scheduling

We begin our analysis of scheduling techniques with an examination of the simplest cluster structure—a cluster with only one processing unit. An example of a single-unit cluster is given in figure 7.1. This diagram shows a cluster in stage N that consists of a single processor (rectangle) and inventories of output materials (lower set of triangles). The unit receives materials from the preceding stage, stage N–1, and in turn, supplies materials to its successor stage, stage N+1. These inventories decouple the schedules for the unit in stage N from the schedules of the units in stage N–1 and N+1.

Figure 7.1 shows one processing unit with two input inventories and three output inventories. A single-unit cluster will always have one processing unit; however, the number of input and output inventories will vary according to individual circumstances. If stage N is the first stage, then the input materials are raw materials from stage 0, which has no associated processing units. If stage N is the last stage, its output inventories directly feed customers.

There is no standard way to schedule a single-unit cluster. However, based on the order in which materials and processors are scheduled, single-unit scheduling techniques can be divided into three major categories. Figure 7.1 helps depict these approaches. We can start in the middle and schedule the processor first. This is the processor-dominated scheduling (PDS) strategy, which was briefly discussed in chapter 3.

In contrast, we could begin scheduling with either the output or input materials. Since materials are scheduled before capacity, this is a material-dominated scheduling (MDS) strategy. If output materials are scheduled first, then output materials are pulled through the processor based on their need dates. This is called a *material pull* approach. On the other hand, if input materials are scheduled first, then input materials are pushed through the processor based on their availabilities and a need for quick processing. This is called a *material push* approach.

The third approach for scheduling single stages is simultaneous scheduling. Simultaneous scheduling uses mathematical programming techniques to concurrently schedule processors and materials. While this approach has proved very effective at the more aggregate production planning level, it is difficult to implement in scheduling systems.

Let's now look at each of these approaches to single-unit scheduling in detail. Because there is no standard way in which all clusters must be scheduled, we will present several examples. For any particular cluster, you will need only one approach. However, you may need to combine the different scheduling approaches illustrated in this chapter when scheduling a process train with multiple stages.

Processor-Dominated Scheduling

The most common processor-dominated scheduling technique is finite forward scheduling. This type of scheduling starts in an initial period (usually period 1) and sequentially loads work through the final period while observing capacity limits. The term *finite forward scheduling* is used because finite capacity limits are observed and schedules are developed by proceeding forward in time. The initial processor schedule commonly uses sequences and lot sizes that efficiently utilize processor capacity or enhance product quality. As mentioned in chapter 6, these lot sizes and sequences are obtained from the scheduling guidelines that are developed as part of the production planning process.

The initial processor schedule assumes that sufficient input material is available from the preceding stage and that scheduled production will meet the demands for the stage's products. This infinite availability assumption is checked in a later scheduling step. The initial schedule also assumes that maximum inventory targets will not be violated for both feed and product. This amounts to an infinite storage assumption that is also scrutinized after developing the initial processor schedule.

If problems arise with either input or output inventories, changes are made to processor or material schedules. Some possible courses of action are

- Adjust lot sizes
- Change production sequence

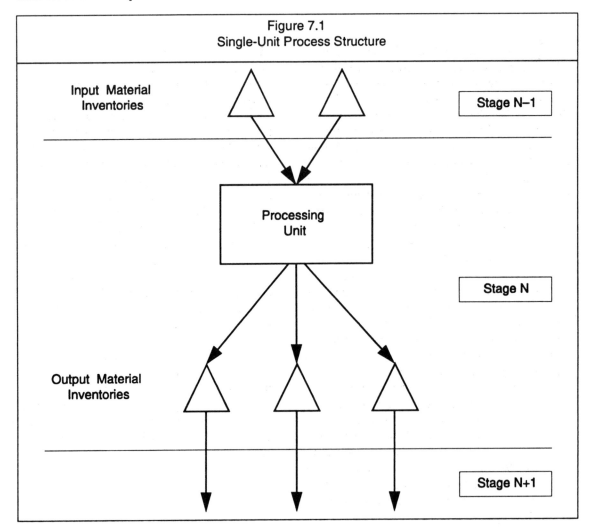

Figure 7.1
Single-Unit Process Structure

Input Material Inventories

Stage N–1

Processing Unit

Stage N

Output Material Inventories

Stage N+1

- Adjust production rate (increase or decrease operating rate, idle time, overtime, extra shifts etc.)
- Defer scheduled maintenance
- Use safety stocks
- Use substitute materials
- Expedite raw materials
- Change schedule for a downstream process
- Ship some orders late
- Decline new orders

Some commercial PFS systems provide algorithms or expert systems to assist schedulers in developing initial schedules or in resolving problems with proposed schedules. However, all commercial and custom systems we have investigated rely heavily on schedulers to adjust computer-generated schedules for current local conditions.

The Polygoo example given in chapter 3 illustrates processor-dominated scheduling for a continuous flow operation. Both reaction and packaging clusters were scheduled using a processor-dominated scheduling approach. The proposed initial schedule used target sequences and lot sizes. This schedule was displayed with a Gantt chart (figures 3.4 and 3.5). After the processor schedule was proposed, inventories were checked. The scheduling procedures described in the flowchart of figure 3.3 illustrate the interactive nature of stage scheduling.

We now present two additional examples of processor-dominated scheduling. The first is for a batch operation with a make-to-stock product, while the second is for a make-to-order environment. Along with Polygoo, these examples illustrate the variety

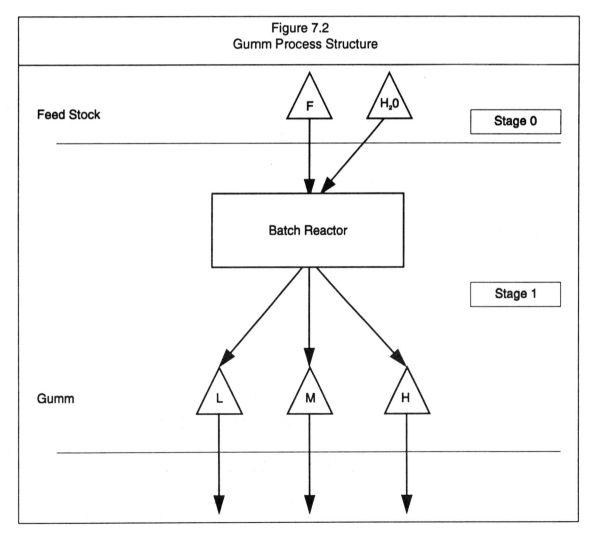

Figure 7.2
Gumm Process Structure

in processor-dominated scheduling techniques for a single stage.

Example 7.1: Gumm-A

Gumm is produced in batches by a single reactor, as shown in figure 7.2. The three types of Gumm are differentiated by their viscosities: low (L), medium (M), and high (H). The reactor represents a single process unit in a single cluster within a single-stage process train. Nothing could be simpler.

Gumm-A is similar to the Polygoo example presented in chapter 3, but it illustrates several important variations. In contrast to the around-the-clock operations for Polygoo, the Gumm reactor only operates eight hours a day, five days per week. When switching products, the Gumm reactor must be shut down and cleaned. This creates a setup time that was not required for Polygoo. Gumm also illustrates scheduling batch operations and uses a lead-time offset. Finally, in the Gumm-A example we explore schedule revisions in greater depth than in the Polygoo example.

Let's now examine the process flow in figure 7.2. A feed stock, F, is reacted with water in 12,000-gallon batches. Although all three products use the same feed stock, each product requires different amounts as shown in figure 7.3(a). Moreover, each product has different processing times as shown in figure 7.3(b).

The setup times for each product depend on the product made in the previous batch. Figure 7.3(c) gives the setup hours for every possible product switch. All the operating data in figure 7.3 can be combined into a production activity table given in figure 7.4. This activity data is one of the scheduling inputs discussed in chapter 6 and illustrated in figures 6.1 and 6.2.

Standard Schedule

The standard weekly schedule shown in figure 7.5 provides a trial reactor schedule. This standard weekly schedule is developed using guidelines from the production plan for target lot sizes and target sequences. The first guideline is that all products will be produced in full 12,000-gallon batches. The

Figure 7.3
Gumm Operating Data

PRODUCT	FEED
LOW	1.1
MED	1.2
HIGH	1.4

(a) Feed Stock Requirements per Gallon of Product

PRODUCT	BATCH TIME HOURS
LOW	4
MED	6
HIGH	8

(b) Batch Times

FROM/TO	SETUP HOURS LOW	MED	HIGH
LOW	0	2	6
MED	4	0	2
HIGH	4	4	0

(c) Setup Times

Figure 7.4
Gumm Production Activities

	ACTIVITY									
	LOW	MED	HIGH	L-M	L-H	M-L	M-H	H-M	H-L	MAINT.
FEED STOCK, GAL.	-1.1	-1.2	-1.4							
REACTOR HOURS	-4.0	-6.0	-8.0	-2.0	-6.0	-4.0	-2.0	-4.0	-4.0	-2.0
LOW VISCOSITY, GAL.	1.0									
MED. VISCOSITY, GAL.		1.0								
HIGH VISCOSITY, GAL.			1.0							

Note: Setup activities are shown by the products involved. Thus, L-M represents the setup for changing from low to medium.

second guideline concerns sequences. Examination of the setup times given in figure 7.3(c) shows that the sequence with the lowest combined setup times is low, medium, high, and then back to low. In addition to these targets, there is also a technologically based operating rule that a batch must be finished on the day it starts.

The standard weekly schedule also uses demand forecasts from the production plan. The forecast is 24,000 gallons per week for both low- and medium-viscosity Gumm. In contrast, the forecast for high-viscosity Gumm is only 12,000 gallons per week. Dividing these forecasts by their batch sizes gives the forecasted batches per week. This results in two batches per week for both low- and medium-viscosity Gumm and only one batch of high-viscosity Gumm. As shown in figure 7.5, these batches fit nicely in the first four days of the week. This leaves Friday for a four-hour major setup (S) to switch from

high-viscosity Gumm back to low, two hours for maintenance (M), and two hours of open time (O).

The standard schedule is now checked for feasibility against the actual demands and current inventory positions. This is done by simulating a period-by-period material balance as presented in figure 7.6. The first row of each time-phased record shows production from the standard weekly schedule. Two 12,000-gallon batches of low viscosity are produced each Monday; one 12,000-gallon medium-viscosity batch each Tuesday and another 12,000-gallon batch each Wednesday; and one 12,000-gallon high-viscosity batch each Thursday.

The receipts row for each record reflects that each batch must be held two days for quality testing before it is available for shipment. These quality tests are not labor-intensive, but involve an aging step that requires two calendar days. Because of these quality testing delays, the 24,000 gallons of

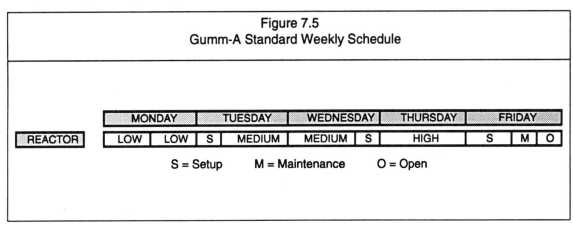

Figure 7.5
Gumm-A Standard Weekly Schedule

REACTOR	MONDAY			TUESDAY	WEDNESDAY		THURSDAY			
	LOW	LOW	S	MEDIUM	MEDIUM	S	HIGH	S	M	O

S = Setup   M = Maintenance   O = Open

low-viscosity Gumm produced on Monday are not available for shipment until Wednesday. Other receipts can be determined by using the two-calendar-day offset for all production quantities. The spreadsheet schedule also assumes that any production on Thursday will not be available until Monday. Although the standard production schedule does not call for any production on Fridays, it is assumed that, if required, any production on Friday will be available for shipment on Monday.

The demand row for each record in figure 7.6 shows the ship dates and quantities for orders that have been booked for the next two weeks. In different production environments, this demand row could show forecasted demands or a combination of forecasts and demands.

The last row, the inventory row, projects future inventory positions. Let's review the calculations by examining low-viscosity inventories. The initial inventory of 48,000 gallons is reduced by the 12,000-gallon demand on Monday of week 1. This results in an inventory of 36,000 gallons at the end of Monday. No receipts or demands occur on Tuesday, so the inventory remains at 36,000 gallons. On Wednesday, 24,000 gallons are received (two batches), and 6,000 gallons are shipped. The resulting inventory is the prior inventory (36,000 gallons) plus receipts (24,000 gallons) minus demand (6,000 gallons) which results in 54,000 gallons in inventory at the end of Wednesday.

These calculations are normally transparent to the scheduler. The scheduler is usually concerned only with the resulting inventories. Figure 7.7 shows

---

Figure 7.6
Initial Schedule Detail

LOW VISCOSITY

UNITS: K Gal.
SAFETY STOCK: 24

		WEEK 1					WEEK 2			
		MON	TUES	WED	THUR	FRI	MON	TUES	WED	THUR	FRI
PRODUCTION		24					24				
RECEIPTS				24					24		
DEMAND		12		6	6		12		6	6	
INVENTORY	48	36	36	54	48	48	36	36	54	48	48

MEDIUM VISCOSITY

UNITS: K Gal.
SAFETY STOCK: 24

		WEEK 1					WEEK 2			
		MON	TUES	WED	THUR	FRI	MON	TUES	WED	THUR	FRI
PRODUCTION			12	12				12	12		
RECEIPTS					12	12				12	12
DEMAND		6	6	6		6	6	6	6		6
INVENTORY	42	36	30	24	36	42	36	30	24	36	42

HIGH VISCOSITY

UNITS: K Gal.
SAFETY STOCK: 18

		WEEK 1					WEEK 2			
		MON	TUES	WED	THUR	FRI	MON	TUES	WED	THUR	FRI
PRODUCTION					12					12	
RECEIPTS		12					12				
DEMAND		12			12				6	6	
INVENTORY	18	18	18	18	6	6	18	18	12	6	6

daily inventory levels as well as the safety stock for each product. Inspection of these charts indicates that low-viscosity inventories are a little high, since they never drop to their safety stock level. Medium-viscosity inventories are about right—they drop to their safety stock levels just before the receipt of a new batch each Thursday.

On the other hand, high-viscosity inventories require further attention. Note that high-viscosity inventories are below the safety stock level at the end of both weeks. The best high-viscosity position exists after a receipt, when inventory reaches its safety stock level. However, since projected inventories do not drop below zero, this schedule is feasible.

Alternative Schedules

Should the scheduler accept this schedule? The schedule is feasible, but it violates safety stock targets. It appears that schedule changes might improve safety stock coverage, but these changes will probably result in higher setup times. This in turn would probably create a need for overtime. What should be done? The answer lies in the competitive priorities (as shown previously in the scheduling guidelines in figure 6.1). If customer service is a higher priority than low operating costs, the higher cost schedule changes should be implemented. On the other hand, if the company competes primarily on price, the risk of a stockout may be acceptable.

Let's suppose that service is relatively important. In this case the initial schedule, with its low inventories for high-viscosity Gumm, is unacceptable.

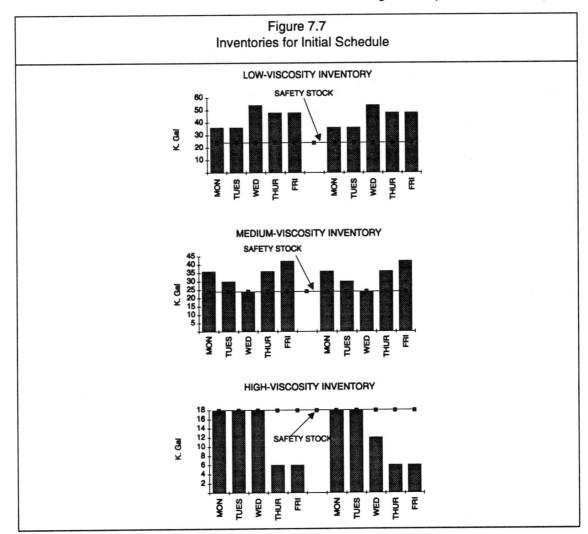

Figure 7.7
Inventories for Initial Schedule

The scheduler must now investigate alternatives. One possibility is substituting a high-viscosity batch for a low-viscosity batch at the beginning of week 1. Figure 7.8 shows this substitution.

Because high-viscosity Gumm requires four more hours for processing a batch and since the switch from high to low requires an additional four hours, the new schedule requires eight more production hours. These eight hours are obtained by using the two hours of open time on Friday in the standard schedule and scheduling six hours of overtime on Saturday. This switch of a high batch for a low batch will increase high-viscosity inventories—but is it enough? Moreover, will low-viscosity inventories drop too low? Let's check their inventories.

Figure 7.9 shows the inventory profiles for the revised schedule. These inventories show that the safety stock targets are now met. Note, however, that six hours of overtime (see figure 7.8, week 1) is required. Is this worth the improved service? Again we must refer to the competitive priorities and a knowledge of the scheduling environment.

Suppose the scheduler checks with sales and learns that additional orders are unlikely in week 1, but are a reasonable possibility in week 2. The scheduler might look for a solution that allows the safety stock target to be violated in week 1, but not in week 2. Figure 7.10 shows one possibility. This schedule uses the standard weekly schedule for the first four days of week 1. On Friday of week 1, however, a second high-viscosity batch is scheduled.

Week 2 also requires a slight deviation from the standard weekly schedule. On Monday, one batch of low-viscosity is replaced with a high-to-low setup and the maintenance that would normally have been performed on the preceding Friday. This, along with one batch of low-viscosity, creates a need for two hours of overtime on Monday. The balance of the week follows the standard weekly schedule.

The resulting inventories for this schedule are shown in figure 7.11. Inspection shows that the only inventory violation is for high-viscosity safety stock in week 1. This violation saves four hours of overtime from the prior schedule. The schedule, however, still requires two hours of overtime. This increased operating cost is justified by reducing the possibility of a stockout in week 2.

Having scheduled the reactor and checked the Gumm inventories, the input material, feed stock F, is checked. We will not show the calculations, but

assume that there is sufficient feed stock in inventory and no problems are projected.

The schedule can now be issued to unit supervisors and operators. The first week of the schedule is frozen and will be executed barring major unforeseen events. The second week of the schedule will serve as the starting point for generating the next schedule in another week. The second week is currently necessary to provide continuity in the scheduling strategies for week 1 and week 2. This is illustrated by the final schedule, which needed to coordinate modifications at the end of week 1 with planned deviations from the standard schedule in the beginning of week 2.

Review of Gumm-A

Let's reexamine the steps that were followed in developing this schedule. The flowchart in figure 7.12 shows the general steps. First, data and guidelines were used to develop the standard weekly schedule. The standard weekly schedule was proposed, and output material (Gumm) inventories were checked. Low-viscosity inventories were a little high, and high-viscosity inventories were a little low. But since the projected inventories were all above zero, the schedule was feasible. Referring to the competitive priority for service, the schedule was not accepted because high-viscosity inventories were too low. Accordingly, the "No" branch was taken from the first decision in figure 7.12.

A revised finite forward schedule was developed. The output materials were evaluated and found to meet the safety stock requirements, but with six hours of overtime. Another possibility was discovered while evaluating this change. Accordingly, the "Yes" branch was taken from the second decision point in figure 7.12. The third schedule had only two hours of overtime, but was below the safety stock level for high-viscosity product in the first week. This compromise between operating costs and stock reliability was judged acceptable, and scheduling moved to the last decision point. Here the input materials were checked, and no feed stock availability problems surfaced. The "Yes" branch from the third decision point was taken and the schedule finalized and issued.

Although Gumm-A has only one processing unit, it still uses the three principles for process flow scheduling. First, the process structure guides scheduling calculations. Following the process structure,

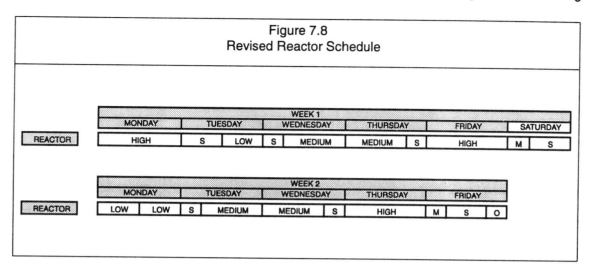

Figure 7.8
Revised Reactor Schedule

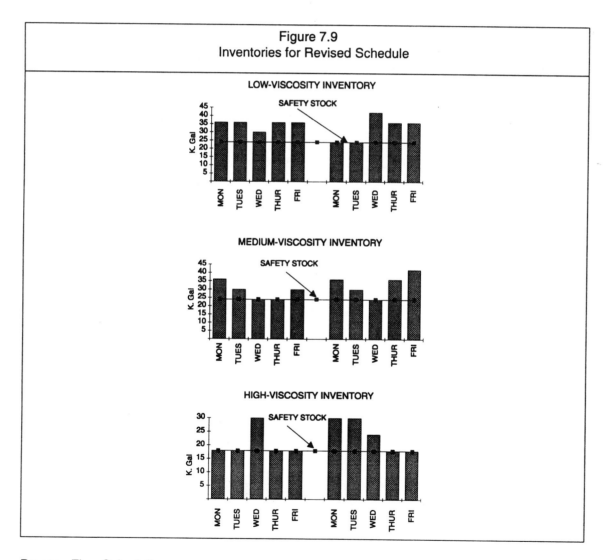

Figure 7.9
Inventories for Revised Schedule

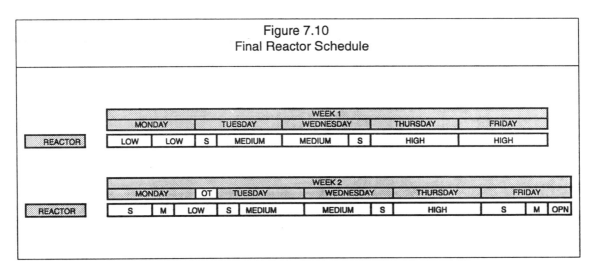

Figure 7.10
Final Reactor Schedule

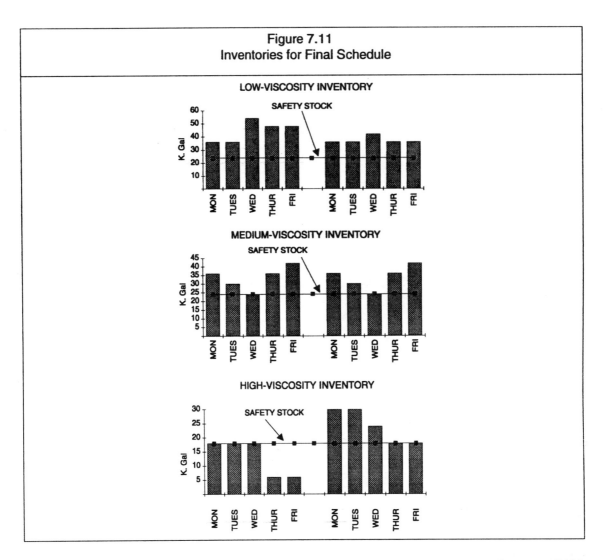

Figure 7.11
Inventories for Final Schedule

the reactor was scheduled, then the output material, and finally the input material. Guided by the second PFS principle, which specifies that stages are scheduled using processor-dominated scheduling or material-dominated scheduling approaches, the reactor was scheduled using processor-dominated scheduling. Moreover, since stage 1 was scheduled before the feed stock in stage 0, a reverse flow scheduling procedure was used. Reverse flow scheduling is one of three options in the third PFS principle.

An important aspect of this example is the interactive development of schedules. As illustrated above, PFS systems generally use a trial-and-error approach. In processor-dominated scheduling, an initial trial schedule is proposed. Then the output and input material inventories are checked. If violations occur, a new processor schedule is proposed. This iterative procedure continues until a satisfactory schedule is obtained.

This example and example 3.1 (Polygoo) both illustrate processor-dominated scheduling in make-to-stock environments. In these examples, the customer service objective was to maintain planned inventories at a level above the safety stock levels. In manufacturing environments where custom products are made to order, there are no safety stocks.

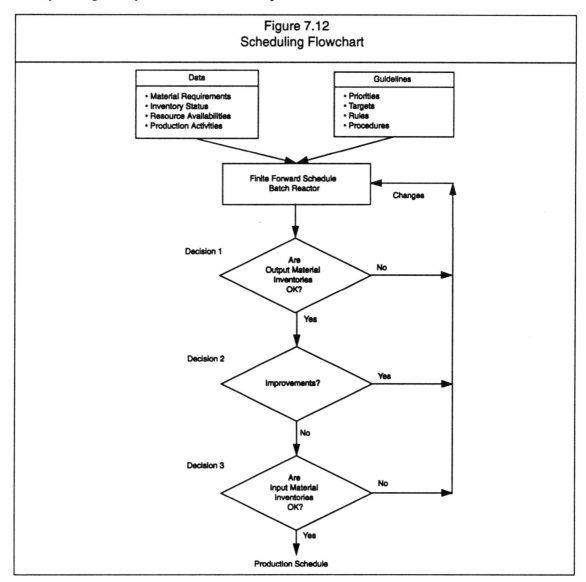

Figure 7.12
Scheduling Flowchart

The next section presents a simple example of scheduling in a make-to-order production environment.

Example 7.2: Colormix-A

The Colormix Company is a custom compounder of plastic resins. Colormix produces plastic resins in any color a customer wants. The process, as shown in figure 7.13, is rather simple. A base resin is mixed with the appropriate combination of pigments in an extruder to produce plastic pellets in the color and quantity ordered. Each order is different; no finished goods inventory is carried in anticipation of future orders. However, some orders may be produced before their due dates and stored until they are shipped. Thus, an inventory of finished goods can exist for orders that have been completed and are awaiting shipment.

The plant typically operates eight hours a day, five days a week. Operating costs are minimized by sequencing customer orders from light to dark colors. The standard operating schedule covers a two-week period in which each color code will be produced only once and colors are sequenced from light to dark. Order promise dates are made with a knowledge of this scheduling sequence. Although the standard color sequence may be broken, it serves as a starting point for developing schedules.

The orders booked for the next two weeks are shown in figure 7.14. The first column gives order numbers that are assigned sequentially in order of receipt. The second column gives the color code assigned when the order is booked. Light colors are given low numbers, and dark colors are given higher numbers. The third column indicates the day the order is due. All orders must be completed by the end of the day given.

The fourth column provides the time required for processing the corresponding order. These job times include a 10-minute setup time for a changeover to the same or a higher (darker) color code. Adding the times in column 4 shows an aggregate load of 72 hours for the next two weeks. However, any setups that involve a changeover to a lower (lighter) color code require additional setup time. This is about

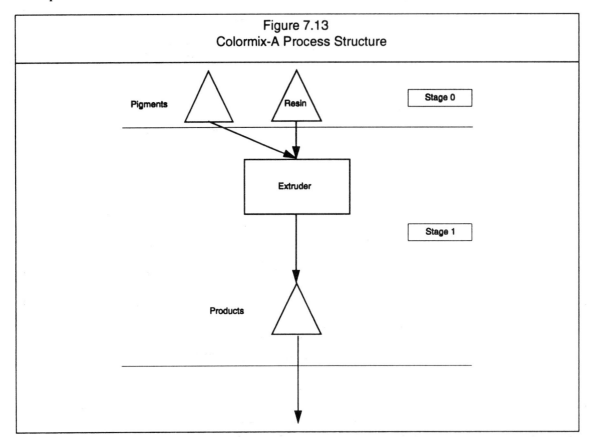

Figure 7.13
Colormix-A Process Structure

one-half hour for each lower color code number. At the end of the normal two-week cycle, therefore, the necessary changeover from code 8 to code 0 results in a four-hour setup. Changeovers from lower to higher color codes involve not only a loss of production time, but also incur costs for additional labor and supplies. Accordingly, these setups should be avoided even when excess extruder capacity exists.

Initial Schedule

The scheduling strategy is not complicated. Using a finite forward scheduling technique, the extruder is scheduled first. An initial schedule is developed by sequencing the orders by color code with the lowest (lightest) code scheduled first. This schedule can now be checked for meeting order promise dates. The schedule is checked by simulating the processing of each order in the specified color sequence. This procedure determines the start time and finish time for each order as well as the amount the order is early or late. Using the data in figure 7.15, the first order is started at shop hour 0 and finishes

at hour 4. This order is due at the end of day 2, which is hour 16. Thus, the first order is early 12 hours.

The second order is scheduled in a similar manner. Since the second order has the same color code as the first, no additional setup time is required. Thus, the second order starts at hour 4, runs for five hours, and finishes at hour 9. This order is also finished before it is due and is seven hours early. The third order takes only two hours and finishes at hour 11. Unfortunately, it is due on day 1 (hour 8) and is projected to be three hours late. The processing of subsequent orders can be simulated in a similar manner. The resulting hours late for each order is given in the last column of figure 7.15. These results indicate that the standard schedule violates the due dates for orders 1 and 12.

The late orders highlight a customer service problem with the initial schedule. Is there an alternative schedule that will resolve these problems? Perhaps. There seem to be a few extra hours that could be used for setups if the target color sequence is violated. Let's see what can be done.

Figure 7.14 Colormix-A Orders			
NO.	CODE	DAY DUE	HOURS
1	1	1	2
2	4	7	11
3	4	6	3
4	3	5	10
5	4	5	4
6	4	9	4
7	4	6	4
8	8	9	9
9	8	8	7
10	0	2	5
11	0	2	4
12	4	2	5
13	1	8	1
14	2	10	2
15	8	7	1

Figure 7.15							
Orders Sequenced by Colors							

ORDER NO.	COLOR CODE	JOB HOURS	HOUR DUE	START HOUR	FINISH HOUR	HOURS EARLY	HOURS LATE
11	0	4	16	0	4	12	
10	0	5	16	4	9	7	
1	1	2	8	9	11		3
13	1	1	64	11	12	52	
14	2	2	80	12	14	66	
4	3	10	40	14	24	16	
12	4	5	16	24	29		13
5	4	4	40	29	33	7	
3	4	3	48	33	36	12	
7	4	4	48	36	40	8	
2	4	11	56	40	51	5	
6	4	4	72	51	55	17	
15	8	1	56	55	56	0	
9	8	7	64	56	63	1	
8	8	9	72	63	72	0	

Alternative Schedules

Instead of sequencing the orders by color, let's try a sequence that schedules the orders by earliest due date. This sequence should tend to minimize late orders. Figure 7.16 shows the resulting schedule. This schedule is not in color sequence, and addi-tional setup time is required when a lighter color is scheduled after a darker color. The additional setup time is given in the fourth column of figure 7.16.

This schedule has three late orders and is not feasible unless overtime is scheduled. Note that the last order finishes at hour 81.5. Since only 80 hours

Figure 7.16								
Orders Sequenced by Due Date								

ORDER NO.	COLOR CODE	JOB HOURS	SETUP HOURS	HOUR DUE	START HOUR	FINISH HOUR	HOURS EARLY	HOURS LATE
1	1	2		8	0.0	2.0	6.	
11	0	4	0.5	16	2.5	6.5	9.5	
10	0	5		16	6.5	11.5	4.5	
12	4	5		16	11.5	16.5		.5
5	4	4		40	16.5	20.5	19.5	
4	3	10	0.5	40	21.0	31.0	9.	
3	4	3		48	31.0	34.0	14.	
7	4	4		48	34.0	38.0	10.	
15	8	1		56	38.0	39.0	17.	
2	4	11	2.0	56	41.0	52.0	4.	
13	1	1	1.5	64	53.5	54.5	9.5	
9	8	7		64	54.5	61.5	2.5	
6	4	4	2.0	72	63.5	67.5	4.5	
8	8	9		72	67.5	76.5		4.5
14	2	2	3.0	80	79.5	81.5		1.5

are available, the schedule is overloaded. Moreover, if the next week is to start with the target code of 0, an additional hour will be needed to clean out after the last order is finished. This means that $2\frac{1}{2}$ hours of overtime will be required. At this point, the standard schedule appears best—it only has two late orders and uses the least-cost color sequence. But what about other alternatives?

Inspection of the initial color-sequenced schedule (figure 7.15) reveals an intractable problem. Order 1 is due at hour 8, and orders 10, 11, and 12 are due at hour 16. These four orders have a combined processing time of 16 hours—just enough to finish the four orders on time. However, the life of a scheduler is seldom blessed with such good fortune. Note that orders 10 and 11 have a color code of 0 and are scheduled before order 1; order 1 will be three hours late. If order 1 is scheduled first, one-half hour setup time will be added for changing back to color code 0. This will add one-half hour to the total processing time; there is no way to schedule these orders and meet their due dates unless overtime is scheduled at the end of day 1.

This analysis does suggest, however, a better solution. Order 1 should be scheduled first because it is due first, at hour 8. A half-hour setup is then required before starting orders 10 and 11, either of which can

be run first. Finally order 12 can be run—but it will be one-half hour late, as shown in figure 7.17. The balance of the orders can be processed in color sequence. This schedule results in the last three orders also missing their due dates. But can this situation be improved?

Examination of the modified schedule shows that the only order due after the finish hour of 74 is order 14. Perhaps moving order 14 to the end of the schedule will improve the situation. Figure 7.18 shows the result. Indeed the overdue orders at the end of the schedule have been eliminated. But the revised schedule has an additional three setup hours. Is this schedule feasible for an 80-hour biweekly schedule period? The finish time for the last order is hour 77. Note however, that the color code for the last job is 2. Thus, only one hour is needed for the final cleanup (assuming a starting color of 0 in the next schedule period). Accordingly, the schedule can be executed in 78 hours and is feasible. The only violation is the delay in order 12 of one-half hour, which is judged acceptable under the circumstances. (The only alternative is for overtime.)

Having arrived at a schedule for the processor (extruder) that yields an acceptable order delivery performance, the scheduling process moves on to check the base resin and pigment inventories. We

---

Figure 7.17
Modified Color Sequence

ORDER NO.	COLOR CODE	JOB HOURS	SETUP HOURS	HOUR DUE	START HOUR	FINISH HOUR	HOURS EARLY	HOURS LATE
1	1	2		8	0.0	2.0	6.	
11	0	4	0.5	16	2.5	6.5	9.5	
10	0	5		16	6.5	11.5	4.5	
12	4	5		16	11.5	16.5		.5
13	1	1	1.5	64	18.0	19.0	45.	
14	2	2		80	19.0	21.0	59.	
4	3	10		40	21.0	31.0	9.	
5	4	4		40	31.0	35.0	5.	
3	4	3		48	35.0	38.0	10.	
7	4	4		48	38.0	42.0	6.	
2	4	11		56	42.0	53.0	3.	
6	4	4		72	53.0	57.0	15.	
15	8	1		56	57.0	58.0		2.
9	8	7		64	58.0	65.0		1.
8	8	9		72	65.0	74.0		2.

will assume that no problems are uncovered and the schedule is finalized.

Review of Colormix-A

The scheduling strategy for this example is similar in many ways to the preceding Gumm-A example. Referring to figure 7.12, which shows a flowchart for Gumm-A, we see that data and guidelines are again needed for Colormix-A. In both examples, scheduling begins by proposing a schedule for the process unit. This is followed by checking product availabilities, identifying problems, and simulating alternative schedules until an acceptable schedule is achieved. Finally raw materials are checked, and if no problems arise, the schedules are finalized. Both Colormix-A and Gumm-A illustrate the interactive nature of process flow scheduling.

The principal difference in the two examples is the nature of product demand. In the Colormix-A example, custom, make-to-order products are produced, and the materials objective is to ship orders on time. In contrast, the materials objective for Gumm-A is to keep inventories above safety stock levels. Many PFS systems are designed to follow inventories and safety stocks in a manner similar to Gumm-A. Other PFS systems are designed to follow orders and due dates like Colormix-A. When selecting or developing PFS software, one needs to make sure that the method of following materials is consistent with the way orders are placed and the plant operates.

The scheduling procedure for Colormix-A uses the three PFS principles. Scheduling is guided by the process structure, a processor-dominated scheduling procedure is used, and since stage 1 is scheduled before stage 0, a reverse flow scheduling procedure is employed.

Finally, it should be noted that we did not discuss work orders in the Colormix-A example. The Colormix-A schedule in figure 7.18 contains all the scheduling information necessary for unit supervisors and operators. The schedule is the authority to produce, and there is no need for work orders, as in an MRP system.

Material-Dominated Scheduling

Single-unit clusters can also be scheduled using a material-dominated scheduling approach. Material-dominated scheduling (MDS) begins by scheduling materials as needed. Then processors are checked to determine if sufficient capacity is available to produce the materials. Thus, this approach initially assumes that infinite processor capacity is available. If

ORDER NO.	COLOR CODE	JOB HOURS	SETUP HOURS	HOUR DUE	START HOUR	FINISH HOUR	HOURS EARLY	HOURS LATE
1	1	2		8	0.0	2.0	6.	
11	0	4	0.5	16	2.5	6.5	9.5	
10	0	5		16	6.5	11.5	4.5	
12	4	5		16	11.5	16.5		.5
13	1	1	1.5	64	18.0	19.0	45.	
4	3	10		40	19.0	29.0	11.	
5	4	4		40	29.0	33.0	7.	
3	4	3		48	33.0	36.0	12.	
7	4	4		48	36.0	40.0	8.	
2	4	11		56	40.0	51.0	5.	
6	4	4		72	51.0	55.0	17.	
15	8	1		56	55.0	56.0	0	
9	8	7		64	56.0	63.0	1.	
8	8	9		72	63.0	72.0	0	
14	2	2	3.0	80	75.0	77.0	3.	

Figure 7.18
Final Schedule

problems arise when the materials schedule is compared with available capacity, the material plan must be changed. Possible courses of action include

- Producing material in an earlier period that has unused capacity
- Increasing capacity by using overtime, extra workers, subcontracting, etc.
- Using safety stocks to defer the need date to a later period
- Splitting lot sizes to reduce the production time required during the overloaded periods
- Deferring demand until a later period with unused capacity

Material-dominated scheduling begins with a schedule based on material need dates. The use of MDS generally indicates that the scheduling environment has ample capacity and that the production sequence is not very important. Material-dominated scheduling is often used in distribution systems where transportation is readily available. Both order point and distribution requirements planning systems (DRP) are material-dominated scheduling systems. Material requirements planning (MRP) systems are also material-dominated scheduling systems.

Let's now examine three examples of material-dominated scheduling for a single-unit production environment. The first two examples—Gumm-B and Colormix-B—are similar to the previous examples, but the production environments are changed to make MDS more appropriate. The use of similar examples helps emphasize how changes in production environment affect scheduling technology.

Example 7.3: Gumm-B

Suppose the Gumm-A example is changed to reflect that the product is expensive when compared to capacity. The scheduling guidelines are revised to give high priority to minimizing product inventories and assign lower priority to maintaining a low cost sequence. This means that additional setup time is now preferred to carrying additional inventory. Since more setups are expected, more capacity is required, and the normal reactor schedule is raised to 12 hours per day. The process structure given in figure 7.2 still applies, as well as the operating data in figure 7.3. Production continues to be for stock, and the same safety stocks are maintained to provide a similar level of customer service. Product demands

and current inventories are also the same as in Gumm-A.

Material Scheduling

Scheduling procedures for Gumm-B use material-dominated scheduling logic. Accordingly, we first determine when materials will be needed. The spreadsheet in figure 7.19 simulates anticipated material transactions. The first row of each record shows the forecasted demand.

The second row gives the projected inventory levels by day. Let us examine the medium-viscosity inventory calculations. The initial inventory is 42,000 gallons. During week 1, the inventory is reduced by the anticipated demands to 24,000 gallons on Wednesday. This is also the safety stock level. On Friday another order is forecasted. This will drive the inventory below the safety stock to 18,000 gallons and trigger the need for 6,000 gallons on Friday. Since production must be in full batches of 12,000 gallons, a receipt of 12,000 is shown on Friday. This in turn brings the inventory up to 30,000 gallons at the end of Friday. Inventories for the second week and for the other two products can be projected in a similar manner.

The last row of the material record shows when production must be started. Remember that a two-day period is required for quality testing. Thus, production must be started two days before a scheduled receipt. Continuing our examination of the medium-viscosity material record in figure 7.19, we note that the receipt of 12,000 gallons on Friday must be started on Wednesday. Other starts are calculated in a similar manner. However, note that production associated with the receipt of low-viscosity Gumm on Monday of week 2 is started on Friday of week 1. This follows from the two-calendar-day aging process for quality testing, which can use weekends.

This material record is similar to a time-phased MRP record. Unlike most MRP implementations, however, this record uses a lead time that reflects only the processing and quality test time of two days. In contrast, most MRP implementations inflate order lead time to allow for interference from other orders. Commonly called queue time, this typically amounts to 90 percent of the total lead time in an MRP implementation. The simple single-unit production environment of our example does not require an allowance for interference from other jobs waiting to be processed.

The net effect of using material-dominated scheduling logic with actual processing lead times is the minimization of inventories. This effect is illustrated in figure 7.20, which shows that inventories are driven to their safety stock levels. After initial excess inventories are consumed, inventories only exceed their safety stock levels because of the difference between the batch size of 12,000 gallons and some lower volume orders.

This initial schedule minimizes inventory, subject to other guidelines such as safety stocks and batch quantities. But is there sufficient capacity to execute the schedule? Let's check.

Processor Capacity Check

Capacity load calculations use the material schedule in figure 7.19 and the operating data from figure 7.3 (or, equivalently, the production activity data from figure 7.4). Again, let us illustrate the calculations using medium-viscosity Gumm.

The material record (figure 7.19) shows batches starting on Wednesday and Friday of week 1 and on Wednesday of week 2. The production activity data (figure 7.4) show that six hours of reactor time is required for each 12,000-gallon batch of medium-viscosity Gumm. Thus, the reactor load for running medium-viscosity product is six hours on each of these three days. This load is graphically depicted in figure 7.21. The bar segments with an "M" show the medium-viscosity capacity requirements. In a similar fashion, the loads for low-viscosity (L) and high-

---

Figure 7.19
Initial Material-Dominated Schedule

LOW VISCOSITY

UNITS: K Gal.
SAFETY STOCK: 24

		WEEK 1					WEEK 2				
		MON	TUES	WED	THUR	FRI	MON	TUES	WED	THUR	FRI
DEMAND		12		6	6		12		6	6	
INVENTORY	48	36	36	30	24	24	24	24	30	24	24
RECEIPTS							12		12		
STARTS						12	12				

MEDIUM VISCOSITY

UNITS: K Gal.
SAFETY STOCK: 24

		WEEK 1					WEEK 2				
		MON	TUES	WED	THUR	FRI	MON	TUES	WED	THUR	FRI
DEMAND		6	6	6		6	6	6	6		6
INVENTORY	42	36	30	24	24	30	24	30	24	24	30
RECEIPTS						12		12			12
STARTS				12		12			12		

HIGH VISCOSITY

UNITS: K Gal.
SAFETY STOCK: 18

		WEEK 1					WEEK 2				
		MON	TUES	WED	THUR	FRI	MON	TUES	WED	THUR	FRI
DEMAND		12			12				6	6	
INVENTORY	18	18	18	18	18	18	18	18	24	18	18
RECEIPTS		12			12				12		
STARTS			12				12				

---

viscosity (H) products can be calculated and graphed.

The capacity requirements must also include setup times. Continuing our detailed examination of the medium-viscosity product, we note in figure 7.21 that the batch on Wednesday of week 1 is preceded by a high-viscosity batch on Tuesday. Using the production activity data, we find that a four-hour setup is required to make this change. This setup can be scheduled for Tuesday, for Wednesday, or split between Tuesday and Wednesday. As shown in figure 7.21 by the segment labeled "H-M," we scheduled it on Tuesday. Assuming no economic or operational penalty for scheduling setups in advance, we elect to schedule all setups as early as possible. This gives a little safety time in case problems arise during the setups.

The reactor load can be completed by calculating the setup requirements for all other required product changeovers. These are also included on the reactor load chart. Finally, we add the two hours of maintenance, which is shown as the "MT" segment on the first Friday in figure 7.21. Note also that the load chart stops on Wednesday of week 2. Since the material schedule stops on Friday of week 2 and there is a two-day quality testing lead time, no batch starts will ever be scheduled for Thursday and Friday of week 2. Thus, the load chart shows capacity requirements for a period two days less than the material planning horizon.

The reactor load exceeds the 12 hours of available capacity on the first Friday and the second Monday. If orders are moved back, shipments will be delayed.

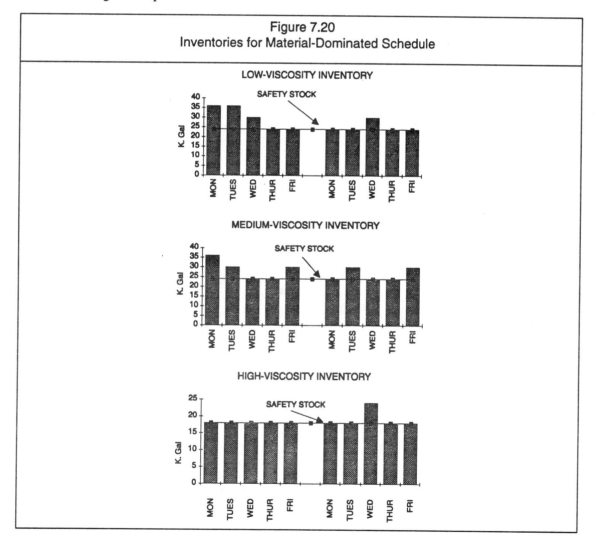

Figure 7.20
Inventories for Material-Dominated Schedule

We should therefore first investigate moving orders to an earlier period.

Many possibilities exist. One possibility, shown in figure 7.22, moves a medium-viscosity batch and a medium-to-low setup from Friday to Thursday. This frees capacity on Friday. Now a low-viscosity batch can be moved from Monday of week 2 to Friday of week 1. As figure 7.22 indicates, these simple schedule revisions also result in a reactor load that meets the daily capacity constraint of 12 hours. The corresponding changes in start dates and receipt dates can now be reflected in the material plan. This material plan (not shown) must be feasible since material orders are processed earlier. These changes will, however, increase inventories.

After product availability and the reactor have been scheduled, the feed stock can also be sched-uled. Production activity data (figure 7.4) are used to determine the amount of feed stock required to support the reactor schedule. Feed stock inventories can be projected and replenishment orders sched-uled to arrive when needed. This scheduling logic closely parallels the logic used previously for the finished products and illustrated in figure 7.19. We will not present details of the feed stock inventory calculations for this example. In addition, we will assume that no material shortages are encountered. This completes the production schedule.

Review of Gumm-B

Gumm-B has a production environment similar to that of Gumm-A, except that excess capacity is available and a scheduling guideline stipulates that inventories should be minimized. Figure 7.23

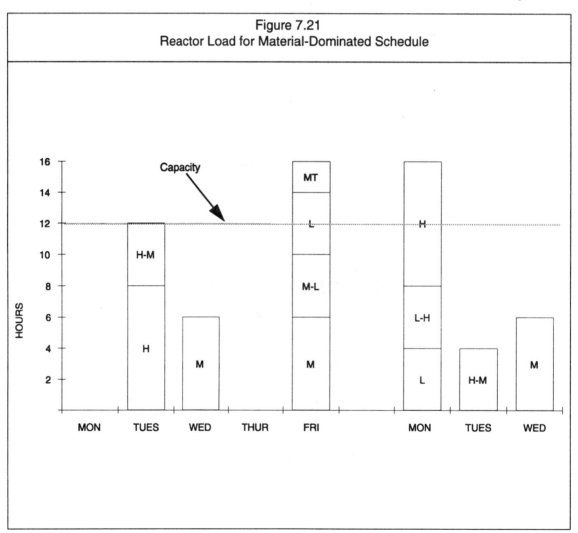

Figure 7.21
Reactor Load for Material-Dominated Schedule

provides an overview of the scheduling process. In order to minimize inventories, an initial infinite-capacity material schedule was developed first. This gave a good view of the best possible material plan.

Next the capacity was checked (decision 1), and a slightly overloaded schedule for Friday and Monday was found. The batch start times were then revised. These changes were reflected in the output material plan. The next capacity check at decision 1 was superficial, since a capacity-feasible schedule was used to develop the new start dates. The schedule was then finalized by checking the input materials.

Gumm-B, like the previous examples, illustrates all three process flow scheduling principles. The process structure guides scheduling calculations, a material-dominated scheduling approach is used,

and since stage 1 is scheduled before stage 0, a reverse-flow scheduling strategy is employed. The Gumm-B example also illustrates the use of an interactive scheduling approach, characteristic of most PFS systems.

Gumm-B uses a material-dominated scheduling approach in a make-to-stock environment. Let's now look at another MDS example—but one that illustrates a make-to-order environment.

Example 7.4: Colormix-B

The production environment for this example is identical to that of Colormix-A except that the extruder is dedicated to one color. Special additives replace the pigments in Colormix-A. These additives are blended with the plastic resin to produce

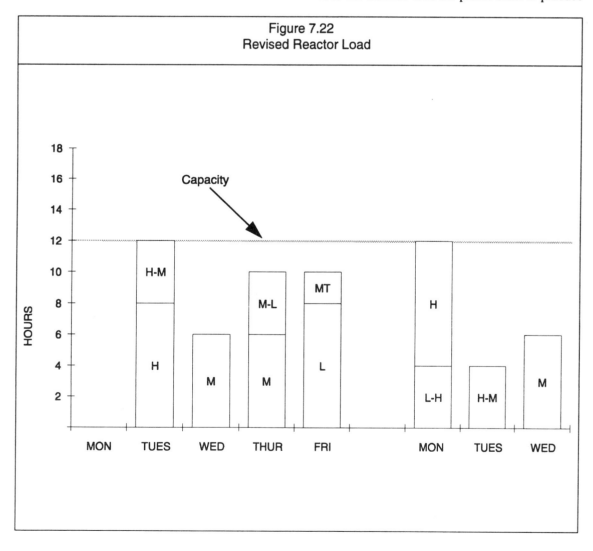

Figure 7.22
Revised Reactor Load

custom plastics. The normal 10-minute changeover is adequate for setups between any pair of products in Colormix-B. Thus, the previous light-to-dark sequence of Colormix-A is not applicable, and products can be sequenced in any order without incurring a setup penalty. As with Colormix-A, production is not scheduled until a customer order is received.

The process flow shown in figure 7.13 for Colormix-A still applies, except that additives replace pigments. We also use the set of orders in figure 7.14, except the color code does not apply.

Scheduling guidelines call for orders to be scheduled as late as possible, but within the limits of eight hours per day of extruder capacity. Overtime will be considered only when the schedule is full.

Scheduling

The calculation of the initial material-dominated schedule is quite easy. The finish time for each order is set equal to the period it is due. Referring to figure 7.24, we see that order 1 is due at hour 8; thus, its finish time is set equal to hour 8. To calculate the start time, subtract the job time from the finish time. Again referring to order 1 in figure 7.24, subtract the job time of two hours from the finish time of hour 8, to give a start time of hour 6. These calculations continue until all jobs have been scheduled.

After a material schedule has been developed, the resulting capacity requirements may be calculated. The lower portion of figure 7.24 shows the load profile for the initial extruder schedule. To determine the number of orders scheduled in any given period, add the orders that have started but have not

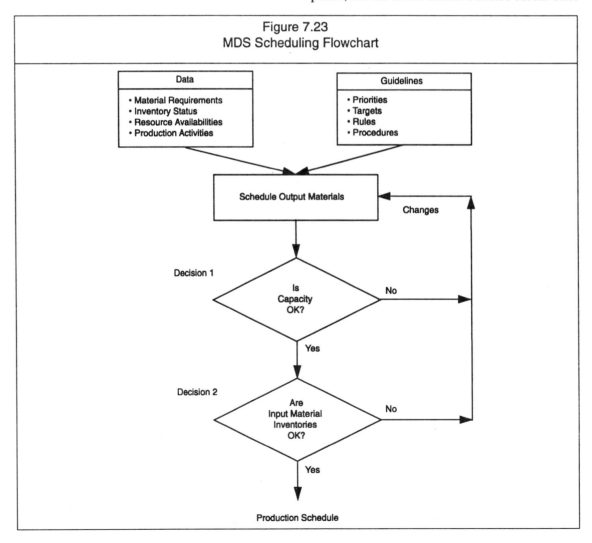

Figure 7.23
MDS Scheduling Flowchart

yet been finished. Consider, for example, hour 11. Inspection of the start and finish times indicates that orders 10 and 12 both start at hour 11 and finish at hour 16. Therefore, both these orders must be running at hour 11. Further inspection of the data reveals that the previous job has already finished and the subsequent jobs have not yet started. Consequently, only two orders (numbers 10 and 12) are scheduled for hour 11. This is shown in the load profile with two orders in period 11.

The load profile shown in figure 7.24 indicates when capacity is needed to produce orders just before they are needed, which eliminates any inventory of preproduced finished orders awaiting shipment on their due dates. Examination of the load profile reveals that if three extruders are available, all orders

can start processing at their latest start times. However, since only one extruder exists, the schedule must be revised.

Assuming that preproduction is preferable to backorders, we will move start dates to an earlier time for some orders. This is accomplished by backward finitely scheduling the order overloads, which levels the schedule to the finite capacity limit of a single extruder. Figure 7.25 shows one of several possible schedules resulting from this process.

The input materials can be scheduled after scheduling orders and the extruder. We again assume that no problems arise in the raw material schedule and do not illustrate these calculations.

Figure 7.24
Extruder Schedule and Load Profile

ORDER NO.	JOB HOURS	HOUR DUE	START HOUR	FINISH HOUR
1	2	8	6	8
10	5	16	11	16
12	5	16	11	16
11	4	16	12	16
4	10	40	30	40
5	4	40	36	40
7	4	48	44	48
3	3	48	45	48
2	11	56	45	56
15	1	56	55	56
9	7	64	57	64
13	1	64	63	64
8	9	72	63	72
6	4	72	68	72
14	2	80	78	80

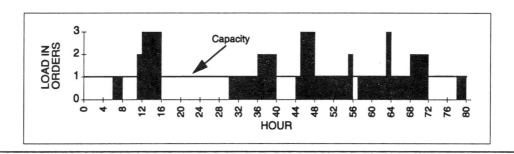

Review of Colormix-B

Colormix-B illustrates material-dominated scheduling in a make-to-order environment. The general scheduling procedure is similar to Gumm-B. Therefore, the MDS scheduling flowchart in figure 7.23 also applies to Colormix-B. As in the previous examples, Colormix-B uses the three PFS principles stated in chapter 3. Also, like all the previous examples, Colormix-B uses an interactive scheduling procedure to resolve problems with the initial schedule.

We have now explored processor-dominated and material-dominated scheduling for make-to-stock and make-to-order environments. The examples all used a demand-driven, reverse flow scheduling approach. Our final example of single-unit scheduling illustrates the use of material-dominated scheduling

with a material push, forward flow scheduling approach.

Example 7.5: Sitka Salmon

Sitka Salmon operates an Alaskan salmon processing plant. When boats arrive with salmon, the fish must be cleaned and frozen within four days. This creates a *material push* on the salmon processing operation. The primary factor driving the schedules is the need to process the fish quickly during the relatively short salmon runs.

The operating data for the processing plant indicate that inventories build quickly during the season and then drop through the year as frozen salmon are sold. Fish can be processed at a rate of 500 kilograms per day. The forecasted demand for frozen salmon is

Figure 7.25
Revised Extruder Schedule and Load Profile

ORDER NO.	JOB HOURS	HOUR DUE	START HOUR	FINISH HOUR	HOURS EARLY
1	2	8	0	2	6
11	4	16	2	6	10
10	5	16	6	11	5
12	5	16	11	16	0
5	4	40	18	22	18
4	10	40	22	32	8
3	3	48	32	35	13
7	4	48	35	39	9
15	1	56	39	40	16
2	11	56	40	51	5
13	1	64	51	52	12
9	7	64	52	59	5
6	4	72	59	63	9
8	9	72	63	72	0
14	2	80	78	80	0

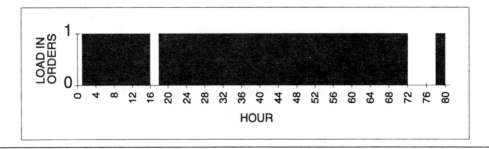

10 kilograms per day. In general, processing capacity is higher than salmon availability during the harvest season. The plant operates 10 hours a day, 7 days per week during the season.

Fish processing yields two products—frozen salmon and fish by-products. Each kilogram of fresh salmon yields 0.6 kilograms of frozen salmon and 0.3 kilograms of by-products. The remaining 0.1 kilograms is waste. The by-products are sold to a pet food processor located nearby. When 800 kilograms of by-product is accumulated, it is shipped to the pet food operation. Again, a forward push of material. The process flow for the salmon processing operation is shown in figure 7.26.

Scheduling

The availability of salmon drives the processing schedules. First, a fresh salmon material plan is developed from the boat schedules during the salmon runs. The plant schedule that consumes the fresh fish is closely coupled to this material plan. Finally, resulting product inventories are projected.

Figure 7.27(a) gives a material plan for fresh salmon. The receipts are based on the scheduled arrival of fishing boats and their forecasted catches. The "use" row shows the fresh salmon consumed in the fish processing operation each day. Consumption depends first on the availability of salmon and second on the available processing capacity. If the prior inventory plus the day's receipts exceeds the daily processing capacity of 500 kg, then 500 kg are

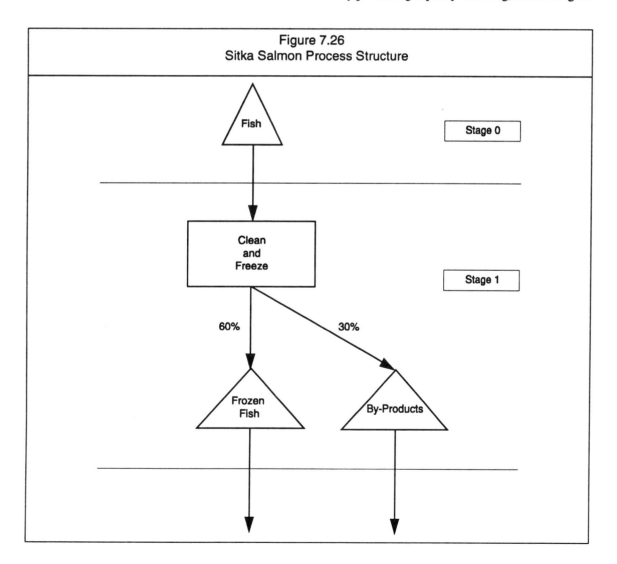

Figure 7.26
Sitka Salmon Process Structure

used. However, if less than 500 kg of salmon is available, only the remaining available fish will be processed.

The last row of the fresh salmon material record shows the run time. The run time indicates the days needed to process the prior inventory and the day's receipts. The run time is calculated only on days when fresh salmon are received. Consider the run time for day 1. The prior inventory is 100, and the receipts are 1,000, giving a total of 1,100 kg of fresh salmon. These salmon will be processed at a rate of 500 kg per day, which requires 2.2 days. The run time is used to check the four-day holding time constraint on fresh salmon.

The plant schedule is obtained directly from the material use row in the fresh salmon material plan.

A Gantt chart showing this schedule appears in figure 7.27(b).

The production of frozen salmon and by-products, shown in figure 7.27(c), is derived from the production schedule. The frozen salmon production is 60 percent of the fresh salmon production scheduled for a day. The demand of 10 kg per day is based on the forecast. The projected inventory is obtained by adding the day's production to the prior day's inventory and then subtracting the day's demand.

The by-product material plan uses a slightly different logic. The production is obtained in a similar manner by multiplying the scheduled fresh salmon processing by 30 percent. However, in place of demand, the by-products are shipped to the pet food processor based on the accumulated amount in

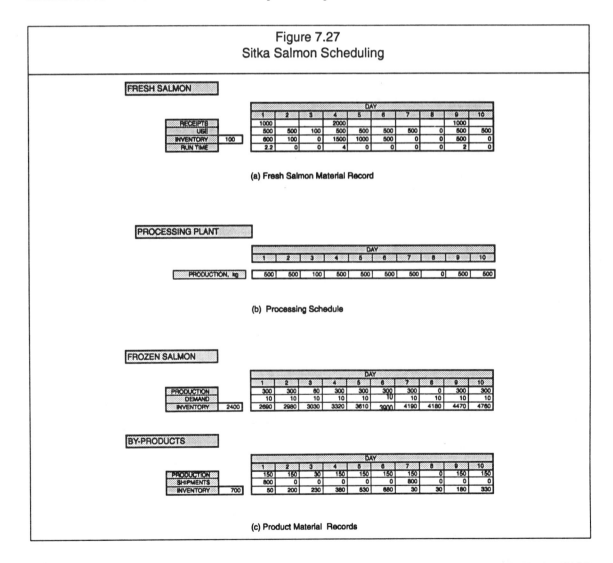

Figure 7.27
Sitka Salmon Scheduling

(a) Fresh Salmon Material Record

(b) Processing Schedule

(c) Product Material Records

inventory. Thus, when 800 kg of by-products is accumulated in inventory, a demand occurs. This is shown in the shipments row of the by-products material record. The resulting inventory is projected in the last row.

Review of Sitka Salmon

Sitka Salmon's scheduling process began with a projection of material receipts. Processing was then scheduled based on both material availability and plant capacity. The resulting schedule was then checked against the four-day holding constraint. Because the constraint was satisfied, neither overtime nor rescheduling of fresh salmon receipts was required. Product and by-product material plans were

then generated. Figure 7.28 summarizes this scheduling process.

This scheduling process differs from previous examples. The operations schedule is driven by the arrival of raw materials—much like the arrival of customers in a service operation.

Even though the scheduling process differs from the preceding examples, it still uses the three process flow scheduling principles. The process structure guides scheduling calculations. These calculations start with the arrival of raw material, move on to scheduling the fish processing operation, and end with developing product material plans. This procedure schedules materials before processors; it is therefore a material-dominated schedule. Finally, since the order for scheduling process stages is the

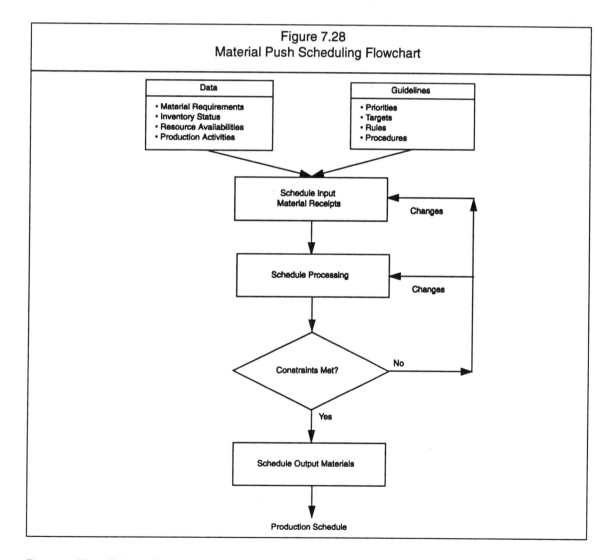

Figure 7.28
Material Push Scheduling Flowchart

Data
- Material Requirements
- Inventory Status
- Resource Availabilities
- Production Activities

Guidelines
- Priorities
- Targets
- Rules
- Procedures

Schedule Input Material Receipts

Changes

Schedule Processing

Changes

Constraints Met? — No

Yes

Schedule Output Materials

Production Schedule

same as the direction in which materials flow, the scheduling process uses a forward flow scheduling strategy.

Simultaneous Scheduling

When scheduling a single unit, processors and materials must be scheduled. The previous sections addressed both processor-dominated and material-dominated scheduling. The examples presented above used iterative procedures in which the processors and materials were scheduled and rescheduled until an acceptable schedule was obtained. Wouldn't it be nice if there were some way to schedule both the processor and materials in one operation, obtain an initial feasible solution, and thereby eliminate all the iterations? Is simultaneous scheduling a real possibility or an academic fantasy?

The technology now exists to develop production plans in this manner. Mathematical programming techniques—for example, linear and integer programming—are commonly used to develop production plans. Mathematical programming models use equations to represent material balances associated with production and consumption—the material-oriented part of the model. In addition, the model includes equations to represent processor capacity constraints—the processor-oriented part of the model. This set of material and capacity equations is solved simultaneously with special computer algorithms and yields a solution that is feasible, i.e., meets product demands within processor capacity constraints. Moreover, the computer algorithm maximizes or minimizes a user-specified objective. For example, a model may be formulated with an objective of minimizing variable operating cost.

As we move from the development of production plans to the more detailed production schedules, creating—as well as solving—the corresponding mathematical programming model becomes much more difficult. More time periods are necessary, more product and process detail must be included, and integer variables are needed to represent product sequencing and setups in the computer models. Further complicating matters is the need for frequent rescheduling in a rapidly changing environment.

Production plans generally range from a single annual time period to 18 monthly time intervals. In contrast, a production schedule may need detail by hour or minute and have hundreds—or thousands—of time intervals. Mathematical programming models use a bucketed framework for modeling time, and a decision variable is needed for each product in each period. Thus, scheduling models have many more decision variables than production planning models.

Obtaining all the required data for a scheduling model also presents problems. Production schedules must include enough detail that operating personnel can execute the schedule. This means that a schedule must indicate the exact item to be produced on each process unit during the scheduling horizon. Production plans, on the other hand, can aggregate products into families and production processes into plants or process trains. Consequently, production schedules have much more product and process detail and require more data than production plans.

Production plans generally do not consider actual production sequences and lot sizes. In contrast, production schedules must specify sequences and lot sizes. To develop a mathematical programming model that includes a representation of product sequencing constraints and the setups associated with lot sizes, integer variables must be introduced. Introducing integer variables into the resulting model makes optimization of the model much more difficult and often impractical.

Because of these factors, scheduling requires frequent solution of extremely large mathematical programming models with integer variables. Developing the models is difficult because large amounts of rapidly changing data—such as current inventory levels and process unit availability—are needed. Solving the resulting large integer-programming models is generally not practical with today's solution algorithms and computers.

The Outlook

We note that technology has progressed to the point where mathematical programming models with three-day to seven-day time intervals have been developed. These models have sufficient product and process detail and consider sequences and setups (lot sizes). However, they usually do not have sufficient time detail for direct use by operating personnel. While some may consider these as schedules, it must be recognized that these "schedules" lack the time detail characteristic of most operating schedules. We prefer to call them production plans.

What is the answer to our question about the feasibility of simultaneously scheduling processors and materials? Unfortunately, simultaneous scheduling with mathematical programming is not generally practical in most scheduling situations today. We nevertheless believe that mathematicians, operations researchers, and computer scientists will someday advance technology to the point where optimal scheduling will become feasible. We must note that some experts in this area are not as optimistic as we are. This is a very difficult mathematical problem.

Bottom line: Don't hold your breath or delay implementing one of today's computer-based scheduling systems while waiting for the development of an optimal scheduling system.

Conclusion

In this chapter we examined the simplest of all scheduling environments—single units. We presented two examples of processor-dominated scheduling and three examples of material-dominated scheduling. These examples illustrated a variety of scheduling approaches, but they do not represent a comprehensive list.

A number of existing scheduling techniques that we have not illustrated are within the domain of single-stage scheduling. Let's examine three of these techniques. A periodic review system is basically a processor-dominated system. Here the period of the review is set by a schedule for the processor. For example, a truck may replenish a particular field warehouse only on Mondays. The material plan is only reviewed weekly to determine how much of each item should be sent to the field warehouse. The scheduling process is dominated by the truck's schedule.

The familiar order-point systems are material-dominated systems. In order-point systems, inventory positions are continuously monitored. When the inventory position drops below a predetermined order point, an order is placed. This in turn creates a demand for processors (transportation equipment or plant equipment). Here we calculate when materials are needed and set processor schedules to meet these needs.

Just-in-Time systems are also material-dominated systems. Ideally, a JIT system will be able to produce orders quickly in any sequence and in lot sizes as low as one item. The JIT ideal requires a flexible manufacturing facility with level customer demand or excess manufacturing capacity. Formal schedules are replaced with visible signs (kanbans) that indicate to line workers what needs to be produced next. No formal, detailed processor schedules are developed. To avoid overloading the JIT cell, the amount of work must be controlled by a production plan that considers processor capacity.

These examples, as well as the detailed examples presented previously, illustrate the flexibility of PFS systems. There are many ways to schedule a single unit. The technique used depends on the manufacturing environment and business strategy. The appropriate technique may even change with the business cycle. When there is excess plant capacity, a material-dominated approach may be appropriate. On the other hand, when the plant is sold out, a processor-dominated approach may be appropriate.

All five examples presented in this chapter use the three basic PFS principles. The process structure, though simple for a single unit, guides scheduling calculations. Moving on to the second principle, we see that the process units are scheduled using either processor-dominated or material-dominated scheduling approaches. Finally, the overall strategy uses a reverse flow scheduling strategy or a forward flow scheduling strategy.

Let us now examine the scheduling of process clusters. Process cluster schedules are built from process unit schedules. However, since a cluster may contain more than a single process unit, many new possibilities exist.

Chapter 8

Process Cluster Scheduling

Process clusters are groups of process units; as you might expect, process units can be grouped and scheduled in many ways. The three principal groupings are (1) single-unit clusters, (2) stockless clusters, and (3) job shop clusters. Single-unit clusters were discussed in the previous chapter. Stockless cluster scheduling is the main topic of this chapter. The last cluster type, job shops, can be scheduled using MRP techniques.

Cluster Structures

A sample process structure for a simple, serial-flow stockless cluster is given in figure 8.1. The first process unit in this figure might be a mixing operation, and the second, a packaging operation. Notice that the two process units in this cluster have no decoupling inventories, and their schedules must be synchronized. This is an example of a *tightly coupled* process cluster.

Figure 8.2 illustrates another type of stockless cluster—two parallel process units that use the same raw materials and produce the same products. Packaging lines often use this type of parallel structure. Notice that the two parallel units do not feed or supply each other. Thus, they do not require the close synchronization of the previously illustrated tightly coupled process cluster. However, because the process units

use the same feed and produce the same products, their schedules require some coordination. A grouping of parallel process units performing a similar operation is called a *loosely coupled* stockless cluster.

Job shop clusters differ from stockless clusters. A job shop cluster is a group of process units organized in a classical job shop configuration. Job shop clusters include all process units that perform a particular process step, e.g., feed preparation. Individual jobs have different routings through the process units, and inventories are used to smooth work loads.

Let us now explore different ways of scheduling stockless clusters by examining two examples. The first example is for a tightly coupled cluster, and the second is for a loosely coupled cluster.

Example 8.1: Chromopaste

Chromopaste is a colored paste that is manufactured in a continuous flow operation with three process steps. Figure 8.3 illustrates Chromopaste's process structure. The capacity for all three process units is balanced at 600 pounds per day. The first process unit, a reactor, produces two types of paste—A and B. The pastes cannot be stored in inventory and are moved immediately to a mixer. The mixer blends pigments with the pastes to make each type of paste in red, white, and blue. Finally, the paste is filled into containers X and Y. The only difference between the two containers is their labeling; both containers hold one pound of paste.

The result of the Chromopaste process is 12 different paste products. A coding scheme identifies each of the pastes. Products are coded first by color (red, white, and blue), second by paste type (A and B), and third by package (X and Y). For example, product RAX is a red paste of type A in package X.

The most difficult changeovers are for different colors. The color mixer and downstream container filler must be completely shut down and washed out before running another color. This color changeover requires one full day. In contrast, changing container types involves only changing the packaging label used in the filling operation. This changeover can be accomplished without shutting down the filler, and no production time is lost.

Changing paste types on the reactor is also relatively easy. Paste changeovers require changing the reactor temperature and are accomplished quickly in the continuous flow reactor. These paste changeovers, like the package changeovers, do not result in any lost production time.

The net effect of this process technology is that the color mixer, having one-day setups, controls the schedule for the entire three-step process string. Since the color mixer controls the cluster's schedules, it is designated the *key unit*. The reactor and filler schedules, which must be synchronized with the mixer, are called *support units*.

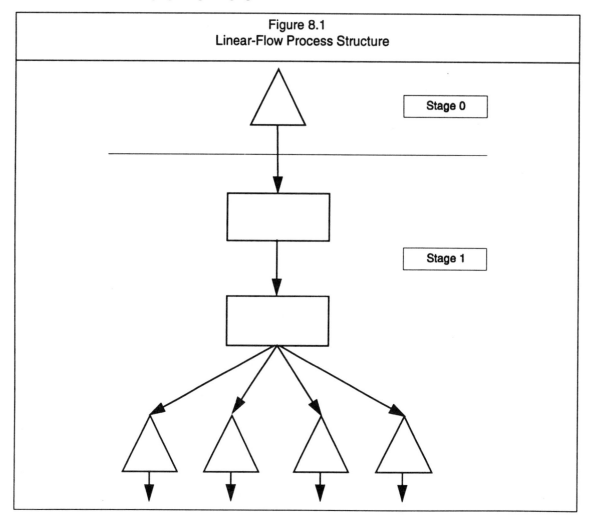

Figure 8.1
Linear-Flow Process Structure

Stage 0

Stage 1

Scheduling Targets

The production plan sets several targets for scheduling product families. First, all products of a given color should be scheduled together to minimize setup time and costs. Second, the scheduling sequence for product families should be red, white, and then blue to minimize color contamination problems. Third, an analysis of cluster capacity and run-length economics reveals that red family runs should be two days; white, three days; and blue, two days.

Other targets concern scheduling individual items. To reduce confusion from too many product changeovers, each product should be produced only once in a family run. In a red family run, for example, each of the four red products should be scheduled only once. This target is flexible because paste and container changeovers are relatively easy.

Another item scheduling target concerns the sequence of production within a product family. Product quality is improved by minimizing the number of paste changes within a color family. Thus, containers X and Y should be switched more frequently than pastes A and B within a product family schedule. The resulting target sequence for the red family is RAX, RAY, RBX, RBY. Similar target sequences are used for the white and blue product families.

Family Scheduling

As discussed above, the production plan specifies a target sequence and run lengths for each color. An initial color schedule is proposed for the entire cluster using these target run lengths and the target

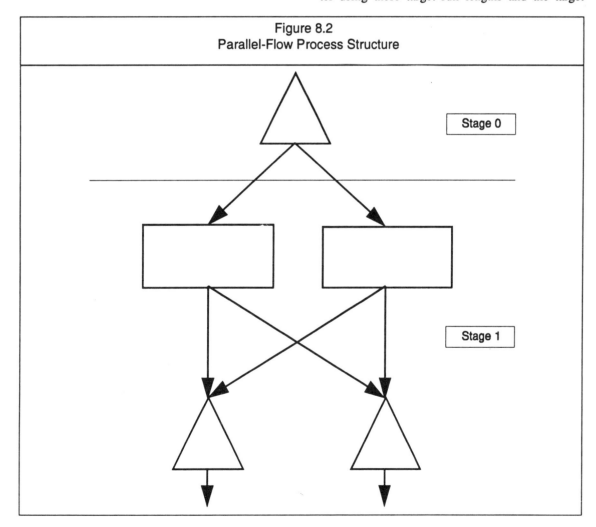

Figure 8.2
Parallel-Flow Process Structure

Stage 0

Stage 1

sequence of red, white, and blue. Figure 8.4 shows this schedule. Since a processor schedule is proposed before a material schedule, this represents a processor-dominated scheduling approach. The PDS approach ensures that target sequences and run lengths are given high priority when developing cluster schedules.

Item Production Requirements

The family schedule must now be disaggregated into a schedule for each item in each product family. To illustrate this process, let us examine the first family production run—a two-day run of the red family. Using the production rate of 600 pounds per day, 1,200 pounds of red products will be produced. There are four red products (RAX, RAY, RBX, and RBY), among which the 1,200 pounds must be divided. One way of allocating production is to equalize the run-out time for each product. This allocation method divides the 1,200 pounds of production so that all four products will reach their safety stock levels at the same future time.

The calculations for the run-out time technique begin with a time-phased projection of material requirements, as shown in figure 8.5. The first row shows the forecasted product demand. The second row gives an inventory projection that assumes no additional production. The last row, titled "CNPR," shows the cumulative net production requirements. This entry represents the amount of production required to bring the inventory up to its safety stock level. The CNPR values are *cumulative*, since no production is assumed in this calculation. The CNPR is *net*, because any existing inventories are netted out.

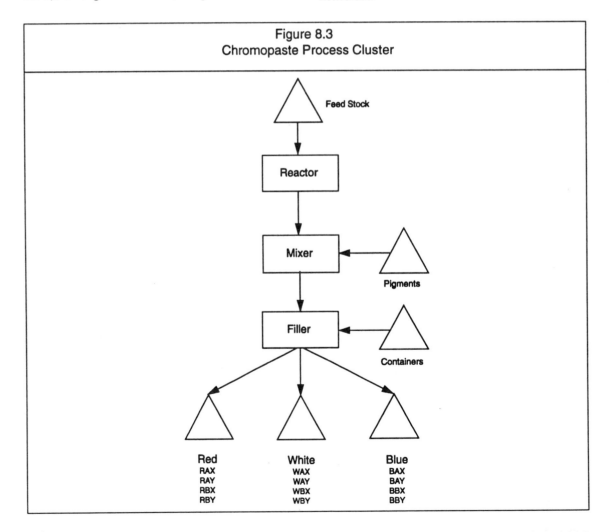

Figure 8.3
Chromopaste Process Cluster

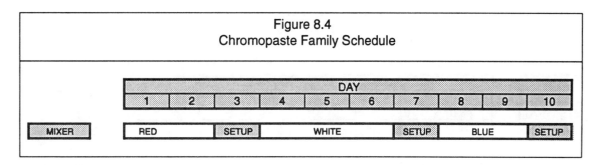

Figure 8.4
Chromopaste Family Schedule

To calculate the CNPR, subtract the current inventory from the safety stock. For example, consider RAX. If inventories exceed the safety stock level, as in periods 1 and 2, then no production is required and a zero is entered for the CNPR. Now look at period 3, with a projected inventory of 200. Since the safety stock is 250, production of 50 is needed to bring the inventory back to the safety stock level.

Thus, the CNPR for period 3 is 50. Skipping the details for a few periods and moving on to period 10, the projected inventory assuming no production is –270. Bringing RAX up to its safety stock level of 250 and covering demand through period 10 will require 520 pounds of production. This is the CNPR value for period 10.

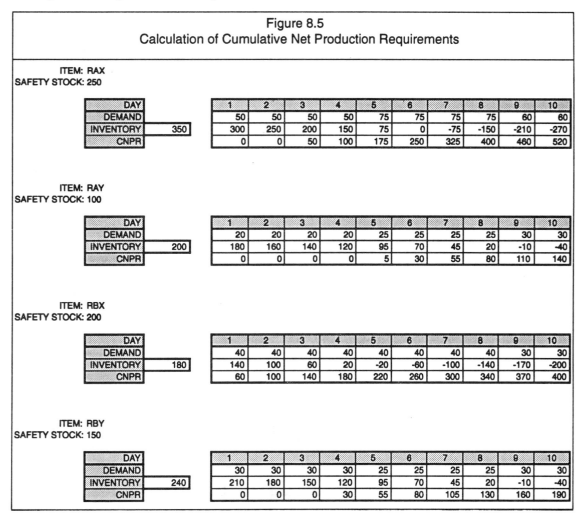

Figure 8.5
Calculation of Cumulative Net Production Requirements

DAY	1	2	3	4	5	6	7	8	9	10
RAX	0	0	50	100	175	250	325	400	460	520
RAY	0	0	0	0	5	30	55	80	110	140
RBX	60	100	140	180	220	260	300	340	370	400
RBY	0	0	0	30	55	80	105	130	160	190
TOTAL	60	100	190	310	455	620	785	950	1100	1250

Figure 8.6
Cumulative Net Production Requirements Summary

The allocation of production among the four products is calculated from the CNPRs. Figure 8.6 summarizes the CNPR values from figure 8.5 in spreadsheet form. In addition, the CNPRs are totaled in the last row. Following across the last row, we see that if 1,100 pounds of the red family is produced, it would last nine days. Similarly, 1,250 pounds of production would last 10 days. Thus, the scheduled 1,200 pounds of production will last between nine and ten days.

The allocation of the 1,200 pounds of production is derived from columns 9 and 10. Let us begin by considering the allocation of the first 1,100 pounds among the four products. This allocation is given by the individual CNPRs in period 9: RAX = 460, RAY = 110, RBX = 370, and RBY = 160. Note, however, that the scheduled two-day production run will produce 1,200 pounds of red paste. This means that there is an additional 100 pounds of paste above the 1,100 pounds required to meet demand through period 9.

The problem now is how to allocate the last 100 pounds, which is only a portion of day 10's demand. The fraction of day 10's demand is calculated as follows:

$$\frac{1,200 - 1,100}{1,250 - 1,100} = 0.667.$$

The allocation of demand among the four products is calculated by adding 0.667 of day 10's demand to the CNPRs for period 9. The demand for period 10 is easily obtained from the difference in CNPRs for periods 9 and 10. This allocation calculation is summarized in figure 8.7 and shows the mix for the 1,200-pound production run of the red family.

The resulting family run-out time can now be checked against the production schedule in figure 8.4. The next proposed run for the red family begins on day 11, and the run-out time is 9.667 days—a problem, but not a big problem. The scheduler must now make a decision. Should a white or blue family run be shortened and the red run moved to an earlier time? Should overtime be scheduled? Or should some of the safety stock be used? Since the run-out time is very close to the next scheduled run, the scheduler decides to use a little safety stock. The scheduler recognizes, however, that it will be necessary to monitor new paste orders closely and possibly revise the schedule.

Process Unit Schedules

The three process units must all share the same underlying schedule, but each unit has differences in the amount of detail. The first unit, the paste reactor,

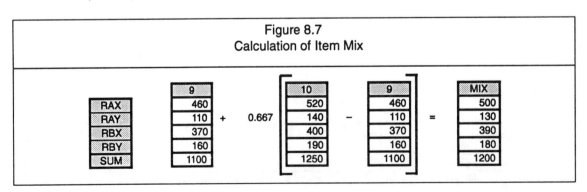

Figure 8.7
Calculation of Item Mix

	9			10		9		MIX
RAX	460	+	0.667	520	−	460	=	500
RAY	110			140		110		130
RBX	370			400		370		390
RBY	160			190		160		180
SUM	1100			1250		1100		1200

only needs to schedule two types of paste—A and B. There is no need to specify the color and package of the finished product where the paste will ultimately be used. The second unit, the color mixer, only needs a schedule that specifies the type of paste and its color. Finally, the filling schedule needs to specify the input material color and paste type as well as the container to be used in each item run.

Let us continue with our analysis of the first scheduled run of the red family. In the previous section, the item mix for the two-day red production run was calculated and the result given in figure 8.7. As also previously discussed, the production plan specifies a target frequency and sequence for items produced in a family production run. These scheduling targets and the item mix provide a starting point for detailed unit scheduling.

Scheduling begins with the filling unit. A spreadsheet schedule for filling is given at the top of figure 8.8. The production mix calculated in figure 8.7 calls for a 500-pound run of RAX. The previously mentioned scheduling guidelines specify that RAX should be produced first and that all 500 pounds should be produced in one run. Accordingly, 500 pounds of RAX is scheduled on day 1 as shown in the spreadsheet.

The next item in the target sequence is RAY. Its run quantity is 130 pounds; however, because of capacity limits on daily production, only 100 pounds can be scheduled for day 1 and the remaining 30 pounds must be carried over to day 2. The 100-pound capacity limit on RAY in day 1 is all that remains of the 600-pound daily capacity after the 500 pounds of RAX is scheduled for day 1. The next two products, RBX and RBY, are scheduled in a

---

Figure 8.8
Process Unit Schedules

FILLING SCHEDULE

	DAY		
	1	2	TOTAL
RAX	500	0	500
RAY	100	30	130
RBX	0	390	390
RBY	0	180	180
TOTAL	600	600	1200

MIXER SCHEDULE

	DAY		
	1	2	TOTAL
RA	600	30	630
RB	0	570	570
TOTAL	600	600	1200

REACTOR SCHEDULE

	DAY		
	1	2	TOTAL
A	600	30	630
B	0	570	570
TOTAL	600	600	1200

similar manner. This completes the filling schedule shown in figure 8.8.

The filling schedule can now be rolled back to develop the mixer schedule. This is easily performed by adding container sizes together in the filler schedule to obtain the mixer schedule. For example, consider the calculation of the amount of red type A (RA) paste to be scheduled on day 1. The filling schedule calls for 500 RAX and 100 RAY on day 1. Adding these together yields 600 pounds of RA for the mixer schedule on day 1. Other mixer entries are calculated in a similar manner and shown in the middle of figure 8.8.

The mixer schedule must be consistent with the family schedule, but it includes more detail. Both the mixer schedule (in figure 8.8) and the red family schedule (figure 8.4) show a two-day run for the red family. Thus, the schedules are consistent. (A lack of consistency would indicate a computational error.) The mixer schedule in figure 8.6 shows the paste type as well as the color being run in the mixer. In contrast, the family schedule in figure 8.4 only shows that the red family is scheduled for days 1 and 2. Thus, the mixer schedule tells operators what type of feed to expect and the complete specification of the mixer's output product for any point in time.

The mixer schedule can now be rolled back to determine the reactor schedule. This procedure is the same as that used for rolling the filler schedule back to the mixer. The bottom of figure 8.8 shows the result. In this figure, the reactor schedule is identical to the mixer schedule because the mixer schedule shows only the two-day run for the red paste family. A mixer schedule for a complete campaign cycle would also show production runs for the white and blue families. In contrast, the reactor schedule never needs to show more than the paste types A and B, as shown in figure 8.8.

Product Inventories

Now that we have detailed production schedules for all process units, the resulting planned inventory levels can be checked. Figure 8.9 gives the material plan for the next 10 days. This 10-day period covers the run-out time for the planned red family run. These inventory projections reveal two problems. First, the inventory for RBX is currently 180, which is below its safety stock of 200. Moreover, RBX inventory drops to 140 in period 1 before being

produced in period 2. The probability that demand will change significantly in the next couple of days is relatively small. Thus, the violation of the safety stock level target is accepted, and no changes are made in the schedule.

Further inspection of the product inventory projections shows that all four red family products drop a little below their safety stock levels in period 10. This is expected, since previous calculations gave a run-out time of 9.667 days. At this time a decision was made to monitor orders and use safety stocks to cover the small anticipated shortfall in meeting demand. Neither inventory problem is serious, and scheduling continues.

Input Material Requirements

After completing processor and material schedules for the cluster, all that remains is to develop an acceptable schedule for feed stock, pigments, and containers. These can be readily calculated from the cluster's production schedule. Since this type of calculation is quite simple and was already illustrated with the Polygoo example in chapter 3, we will not show these calculations. Moreover, for this example we assume that no problems surface while scheduling these raw materials. This completes scheduling for the red product family's two-day production run.

Scheduling continues by making similar calculations for the white and blue product families. If problems appear, the red family schedule may need revision. After satisfactory schedules for red, white, and blue have been developed, the first campaign cycle schedule is complete. Additional campaign cycles can be scheduled through the desired schedule horizon.

Review of Chromopaste

Chromopaste illustrates scheduling procedures for a tightly coupled stockless cluster. An important concept is the designation of one of the process units as the key unit. Since the process units are not decoupled, the same basic schedule must be used for all three process units. The key unit sets the underlying schedule for the entire cluster. In the Chromopaste example, the color mixer is the key unit, and the color mixing schedule dominates the reactor paste and the container filling schedules.

The flowchart in figure 8.10 provides a review of the scheduling steps for Chromopaste. Using the scheduling data and guidelines, a family schedule is developed by color. This schedule is a processor-dominated schedule that uses the run-length and sequencing guidelines. The initial schedule shows only product families and must now be disaggregated into an item schedule. Each family's production is then allocated among individual items so that items in a family will run out at the same time. The resulting run-out time is used to check the family inventories. Since the run-out time for the red family occurs before the next scheduled red family production run, a problem is highlighted. The problem is not severe, and safety stocks will be used to cover the minor projected inventory shortfall.

Next, using the previously calculated item production requirements, a detailed production schedule is developed for each process unit. This process starts with the last process unit—the filler, and the schedules are rolled back to the first unit—the reactor. Product inventories are then checked to see whether safety stock targets have been met. Two minor problems surface, and it is decided to again use safety stocks. Finally, the input material requirements for feed stock, pigments, and containers are calculated, and no problems are encountered. This completes the schedule.

As with all previous examples, Chromopaste scheduling uses the three process flow scheduling principles. The cluster's process structure guides the scheduling steps, processor-dominated scheduling is employed, and a reverse flow scheduling approach is used.

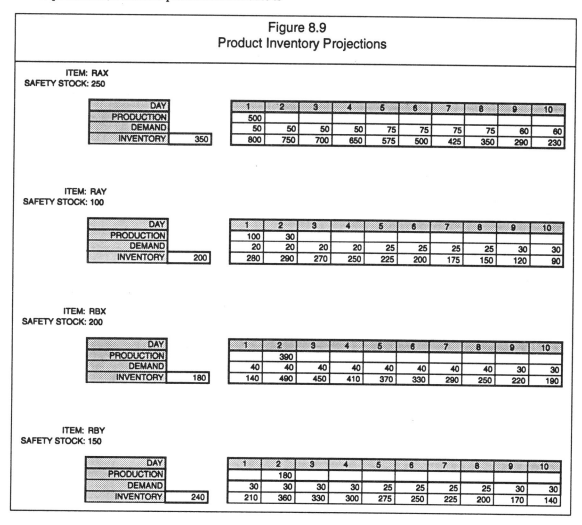

Figure 8.9
Product Inventory Projections

ITEM: RAX
SAFETY STOCK: 250

DAY		1	2	3	4	5	6	7	8	9	10
PRODUCTION		500									
DEMAND		50	50	50	50	75	75	75	75	60	60
INVENTORY	350	800	750	700	650	575	500	425	350	290	230

ITEM: RAY
SAFETY STOCK: 100

DAY		1	2	3	4	5	6	7	8	9	10
PRODUCTION		100	30								
DEMAND		20	20	20	20	25	25	25	25	30	30
INVENTORY	200	280	290	270	250	225	200	175	150	120	90

ITEM: RBX
SAFETY STOCK: 200

DAY		1	2	3	4	5	6	7	8	9	10
PRODUCTION			390								
DEMAND		40	40	40	40	40	40	40	40	30	30
INVENTORY	180	140	490	450	410	370	330	290	250	220	190

ITEM: RBY
SAFETY STOCK: 150

DAY		1	2	3	4	5	6	7	8	9	10
PRODUCTION			180								
DEMAND		30	30	30	30	25	25	25	25	30	30
INVENTORY	240	210	360	330	300	275	250	225	200	170	140

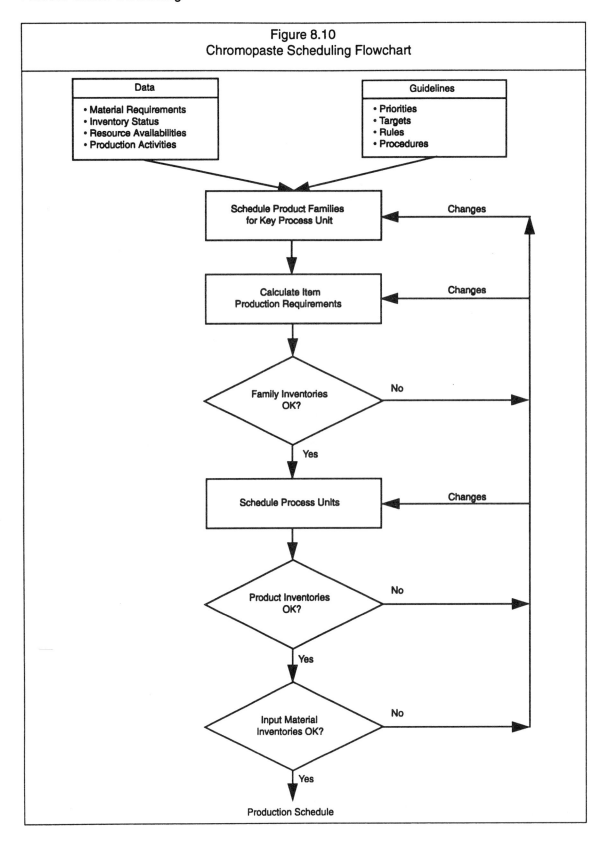

Figure 8.10
Chromopaste Scheduling Flowchart

Tightly Coupled Stockless Clusters

The Chromopaste example illustrates scheduling a cluster with a tightly coupled structure. This structure, given in figure 8.3, is a serial structure (sometimes called a string) in which each successive process unit directly feeds the next downstream unit. Figure 8.11 illustrates two other simple process structures. The top structure shows a split-flow cluster that might be found in a separation process where a co-product or a by-product is produced. Note that units B1 and B2 obtain different materials from A1's separation process and that B1 and B2 produce different products. The bottom structure in figure 8.11 shows a merged-flow structure that might be found in a blending or assembly operation. Here process units A1 and A2 provide different input materials to unit B1.

The basic strategy for scheduling split-flow and merged-flow structures is the same as previously illustrated for serial-flow structures with the Chromopaste example. The key process unit is identified first; a family schedule based on the key unit is then proposed. The next step is to determine item-level requirements that are consistent with the family sequences and run lengths for the key unit. Finally, the item schedules are rolled back and/or pushed forward through the cluster's process structure until all units are scheduled.

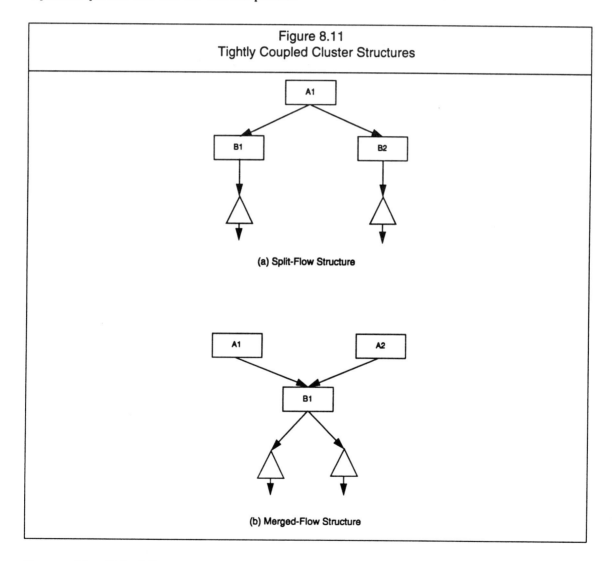

Figure 8.11
Tightly Coupled Cluster Structures

(a) Split-Flow Structure

(b) Merged-Flow Structure

This concludes our brief introduction to scheduling tightly coupled process clusters. Let us now investigate scheduling loosely coupled cluster structures. We will introduce this topic with another example and then explore variations.

Example 8.2: Show Glow Packaging

Show Glow is a liquid wax that is produced in large and small bottles. The daily demand forecast is 1,100 small bottles and 1,600 large bottles. As shown in figure 8.12, the Show Glow packaging cluster consists of three identical packaging lines. A bulk liquid wax (W) inventory feeds all three bottling lines. These in turn produce the small (S) and large (L) bottles of Show Glow wax. Each bottling line can fill 1,000 bottles per day of either size. One day is required to change a line from one bottle size to the other.

The production plan specifies guidelines for scheduling. One guideline is a rule that line 1 will always run small bottles, line 3 will always run large bottles, and line 2 will run both sizes by alternating between bottle sizes. Another guideline is a rule that specifies

a minimum run length of one day on line 2 for either bottle size. One more guideline specifies that the target maximum inventory for each product is 10,000 bottles and the target minimum for each is 4,000 bottles.

Target Schedules

The above guidelines determine the target schedules for lines 1 and 3. Line 1 runs small bottles at its capacity of 1,000 bottles per day. In a similar manner, line 2 runs large bottles at its capacity of 1,000 bottles per day. The remaining demand, 100 small bottles per day and 600 large bottles per day, is assigned to line 2.

The target campaign cycle length for line 2 is derived from the one-day-minimum-run-length rule. In one day, line 2 can produce 1,000 small bottles. This production will be consumed at a rate of 100 bottles per day, which is the small-bottle demand assigned to line 2. Dividing the minimum lot size of 1,000 by the demand of 100 shows that the small-bottle production lot will last 10 days. If more than one lot is produced within a 10-day period, production will exceed demand and inventories will increase. Since 10 days is required to work off the minimum lot size of 1,000 bottles, the minimum

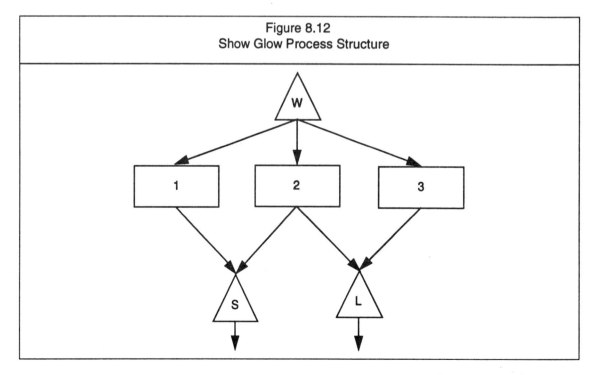

Figure 8.12
Show Glow Process Structure

time between small bottle runs is 10 days. This in turn sets the minimum campaign cycle length.

The production run length for large bottles must be sufficient to cover demand during the 10-day campaign cycle. The large bottle allocation for line 2 is 600 bottles per day. Thus, a six-day production run producing 6,000 large bottles will be needed every 10 days. Each campaign cycle must also include one day to switch from small bottles to large and another day to switch back.

Using the above data, we see that the 10-day campaign cycle should include one day for a small-bottle run, six days for a large-bottle run, and two days for line changeovers. This leaves one day of planned idle time, which can be used as a capacity cushion. The resulting target schedule for line 2 is given at the top of figure 8.13.

Scheduling

Scheduling uses the target schedule, other guidelines, and data on the current inventory levels. Scheduling begins by proposing the target schedule given in figure 8.13. Next, product availability is checked against target minimum and maximum inventories. The results are given by the graphs at the bottom of figure 8.13. These inventories are within the inventory guidelines' acceptable ranges of 4,000 to 10,000 bottles for both products.

The final step checks input material (bulk wax) to ensure that a sufficient quantity is available to support the proposed schedules for lines 1, 2, and 3. This bulk wax schedule will not be shown, and we will assume that no problems surface. This completes scheduling of processors and materials for the Show Glow packaging cluster.

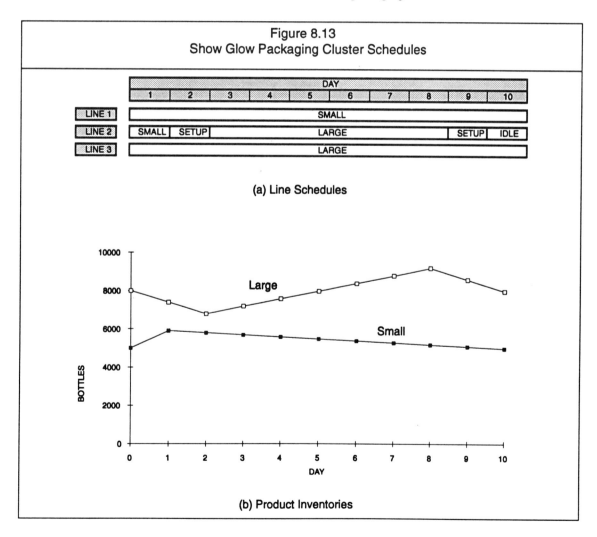

Figure 8.13
Show Glow Packaging Cluster Schedules

(a) Line Schedules

(b) Product Inventories

Scheduling a cluster of parallel process units is similar to scheduling individual process units. The Show Glow example uses a processor-dominated scheduling procedure similar to that used in example 7.1, Gumm-A. The flowchart given for Gumm-A in figure 7.12 also applies to Show Glow. The major difference between these two examples is the need to allocate demand among each of the three process units in the Show Glow example.

Loosely Coupled Stockless Clusters

Show Glow illustrates scheduling loosely coupled stockless clusters. The process structure presented in figure 8.12 is a parallel unit structure. Units in loosely coupled structures perform similar tasks. They may also be linked by using the same or similar input materials or by producing the same or similar output materials.

A key issue in scheduling parallel units is allocating demand among process units. Scheduling guidelines from the production plan set the basis for this allocation. The procedure for allocating demand depends on the particular scheduling environment. In some cases, the allocation is based on differences in the processing capabilities of the units. For example, a packaging line may only be able to produce certain package sizes.

In other cases the demand allocation is based on differences in marginal operating costs. For example, a new packaging line may be more automated and require less labor than an older line. The guidelines might then specify that the new line should be fully used and any remaining production should be assigned to the older line. Another factor to consider in assigning production to lines is product groupings. Thus, light-colored products might be assigned to one line and dark-colored products to another.

After production among parallel process units has been allocated, the scheduling problem is essentially a set of single unit scheduling problems. However, if problems arise with common output or input materials, adjustments to the schedules for one unit may affect the schedules for another unit. Consequently, the schedules of the parallel process units are loosely coupled.

Complex Stockless Cluster Structures

The simple stockless cluster structures previously presented can be combined into more complex process structures. Figure 8.14 shows two examples of more complex structures. The top figure shows two parallel strings in the same cluster. Grouping the two strings into a single cluster indicates that they perform similar operations. For example, these might be two packaging lines. On the other hand, if the processes are different, then the two strings should be grouped into two separate process clusters.

Another, far more complex, structure is given at the bottom of figure 8.14. Complex cluster structures such as this are rare. The lack of inventories in this system means that the process unit schedules must be coupled. When schedules are rolled back or rolled forward, intractable conflicts may arise. The solution is to decouple the process units with inventories. This creates another process stage, with inventories decoupling the schedules of the simpler clusters resulting from dividing the large, complex cluster.

Job Shop Clusters

Job shop clusters differ markedly from stockless clusters. A job shop cluster is a group of process units that performs one step in a multistage process. These clusters operate as job shops and can be scheduled with traditional MRP techniques. Since MRP systems schedule materials before processors (capacity), job shop clusters are scheduled using a material-dominated scheduling approach.

MRP systems are thoroughly discussed in many texts, including Orlicky 1975 and Vollmann, Berry, and Whybark 1992. Consequently, we will limit our coverage of job shop clusters to a review of the Kodak case in chapter 4. This case illustrates the use of job shop clusters in a PFS environment.

Kodak's Colorado film plant has three single-cluster stages. The first cluster prepares chemicals and emulsions in a job shop. The next cluster, a film coating process, operates as a single-unit stockless cluster. It is scheduled using a processor-dominated scheduling technique. The third cluster, the finishing step, also operates as a job shop. This final cluster cuts, perforates, and packages wide rolls of film from the coater.

Kodak integrates these three clusters into a single process train. The chemical and emulsion job shop performs the initial processing. All jobs pass through this step and the film coating step before being processed in the finishing job shop. Thus, there is a directed *flow* through the three stages of the process train, but variable routings within each of the two job shop clusters.

The Kodak case illustrates the use of MRP as a single-cluster scheduling technique in a PFS system. One large MRP system could be used to schedule the entire system. However, scheduling is simplified by exploiting the process structure and dividing the full scheduling problem into three simpler, but linked, cluster scheduling problems.

Conclusions

Process clusters have many structures; as a result, they can be scheduled in many different ways. In chapter 7, we investigated different ways of scheduling single-unit process clusters. This chapter has extended the analysis to include multiunit process clusters. Process units in tightly coupled clusters have schedules with the same basic sequences and lot sizes. These tightly coupled schedules are created by rolling schedules backward, forward, or backward and forward through the process structure.

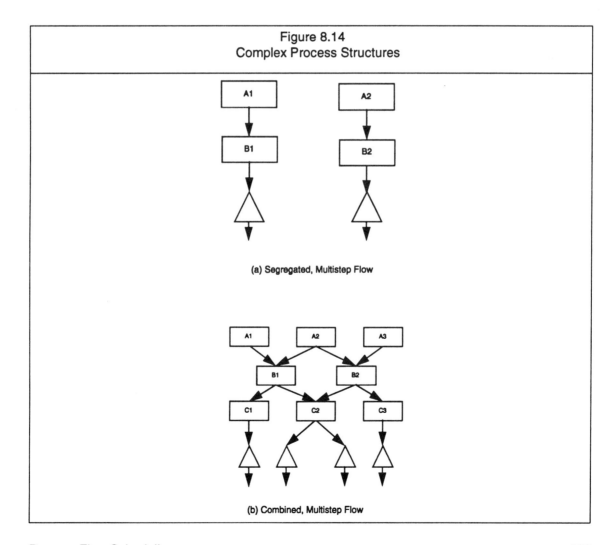

Figure 8.14
Complex Process Structures

(a) Segregated, Multistep Flow

(b) Combined, Multistep Flow

Process units in loosely coupled clusters perform similar operations and are connected, if at all, by common input or common output materials. Scheduling loosely coupled, parallel process units is similar to scheduling single-unit clusters. The principal difference is the need to determine guidelines for allocating production among the process units in a parallel structure. Complex stockless process clusters are unusual because of the difficulty in scheduling and operating process units having different schedules but no decoupling inventories. Job shop clusters are scheduled using MRP techniques within a PFS framework.

Process cluster schedules emphasize the first two process flow scheduling principles: (1) the process structure guides scheduling calculations, and (2) process clusters are scheduled using processor-dominated or material-dominated scheduling. The third principle—process stages are scheduled using forward flow scheduling, reverse flow scheduling, or mixed-flow scheduling—is most important in situations with multiple process stages. This is the topic of the next chapter.

References

Orlicky, J. 1975. *Material Requirements Planning*. New York: McGraw-Hill.

Vollmann, T.E., W.L. Berry, and D.C. Whybark. 1992. *Manufacturing Planning and Control Systems*. 3d ed. Homewood, Ill.: Irwin.

Chapter 9

Process Train Scheduling

The basic concepts for scheduling process trains have already been presented in previous chapters. Chapter 3 uses the Polygoo example to introduce process flow scheduling calculations. The Polygoo example shows the details of linking multiple stages together in a process train. Later in chapter 3, the three PFS principles were introduced. The third principle gives alternative strategies for scheduling process trains: reverse flow scheduling, forward flow scheduling, and mixed-flow scheduling. All three train scheduling strategies were discussed, and scheduling flowcharts were presented for reverse flow and mixed-flow strategies.

The 10 cases presented in chapter 4 and appendix A illustrate process train scheduling in a variety of production environments. Flowcharts for each of the 10 cases illustrate different ways for scheduling process trains. These 10 cases focus on the overall train scheduling strategies, but lack detail on scheduling process clusters or individual process units. This detail is provided in the examples given in chapters 7 and 8.

Since you have already been exposed to many concepts and examples of process train scheduling, this chapter is rather brief. After analyzing the different types of process train structures, we examine reasons for creating multiple process stages. Following this is an overview of train scheduling approaches. We next introduce the concept of master clusters. The chapter concludes with a brief presen-

tation and analysis of scheduling strategies for process trains.

As mentioned above, the material in this chapter builds on train scheduling concepts presented in earlier chapters. You may want to review some of the previous material before proceeding with this chapter.

Process Train Structures

A process train is a set of process clusters that are grouped in process stages. An example of a fairly complex process train structure is shown in figure 9.1, which uses hexagons to represent process clusters. A hexagon could be a single process unit, a tightly coupled cluster, a loosely coupled cluster, a complex cluster, or a job shop cluster. Also note that the triangles in figure 9.1 may represent inventories of more than one item.

Stages separate groups of process clusters with inventories. These inventories decouple a cluster's schedule from cluster schedules in other stages. In the ideal plant, all process units would be part of a single continuous-flow cluster, and there would not be any decoupling inventories. However, many plants have clusters with unsynchronized schedules, which forces the use of decoupling inventories and creates multiple process stages. The reasons for unsynchronized schedules and decoupling inventories will be discussed in a later section.

The numbering of stages shows the direction of material flow through the process train. Raw materials are the only element in the initial stage, which is labeled "stage 0." Subsequent stages are numbered sequentially in the direction of material flow. Stages near the beginning of the process flow therefore have low numbers, and stages near the end of the process flow have higher numbers.

Process trains have a variety of structures. Let's examine a few of the major types of process structures. Figure 9.2 illustrates a simple linear structure. The Polygoo example in chapter 3 and all five case descriptions in chapter 4 illustrate linear process trains. While linear process structures are common,

more complex process structures are frequently encountered.

Simple diverging and converging structures are illustrated in figures 9.3 and 9.4. A diverging structure arises when a raw material is separated into several different products that require further processing. For example, in the corn refining industry, corn is initially separated into fiber, starch, gluten, and oil. In subsequent process stages, each of these components is processed in different clusters.

A converging process structure results when several items join to make a finished product. One common converging process structure occurs when packaging is made in the same process train where it is used. For example, a food processor makes cans in addition to processing fruits and vegetables in a

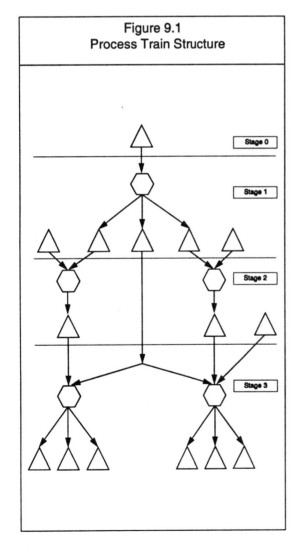

Figure 9.1
Process Train Structure

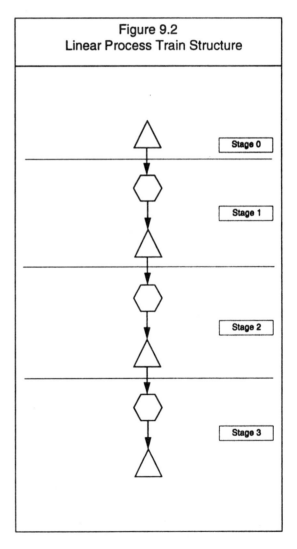

Figure 9.2
Linear Process Train Structure

single process train. The principal process flow is through the food processing cluster and the packaging cluster. However, another branch of the process flow comes from the can manufacturing process and converges with the processed food in the packaging cluster. Converging process trains are also found in mixing, blending, and assembly operations.

The simple linear, diverging, and converging process structures can be combined to form more complex process structures. A feeder-line structure is illustrated in figure 9.5. Here the converging structure is repeated with feeder lines joining the process train's main line. The Sylvania Lighting case in appendix A illustrates a feeder-line process structure.

A by-product/co-product process structure is shown in figure 9.6. These structures can be formed

by repeated use of the diverging process structure. Each secondary line produces a by-product or co-product, while the principal product is made on the main line. Sawmills have a by-product process structure. The main line produces lumber; the by-product lines process bark, chips, and sawdust.

Process structures can become intertwined into complex structures, as shown in figure 9.7. Oil refineries have complex process train structures that combine diverging and converging process structures. Diverging process structures arise in the distillation of crude oil and in processing operations, such as catalytic cracking, that split large hydrocarbon molecules into smaller molecules. Converging process structures arise in blending operations to make gasoline, heating oil, jet fuel, and other products. Converging structures also occur in processing

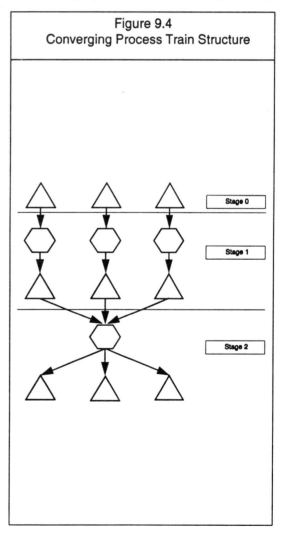

Figure 9.3
Diverging Process Train Structure

Stage 0

Stage 1

Stage 2

Figure 9.4
Converging Process Train Structure

Stage 0

Stage 1

Stage 2

operations, such as alkylation and polymerization. The operations chemically combine small hydrocarbon molecules to form larger molecules. Oil refineries closely coordinate the operations of various process units; however, storage tanks are still required to decouple the processes.

The linear, diverging, converging, feeder-line, by-product/co-product, and complex process structures describe the full range of process train structures. These process structures are set by the process design and physically incorporated in a plant's processing and storage facilities. Because process structures guide scheduling calculations, they are an important input to train scheduling procedures.

Reasons For Multiple Process Stages

The ideal manufacturing plant is a continuous flow operation with a single stage. However, many plants do not or cannot synchronize process unit schedules. This lack of synchronization results in a need for inventories to decouple the schedules of the process units in different stages. Let's examine some of the reasons for decoupling process units.

Equipment Utilization

In some production environments, equipment utilization can be improved by accumulating an interme-

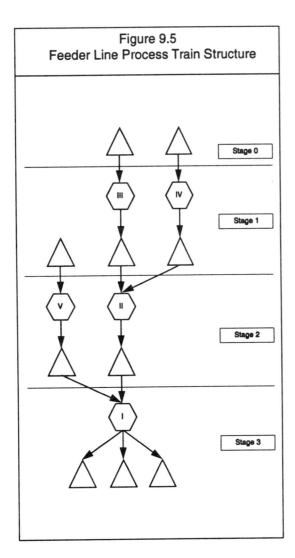

Figure 9.5
Feeder Line Process Train Structure

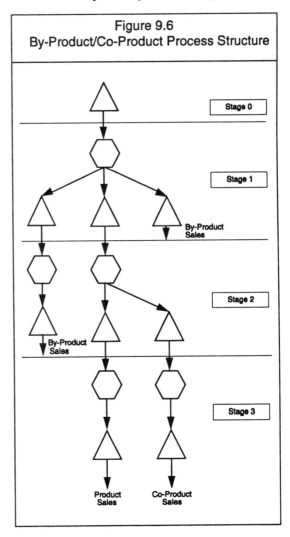

Figure 9.6
By-Product/Co-Product Process Structure

diate product in inventory to satisfy peak demand requirements from a downstream unit. Let's consider an example. The process structure shown in figure 9.8 does not have a decoupling inventory between units A and B. Suppose that process unit B operates continuously, and it periodically requires materials from unit A. Thus, B pulls materials from A, and the schedules for A must be synchronized with the schedules for B. The techniques for tightly coupled clusters as discussed in chapter 8 apply in this environment. Note, however, that without the ability to accumulate inventory, unit A must have sufficient capacity to meet the peak requirement from B.

Now consider the similar process structure shown in figure 9.9. Here process unit Y periodically pulls material from X; however, an inventory now decou-

ples Y from X. This permits X to produce feed continuously for Y and results in much higher utilizations for X than was possible for A in the previous situation.

Which of these two designs is best? The decision involves a trade-off between the cost of extra, underutilized capacity for the upstream stage and the cost of carrying intermediate inventory. If capacity for the upstream stage is inexpensive when compared to the cost of carrying inventory, the process train should be designed and scheduled as one cluster, as shown in the first design. However, if capacity for the upstream stage is relatively expensive and the cost of carrying intermediate inventory is relatively low, the two process units should be decoupled with inventory, as in the second design. Thus, the optimal

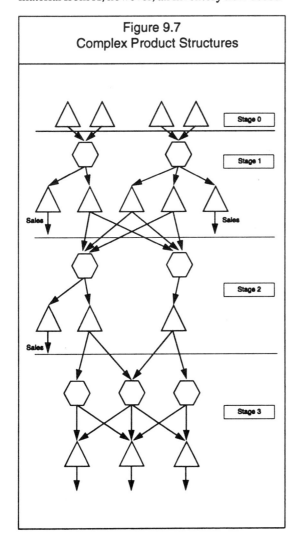

Figure 9.7
Complex Product Structures

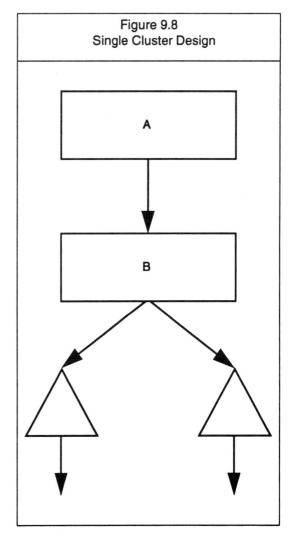

Figure 9.8
Single Cluster Design

process design depends on the relative costs of idle capacity and of carrying inventory.

The above example illustrates how a decoupling inventory can improve equipment utilization. A similar situation occurs when a single support unit periodically feeds two key downstream units. Occasionally, the upstream unit may need to supply both downstream units at the same time. Without intermediate inventory, the upstream unit needs to be designed for the maximum simultaneous demand from both downstream units. This again results in a need to either oversize the upstream unit or create an intermediate inventory.

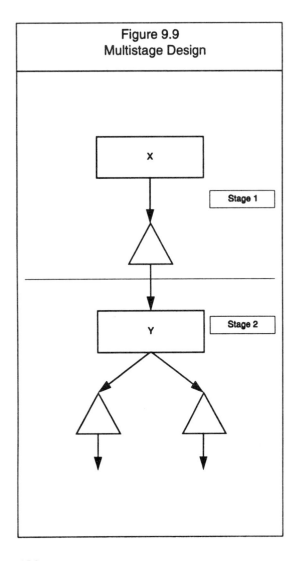

Figure 9.9
Multistage Design

Different Production Rates

When items have different production rates in sequential processes, decoupling inventories are required. Look at figure 9.9 again, but now assume a different production environment. Suppose that both process steps are continuous flow processes and that the output of the first process can be immediately processed in the second process. Furthermore, suppose that a 1,000-liter run of product P requires one hour in stage 1 and 10 hours in stage 2. At the end of one hour, all 1,000 liters will have completed processing in the first stage; however, only 100 liters will have been processed in the second stage. This leaves 900 liters that must be stored until they can be processed in stage 2. This situation requires an intermediate inventory to decouple the two process units. Because of the different production rates, the two units must have separate schedules, and a decoupling inventory is required.

A similar situation occurs when the production rates are reversed. Suppose a 1,000-liter run of product Q requires 10 hours in the first stage and one hour in the second. In addition, let us assume that the second stage cannot be throttled and must run all 1,000 liters in a single one-hour run. Now stage 1 must run product Q for nine hours and accumulate 900 liters in inventory before stage 2 is started. Both stages will finish the 1,000-liter run at the end of hour 10. In product Q's environment, an intermediate inventory is required to accumulate inventory for the faster second stage. Again, the process units must have different schedules, and a decoupling inventory is required.

Different Sequences

Decoupling inventories are also needed to facilitate different sequences in sequential process clusters. Consider again the process structure shown in figure 9.9, but with yet another production environment. Suppose that the first process unit produces slabs of 10 different metal alloys, each of which has a different chemical composition. The process runs continuously, and the production sequence is based on alloy compatibilities. Violating the target production sequence results in adjacent production of incompatible alloys. This sequence increases the off-specification material during alloy transitions—

a costly situation. Thus, there are strong economic incentives to follow the target alloy sequence.

Let us further suppose that the second stage is a rolling mill that makes 20 widths of metal coils. Rolling the metal alloys leaves a groove on the roller at a coil's edge. If a wider coil is rolled next, the groove in the roller will impart a groove to the coil. The roller groove can, however, be removed by machining—an expensive operation. Machining is minimized by sequencing production from wide to narrow coils. In this situation, machining is only required when the sequence "jumps" from the narrowest coil back to the widest coil. The end result of this process technology is that the rolling operation has a sequence that must be observed or high machining costs will follow.

Now we have two sequential operations, each requiring its own technologically based sequence. Which sequence should dominate? The answer is neither. By using a decoupling inventory of alloy slabs, the target sequences for both operations can be observed. The Inland Steel case in appendix A uses an approach similar to this simplified example.

Decrease Delivery Times

Another justification for decoupling inventories is to shorten delivery times. Consider the two-stage converging process train shown in figure 9.4. Let us suppose that this process train produces specialty chemicals. Each of the three process clusters in stage 1 makes a family of five different intermediate products, and the processing times for the 15 intermediate products range from 4 to 20 days. These intermediate products are stored and blended to customer order in stage 2. The blending operation only requires a few hours of lead time, and customer orders are shipped the next day.

This example illustrates the use of decoupling inventories to decrease delivery times. The specialty chemical process has a cumulative processing time of about 21 days. Twenty days are for the intermediate product with the longest lead time. The remaining one day is for blending and shipping. However, by stocking the 15 intermediate products, an infinite number of blends can be produced and shipped the next day. This gives an order lead time of one day.

The Coors Brewing case presented in chapter 4 uses a similar strategy. Coors produces seven brews to stock and packages these brews in a variety of

containers and labels to make several hundred finished products.

The above examples show the varied reasons for designing process trains with multiple stages. Improved equipment utilization justifies the extra decoupling inventory in some cases. In other situations, the intermediate inventory is needed to link processes with different production rates or processes requiring different sequences. In yet other situations, decoupling inventories are used to cut delivery lead times.

Process Train Scheduling Approaches

Theoretically, there are two basic approaches for developing process schedules. The first is a global approach, and the second is a decomposition approach. The global approach simultaneously schedules material and capacity in all process clusters. While a global approach can be used in less detailed production plans, global scheduling is seldom feasible in plant scheduling. As discussed in chapter 7, it is generally not feasible to simultaneously schedule capacity and materials for a single unit. The global scheduling approach tries to extend simultaneous scheduling to include more than one stage. Scheduling problems are usually so complex that global approaches are not feasible, and a decomposition approach must be used.

The decomposition approach breaks process train scheduling into a set of single cluster scheduling problems. Train schedules are built by scheduling one process cluster at a time. One cluster is initially scheduled; subsequent clusters are scheduled by branching out until a network encompassing the entire process train is scheduled. For example, the process train in figure 9.5 could be scheduled in the order indicated by the Roman numerals. First, cluster I at the end of the train is scheduled, then clusters II and III. After the main line has been scheduled, the two feeder lines (clusters IV and V) are scheduled.

As schedule building proceeds, problems may arise, and previously scheduled stages may need rescheduling. Thus, if a shortage of material arises when scheduling cluster IV in figure 9.5, changes may be required in the initial schedule for cluster II, which in turn triggers a need to reschedule clusters I and III. This type of interactive rescheduling to solve problems was illustrated for a single stage in chapter 7 for Gumm-A and Colormix-A. The resolution of problems becomes more complex as more clusters become involved in the schedule.

Master Process Clusters

A process train is a connected group of process clusters whose schedules are decoupled with inventories. Process clusters can vary widely in level of independence. As decoupling inventories are increased, the cluster schedules become more independent of each other. Conversely, when decoupling inventories are decreased, the cluster schedules become more dependent, more scheduling problems arise, and rescheduling is more frequent.

Process clusters that are initially scheduled independently from the other clusters are called *master process clusters,* and their schedules are called *master schedules.* The first process cluster scheduled is always a master process cluster. In some cases, the schedules of two or more clusters must be strongly decoupled and multiple master clusters created. This is done by increasing the decoupling inventory so that the linkages between individual cluster schedules are very weak.

A simple test determines whether there is more than one master process cluster in a process train. Any cluster that can be scheduled first must be independent of other clusters and is a master cluster. In contrast, any cluster that cannot be scheduled first is dependent on another cluster's schedule. These clusters are called *support clusters.* A support cluster must be scheduled after the master cluster to which it is linked.

After scheduling a master cluster, a choice may exist as to which of several support clusters should be scheduled next. For example, figure 9.3 shows a simple diverging process train structure. Let us assume that the single cluster in stage 1 is the only master cluster and the four clusters in stage 2 are support clusters. After scheduling the master cluster, there is a choice of four support clusters. Which should be scheduled first? The cluster that is most likely to require changes in the master schedule

should be scheduled next. This is the hardest cluster to schedule. Train scheduling is an iterative process; resolving difficult problems as early as possible tends to reduce the amount of rescheduling.

Scheduling Strategies

The decomposition approach for scheduling uses three basic strategies for scheduling process trains: reverse flow scheduling, forward flow scheduling, and mixed-flow scheduling. Reverse flow scheduling proceeds from the last stage backwards through the process structure to the first stage. Reverse flow scheduling requires that all the clusters in a stage be scheduled before scheduling the next upstream stage. Since a reverse flow strategy schedules the stage closest to customer demands first, it is responsive to changes in customer demands. Any problems arising because of unusual demands are quickly resolved by scheduling the final stage first. Reverse flow scheduling applies to any type of process structure, but works best with simple process structures. The Polygoo example in chapter 3 and the Exxon Chemical case in chapter 4 both illustrate reverse flow scheduling.

Forward flow scheduling proceeds from the first stage forward through the process structure to the last stage. As with reverse flow scheduling, forward flow scheduling requires scheduling all the clusters in a stage before proceeding to the next stage. Forward flow scheduling also works best in environments with simple process structures. Since forward flow scheduling begins with the first stage, this strategy is particularly effective when schedules are closely tied to raw material receipts. By starting with the first stage, many problems caused by too much or too little raw material are resolved before scheduling downstream stages. The EG & G case in chapter 4 illustrates forward flow scheduling.

Mixed-flow scheduling, the last process train scheduling strategy, has many variations. One variation is the inside-out strategy, which begins scheduling with an internal cluster and then works its way out. This strategy, which is particularly effective for scheduling a process train with an internal bottleneck, master schedules an internal cluster and gives it priority over the outside clusters. The Eastman

Kodak case in chapter 4 illustrates the inside-out strategy.

Another variation of mixed-flow scheduling is the outside-in strategy. The outside-in strategy master schedules clusters at both the beginning and ending process stages. Scheduling then proceeds from both ends toward an internal reconciliation point. The outside-in strategy is useful in environments where products are finished-to-order. In this environment a few intermediate products are produced to stock before being blended, mixed, packaged, or assembled to make many finished products. These finished products may be custom items that are only made upon receipt of a customer order. Alternatively, these finished products may be a wide variety of items that are produced to fill short-range demand forecasts. The Coors brewing example in chapter 4 is an example of the outside-in strategy.

The main-line strategy is another major type of mixed-flow scheduling strategy. This strategy fits well with the feeder line train structure (figure 9.5) or the by-product/co-product train structure (figure 9.6). In both of these situations a principal, linear subtrain is scheduled first using reverse flow, forward flow, inside-out, or outside-in strategies. After scheduling the main line, clusters in the secondary feed, by-product, and co-product lines are scheduled. The Sylvania Lighting case in appendix A illustrates a main-line strategy with feeder lines.

In complex process train structures, a hub-and-spoke scheduling strategy can be useful. This strategy initially master schedules several critical clusters—the hubs. Schedules are then built by linking additional clusters until all support clusters in the train are scheduled. Complex structures tend to have large decoupling inventories. This tends to reduce the probability that problems will arise and rescheduling will be necessary.

Mixed-flow scheduling is flexible, and many variations are possible. When building process train schedules, any unscheduled master cluster or any support cluster linked to a previously scheduled cluster may be scheduled. The order of scheduling clusters should be selected to minimize the amount of rescheduling required to build a satisfactory, feasible schedule. This order may change as the scheduling environment changes. During a period of slack demand, for example, a scheduler might use a reverse flow scheduling strategy that is closely tied to demand. When demand picks up, an internal bottleneck may surface. In this environment, the scheduler may switch to an inside-out strategy. This would help optimize the utilization of the bottleneck cluster, thereby increasing the process train's output.

Summary

Process structures guide scheduling of process trains. Since there are many different process structures, there are many ways to schedule process trains. Process train scheduling is similar to process cluster scheduling; however, process trains have intermediate inventories that decouple schedules. Process train scheduling begins by master scheduling one or more master clusters. Scheduling proceeds by using a reverse flow, forward flow, or mixed-flow scheduling strategy. The mixed-flow strategy has many variations. Four principal types of mixed-flow strategies are inside-out, outside-in, main line, and hub-and-spoke.

This concludes our four-chapter presentation of scheduling concepts and calculations. You should now know (1) several ways to schedule single process units, (2) methods of linking unit schedules into cluster schedules, and (3) ways of combining cluster schedules into a process train schedule. Since your introduction to process flow scheduling is now complete, let's review and reflect on these concepts in the final chapter.

Chapter 10

Conclusion

Now that you have been introduced to process flow scheduling, let's take a moment and reflect on what you have learned about PFS, how it relates to other scheduling frameworks, and how you can use PFS.

Review of PFS

The first PFS principle states that scheduling calculations are guided by the process structure. To facilitate this process, we have proposed a taxonomy consisting of trains, stages, clusters, and process units. This hierarchy is shown in figure 10.1.

Process Trains

Process trains come in all sizes and shapes. The simplest train structure is a linear structure. Slightly more complex are the diverging and converging structures. These can be combined to form feeder-line and by-product/co-product structures. Finally, we have complex structures.

Train structures are used to link steps in the overall scheduling process. As shown at the top of figure 10.2 and specified by the third PFS principle, process trains are scheduled with reverse flow scheduling, forward flow scheduling, or mixed-flow scheduling. These strategies specify a general plan of attack, but more detail is required before sched-

uling can begin. Thus, we need to look at process structures in more detail.

Process Stages

Process trains consist of process stages containing process clusters that, in turn, consist of process units. Process clusters within a stage are decoupled from clusters in preceding and succeeding stages by inventories. At a minimum, a process stage has a single cluster, containing a single process unit and an inventory of the process unit's output material. The one exception to this is stage 0, which contains only raw materials and has no processors.

The primary function of process stages is to provide order to the process structure. Stages are numbered beginning with the raw material stage as stage 0 and successively numbering stages until the final process stage is reached. Unlike process trains and clusters, stages do not guide the scheduling calculations; and unlike process units, stages are not scheduled. However, when a stage has only a single cluster containing a single process unit, scheduling the process unit is the same as scheduling the stage.

Process Clusters

Like process trains, process clusters have many different structures. The simplest cluster structure has only one process unit. A process unit may combine several production processes, but all these processes must share the same schedule. The Simplot example in chapter 4 provides a good example of a single-unit cluster. Although potato processing operations covered the full range from peeling to packaging, all operations in a production line share the same schedule and thus, from a PFS view, constitute a single process unit, a single cluster, a single stage, and a single train.

Scheduling Single-Unit Clusters

Single-unit clusters can be scheduled in many ways and tailored to the needs of a particular environment. Single-unit clusters can be scheduled using processor-dominated scheduling as in the Polygoo reactor, Gumm-A, and Colormix-A examples. Alternatively, single-unit clusters can use a material-dominated scheduling approach as in the Gumm-B, Colormix-B, and Sitka Salmon examples.

PFS can be used in many different process unit environments. The process units can be continuous-processing equipment, as illustrated by the Polygoo reactor, or batch-processing equipment, as illustrated in the other examples. Single units can be scheduled for either make-to-stock (e.g., Gumm-A, Gumm-B, and Sitka Salmon) or make-to-order (e.g., Colormix-A and Colormix-B) environments. Schedules are driven by the arrival of a raw material, as in the Sitka Salmon example or the EG & G case; by customer orders, as in the Colormix examples and the Inland Steel case (appendix A); or by the need to maintain minimum inventory levels, as in the other

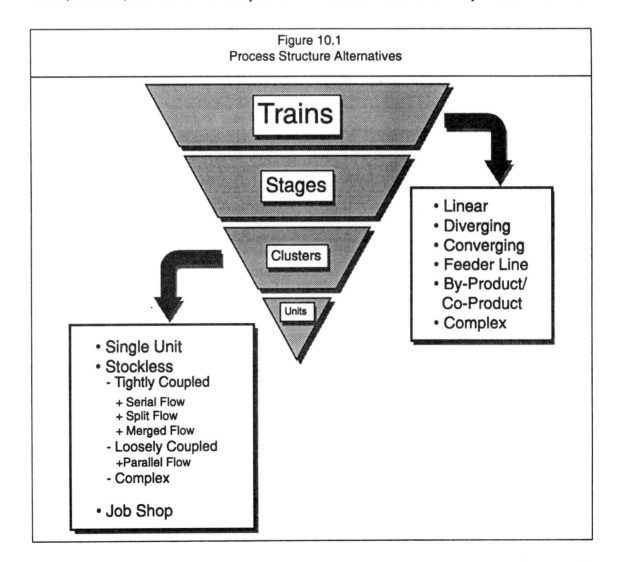

Figure 10.1
Process Structure Alternatives

Trains

Stages

Clusters

Units

- Linear
- Diverging
- Converging
- Feeder Line
- By-Product/ Co-Product
- Complex

- Single Unit
- Stockless
  - Tightly Coupled
    + Serial Flow
    + Split Flow
    + Merged Flow
  - Loosely Coupled
    +Parallel Flow
  - Complex

- Job Shop

examples and cases. Indeed, PFS can use a wide variety of cluster scheduling techniques to best fit any one of a wide variety of cluster scheduling environments.

One alternative to PDS or MDS scheduling approaches is simultaneous scheduling. This approach uses mathematical programming techniques to schedule both material and capacity in one step. While simultaneous scheduling is appealing, it is not practical today in most scheduling environments. The mathematical procedures bog down in evaluating all the alternatives for even moderately sized scheduling problems. Nevertheless, we are hopeful that simultaneous scheduling will become useful as optimization and computer technology improve.

Scheduling Stockless Process Clusters

Some process clusters have more than one process unit. Tightly coupled process clusters consist of a group of process units that are not decoupled by inventories. If a group of process units all share the same schedule, they should be considered a single unit. However, the units will sometimes share the same basic schedule but require different amounts of detail. This was illustrated by the Chromopaste example, where the reactor schedule only needed paste type detail, the mixer schedule needed to specify both paste type and color, and the packaging schedule needed paste type, color, and container type. Even though all three schedules were different, they shared the same basic schedule.

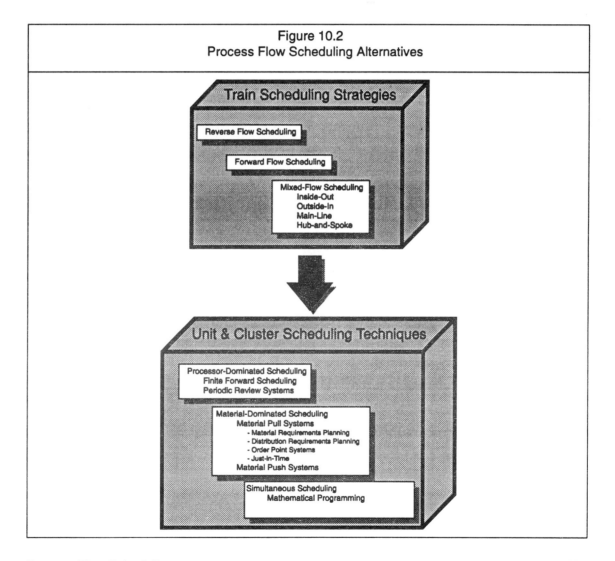

Figure 10.2
Process Flow Scheduling Alternatives

Another type of stockless process structure is the loosely coupled cluster with parallel process units. Here the process units perform similar process steps, as in a set of packaging lines. The schedules for process units in a loosely coupled cluster are linked, if at all, by using common feed materials or by producing common products. A major issue in scheduling parallel process units is the allocation of demand among the units. This is usually performed in the production plan and passed on to the schedule as an allocation guideline. The Show Glow example illustrated scheduling loosely coupled process clusters.

Although more complex stockless process clusters are possible, the lack of decoupling inventories makes them difficult to schedule. When a decoupling inventory is introduced into a complex cluster, the cluster divides into simpler clusters that form two or more process stages.

Scheduling Job Shop Clusters

One last category of process clusters is a job shop. These clusters have jumbled material flows created by different routings for each product. A job shop cluster may be only one stage of a multistage operation. The Kodak cases illustrate this situation. Job shop clusters might best be scheduled using an MRP approach.

PFS concepts suggest a way of simplifying MRP systems for manufacturing environments with two or more job shop clusters. For example, suppose that a manufacturer has three fabrication operations that produce parts for a final assembly operation. One parts fabrication operation produces plastic parts, another produces metal parts, and a third, ceramic parts. Each of these operations has a job shop layout, but no equipment is shared by the three operations.

A traditional MRP approach would schedule materials for the whole plant before checking equipment loads. On the other hand, a PFS philosophy decomposes the large scheduling problem into four cluster scheduling problems. The assembly line might be scheduled with JIT and the upstream parts fabrication operations scheduled with three separate MRP systems. Inventories of parts would decouple the three parts-fabrication operations from the assembly schedule.

PFS Flexibility

Process flow scheduling is an extremely flexible scheduling framework. Given the variety of train scheduling strategies shown in figure 10.2 and the various train structures shown in figure 10.1, process trains can be scheduled in many ways. Moreover, process clusters have many structures and employ a wide variety of scheduling techniques. This results in a framework that encompasses many scheduling techniques. The net effect is that process flow scheduling provides an integrative framework for customizing scheduling systems for a wide variety of different flow manufacturing environments.

Framework Comparison

For those of you who have spent some time in the production and inventory management field, an inevitable question remains: How does PFS differ from other planning/scheduling systems? Over the past 20 years, a number of systems have been proposed. Paramount among these are three: MRP (material requirements planning), JIT (Just-in-Time), and TOC (theory of constraints). Let's now examine some similarities and differences in these systems. Warning: We are assuming you already are familiar with these other frameworks. If you are not familiar with them, you may have some difficulty following parts of this section and may want to skip it.

Scheduling Frameworks

The four frameworks mentioned above use different approaches for scheduling. PFS schedules clusters using processor-dominated scheduling or material-dominated scheduling. Generally both material and capacity are scheduled for a cluster before scheduling begins for the next cluster. These cluster schedules are linked together using one of the train scheduling strategies: reverse flow scheduling, forward flow scheduling, and mixed-flow scheduling.

In contrast, MRP systems schedule all materials before checking capacity. Material scheduling begins by setting due dates for all end item orders. Start times are calculated next by using the lead times to schedule backwards from the due dates. Product structures are then used to determine the material needs from the next lower level in the bill of material (a bill of material explosion). Scheduling proceeds in this manner until all levels are scheduled. Following the development of the material schedule, capacities are checked using the material schedule's due dates, processing times for individual operations, and routings for each part. If problems are found, the material schedule is revised.

TOC is similar to MRP, but it does not directly use order due dates. Schedule dates at the constraint operation, rather than end item order due dates, drive the schedule. These schedule dates are, however, linked to the order due dates. Lead times of operations upstream from the constraint operation are added to a time buffer in front of the constraint to determine the timing of material releases to the gateway operation. In this sense TOC backward schedules from the constraint operation to upstream operations. On the other hand, downstream operations and material priorities are driven by the availability of material from the constraint operation. Material is processed on a first-come, first-served basis as it is received from the upstream constraint operation. Variations from the above description exist.

JIT systems use a material pull, backward scheduling strategy. However, JIT systems do not use lead times, work orders, or formal schedules. Instead, downstream empty kanbans (cards, squares, shelves, etc.) authorize upstream operations to produce. The overall production lead time is controlled by the number of kanbans, but lead times are not used to determine a production schedule.

Usage Domains

The use of either the process or the product structure for guiding scheduling calculations affects the choice of a scheduling technique. Process flow scheduling uses the process structure and works only in flow manufacturing environments. Although the process flow may be complex, there must be a discernable, directed flow through one or more process trains in a PFS system.

In contrast, MRP will work in many manufacturing environments; however, it fits best in job shops. Each order in a job shop can have its own routing. Thus, there is no discernable directed flow on which to base PFS scheduling calculations. On the other hand, MRP systems model job shops quite closely by giving each unique part its own routing. MRP

systems can also be used for flow manufacturing environments; however, other frameworks are generally more efficient and effective.

TOC is similar to MRP's focus on product structures, and we therefore also find most applications of TOC in job shop environments. However, TOC's use of product structures differs somewhat from MRP's use of bills of material. Since the focus of TOC is on constraints and the subordination of non-constraint schedules to the constraint's schedule (the drum and the rope), TOC fits better in flow environments than does MRP. Unfortunately, the literature of TOC does not clearly explain how to make this adaptation to flow manufacturing environments.

JIT systems strive for a continuous flow, and, like PFS, these systems work best in manufacturing environments with consistent, well-defined process flows. As material flows become more variable, JIT will still work, but more inventory is required.

Guiding Scheduling Calculations

The first PFS principle states that scheduling calculations are guided by the process structure. Let's now briefly examine what guides the scheduling calculations in other frameworks. MRP and TOC systems use the product structure (bill of material) to guide scheduling calculations and differ in this regard from PFS systems. JIT systems, on the other hand, do not have any scheduling calculations. However, the flow of kanbans and materials is guided by the process structure.

Capacity

Each of the four frameworks has a different approach for dealing with capacity. PFS schedules each cluster using either processor-dominated scheduling or material-dominated scheduling. In either case, both capacity (equipment and labor) and materials are generally scheduled for a cluster before the next cluster is scheduled. This results in a cluster-by-cluster reconciliation of materials and capacity.

MRP initially assumes infinite capacity is available. It is only after the initial material schedule is created that one reviews the capacity load and manually intercedes to alter either the material schedule or the available capacity. In this regard, MRP uses a material-dominated scheduling approach.

JIT also uses a material-dominated scheduling approach. JIT does not pay any real attention to capacity except during the design of the line and in production planning where an upper limit may be placed on the number of order kanbans. During the design phase, excess capacity is built into the production line to handle demand variations. Thus, when a JIT line is operating, capacity is secondary to the signals for material movement.

TOC uses a capacity treatment more closely aligned to PFS than to MRP or JIT. Most TOC examples use a material-dominated scheduling approach to finitely schedule material on the constraint. This procedure is similar to that illustrated in the Colormix-B example. However, TOC does not preclude the use of processor-dominated scheduling for the constraint. In either case, the objective is to maximize constraint throughput while maintaining level product flow to avoid creating temporary bottlenecks.

TOC schedules only materials at stages considered nonbottlenecks. This follows from the assumption that throughput is limited by a single constraint and that nonconstraints will not have any capacity problems. This assumption must be challenged in many flow shops. The initial design of many flow shops balances capacity among the clusters within a process train. Under these conditions, the existence of a single constraint may not be valid. For example, when running product A, the constraint may be in cluster I; however, when running product B, the constraint may shift to cluster II. In this situation, scheduling should check capacity at both constraints using a PFS approach.

Authority to Produce

After a schedule is developed, it must be communicated to unit supervisors and line workers. The four frameworks all use different methods for authorizing production. PFS authorizes production by issuing a production schedule. Only the *frozen* part of the schedule is executed. Periods further out provide a look ahead, but new schedules are issued before periods beyond the frozen schedule need to be executed.

MRP releases production orders to workstations identifying what must be produced, along with start dates, due dates, materials needed, etc. Production is authorized in a JIT system by an empty kanban. TOC authorizes work at the constraint by the release of a constraint schedule. Nonconstraint activities are authorized by a first-come, first-served prioritization of work and an attitude of work if and only if you have work to do.

Costs

Most implementations of all four scheduling frameworks do not directly incorporate costs or optimization in their scheduling calculations. Optimization and cost considerations are factors in process design and in developing production plans. On the other hand, scheduling is concerned primarily with finding an acceptable, feasible solution—one that meets demands without violating too many guidelines. However, some scheduling guidelines, such as lot-size targets for PFS systems, are based on optimizations performed as part of the earlier production planning process.

Application

You may now be wondering which of the above frameworks best fits your manufacturing environment. Fortunately, you are not constrained to using just one framework. Thus, one part of your plant may be able to use JIT. If so, do it. JIT, which is simpler than the other frameworks, should be used if it fits your environment. Another part of your operation may need to operate as a job shop; you should probably use MRP here. Finally, you might want to optimize the use of a bottleneck cluster with a finite forward scheduling technique. All these techniques may be combined into one unified system using PFS concepts to link the three clusters together.

Process flow scheduling provides a new framework based on the scheduling practices of many firms. It is a flexible framework that can be molded to fit most—if not all—flow manufacturing environments. This flexibility allows firms to customize their scheduling systems for specific circumstances. Process flow scheduling allows firms to break from the MRP philosophy of *one size fits all.* PFS systems exploit the flows in a process structure to simplify scheduling calculations and to improve the resulting schedules.

How you use process flow scheduling depends on where you sit or what hat you are wearing. If you are a practitioner, your challenge is to analyze your manufacturing environment and process structures, review your current scheduling practices, and determine how to make your scheduling processes more effective and efficient. PFS provides a new way of viewing scheduling that we believe will help in evaluating your existing system and designing improved systems.

If you are a software vendor, your challenge is to develop software that can be customized but fits the needs of many flow-manufacturing firms. There is a need for scheduling software that allows the user to select from a wide variety of cluster scheduling techniques and combine them into an integrated system. More attention needs to be given to integrating production plans with production schedules. Challenges also exist in improving technology for maintaining scheduling system databases and in incorporating, to the extent currently feasible, optimization and expert systems technology in your planning and scheduling systems.

Those of us who are educators can use PFS concepts to help integrate many seemingly unrelated planning and scheduling techniques. On occasion, scheduling educators have been accused of merely offering a bag of tricks. This accusation is not without justification. PFS provides a framework for linking many planning and scheduling techniques presented in the literature. PFS is an integrative concept that ties together the diverse scheduling practices of many firms.

Finally, let's consider the implications of PFS for researchers—be they academicians, practitioners, or software developers. As you study PFS systems and scheduling techniques, problems will arise that have not been adequately addressed in the literature. Do not be surprised. There is still much to learn about scheduling. Consider a few examples of questions not addressed in this book: How much decoupling inventory is required? How do you best schedule complex process clusters? And how can multiple clusters be scheduled simultaneously? Indeed, this book is but an introduction, and many good questions remain to be answered.

Conclusion

Epilogue

Clearly much remains to be done by all of us to improve our planning and scheduling systems. This improvement process can be accelerated by sharing ideas. We invite you to join with us in the activities sponsored by APICS and especially by the Process Industry Specific Industry Group. We look forward to hearing from you about your experiences, questions, and suggestions for improving on the PFS framework.

Appendix A

Supplemental Cases

Scott Paper

Scott Paper is a major producer of facial tissues, toilet tissues, napkins, and paper towels. This case is based on Scott's paper mill in Hull, Quebec; figure A.1 gives an overview of its process flow.

The first stage is the conversion of high-quality recycled paper into pulp. This pulp is blended with virgin pulp and used to feed three paper machines. The paper machines convert pulp into parent rolls, which are typically 70 inches wide and 60 inches in diameter. The parent-roll inventory buffers the paper-machine schedules from the converting-line schedules.

There are more than 30 converting lines. A typical toilet tissue line consists of (1) a winder, where the parent roll is rewound to a 4¼-inch-diameter log; (2) a slitter, where the log is cut to a 4½-inch length; (3) a wrapper; and (4) a case packager. Similar operations are performed on other converting lines and might also include folding (napkins and facial tissue), printing, and embossing.

The scheduling procedures, shown in flowchart form in figure A.2, use a commercial finite scheduling package, Schedulex from Numetrix Ltd., to schedule stages backward through the process structure. The scheduling procedure is similar to the Polygoo example in chapter 3.

Scheduling begins by using an item forecast to develop a schedule for the converting lines. The converting lines are scheduled forward in time and within finite capacity limits (finite forward scheduling) using Gantt charts. Since the equipment within a converting line is not decoupled by inventory, all equipment in a particular line is scheduled as a single entity. Line graphs showing inventory versus time track finished goods inventory levels and identify run-out times.

The line graphs represent an approach many companies use to evaluate the impact that their scheduling decisions will have on inventories. Scheduled production increases the projected finished goods inventory, and actual or forecasted demand decreases the same projected inventory. The scheduling objective is to maintain the finished goods inventory above minimum safety stock positions while not carrying too much inventory; i.e., below maximum inventory positions.

After obtaining a feasible schedule for the converting lines, a similar procedure is used for the three paper machines. Production requirements for the paper machines are determined by the need to replenish parent roll inventories, which are depleted by the converting lines' feed-roll requirements. When a paper machine schedule is created, products are sequenced to the extent possible according to color (light to dark), pulp quality, and basis weight. The scheduler interactively simulates alternative schedules on the computer until a satisfactory paper machine schedule is obtained that meets target minimum and maximum inventories for the parent rolls. In other words, the scheduler keeps enough inventory to meet future demands for the parent rolls but does not overstock the product either.

The paper machine schedules are then used to determine pulp requirements. An attempt is initially made to maximize pulp production from the secondary fiber system, since it uses recycled paper. The remaining pulp requirements are purchased. If sufficient pulp of the proper quality is not available, then prior schedules, or possibly the forecast, must be revised.

Scott Paper's planning procedures illustrate the use of the process structure for guiding scheduling calculations. The procedures use commercial software to assist in the iterative stage-by-stage balancing of equipment schedules and inventory levels. Scott's procedures are a good example of reverse flow scheduling, since the stages are scheduled in the reverse order of the material flow. Since each stage is finitely forward scheduled, Scott also demonstrates processor-dominated scheduling approaches. Summarizing Scott Paper, we see the following conditions:

- Gantt charts and line graphs are used in finite forward scheduling each process stage.
- Capacity and materials are reconciled in each stage before the next stage is scheduled.
- Reverse flow scheduling is used.
- Processor-dominated scheduling approaches are employed.

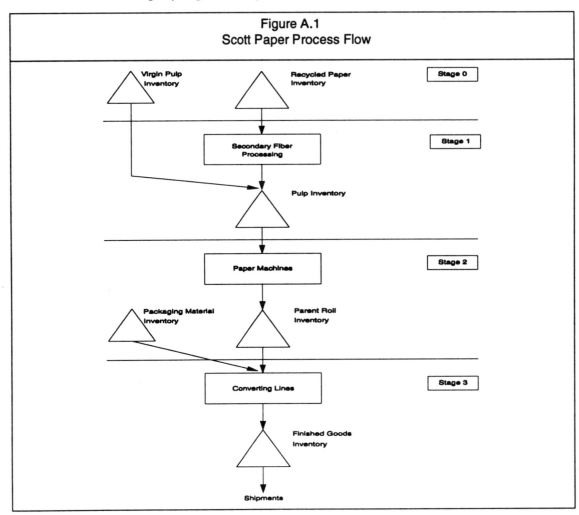

Figure A.1
Scott Paper Process Flow

Eastman Kodak: Kodak Park

The process flow for Eastman Kodak's black-and-white film manufacturing at Kodak Park, Rochester, New York, is shown in figure A.3. Stage 1 is a specialty chemical job shop with many batch operations. In this stage, solutions and emulsions are prepared for use in the coating operation.

Stage 2 consists of several coating machines that apply chemicals to film backing (support) and produce wide rolls of sensitized film. This stage operates as a flow shop with several parallel processors. The final stage is finishing. Here the wide rolls are slit, perforated, and packaged into finished goods.

Kodak's planning and scheduling system uses an effective combination of PFS and MRP scheduling techniques. While it would theoretically be possible to schedule all processes simultaneously with one MRP system, Kodak decomposes plant scheduling into three scheduling systems, as figure A.4 shows.

Stage 3, finishing, is scheduled first, using orders from a distribution requirements planning (DRP) system. Finishing operations are scheduled with an MRP system. The finishing schedule creates requirements for wide rolls from the coaters in stage 2.

A custom finite forward scheduling system (programmed with a spreadsheet language) is used to schedule the coaters. This schedule, in turn, creates requirements for solutions and emulsions in stage 1. Since stage 1 is a job shop, MRP is again used. As shown in the flowchart, a previously scheduled stage

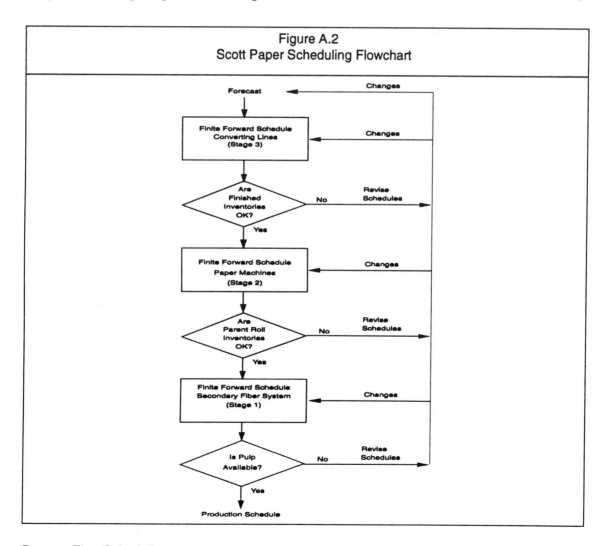

Figure A.2
Scott Paper Scheduling Flowchart

may need to be rescheduled when problems arise in integrating the stage schedules.

Kodak's use of PFS illustrates several points:

- A reverse flow scheduling approach is used.
- PFS principles can integrate MRP and finite forward scheduling techniques in a single scheduling framework.
- MRP (which schedules materials and then checks capacities) is a material-dominated, single-stage scheduling technique.
- Finite forward scheduling (a processor-dominated scheduling technique) facilitates developing schedules that improve quality, increase coater capacity, and reduce costs.

Armstrong

Armstrong World Industries produces floor coverings and ceiling panels in plants located in Lancaster, Pennsylvania. Figure A.5 shows the process flow for a typical process train at Armstrong. The four stages for a floor covering process train are (1) chemical mixing and base coating, (2) printing, (3) top coating and fusing, and (4) inspection and packaging.

The planning and scheduling process at Armstrong is a three-level hierarchy. The top level is the production plan, which uses demand forecasts, production rates, and inventory targets to develop a plan for output by product family by month.

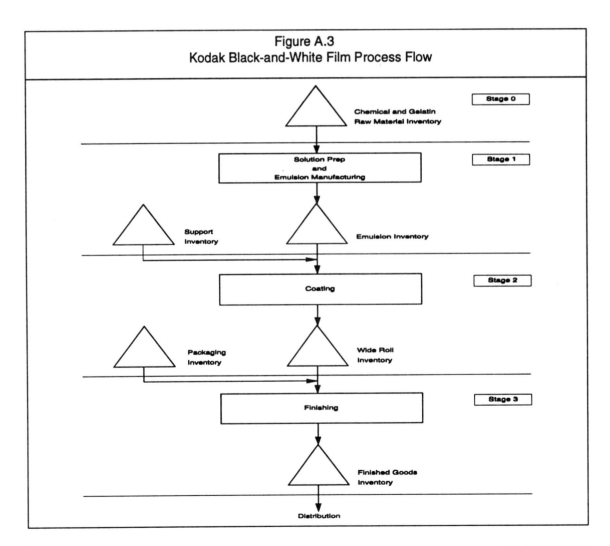

Figure A.3
Kodak Black-and-White Film Process Flow

148

The second level dissaggregates the monthly production plan into a weekly master production schedule. An important part of master scheduling is a production cycle analysis for each product family. This analysis determines the frequency of production for each product family; it is based on lot-sizing considerations and minimum batch quantities. The second level also calculates purchased materials requirements needed to support the master production schedule. An MRP system is used to calculate these requirements, and capacities are checked at key process steps.

The third level is a detailed schedule with shift, process unit, and item level of detail. This detailed scheduling activity is based on PFS concepts. A flowchart describing the scheduling process is given in figure A.6. A mixed-flow scheduling technique is used to schedule the process.

The constraint stage is scheduled first to ensure that resource utilization is maintained at the highest level possible. Demands and demand forecasts are translated into requirements for the constraint stage. Using this demand information, finite schedules are created, paying attention to efficient product sequencing and economic run length strategies.

After the constraint stage has been scheduled, the upstream and downstream stages are scheduled and inventories are checked for feasibility. In other words, reverse flow scheduling is used to schedule upstream stages, and forward flow scheduling is used to schedule downstream stages. If problems arise, the previous constraint schedules may need to be revised. In extreme cases the master schedule and/or production plan must be revised.

Several items are worth noting about Armstrong's use of PFS:

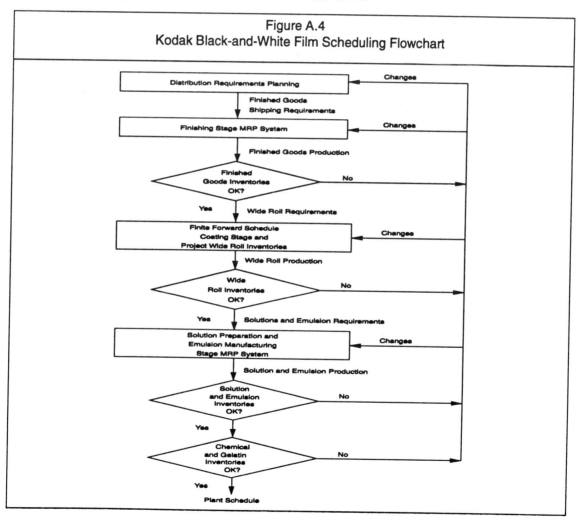

Figure A.4
Kodak Black-and-White Film Scheduling Flowchart

- Finite forward scheduling, which is a processor-dominated scheduling technique, is used to sequence product families efficiently at each stage.
- Mixed-flow scheduling is used to put the highest priority on efficiently scheduling stage 2, the constraint stage.
- Both MRP and PFS are used. MRP is used as a planning system to determine purchased material requirements. MRP is not used for plant scheduling. The PFS schedules are the authority to produce. These schedules replace both work orders and dispatch lists from an MRP system. Thus, PFS significantly reduces the number of transactions (opening and closing of work orders) that are required by MRP systems.

Inland Steel

Inland Steel Flat Products Company produces flat rolled steel coils and sheets in its East Chicago, Indiana, mill. As figure A.7 indicates, steel coils are produced in a three-stage operation. Stage 1, steel making and slab casting, consists of three steps. The first step is production of steel from molten iron and scrap steel in a basic oxygen furnace or an electric furnace. This is generally followed by a ladle metallurgy step where alloys are added to the steel. The final step is continuous casting, where the molten steel is cast into slabs.

Stage 2 is hot rolling, where 32-foot-long, 10-inch slabs are rolled in a hot strip mill. The computer-controlled hot mill, which is about one-half mile long,

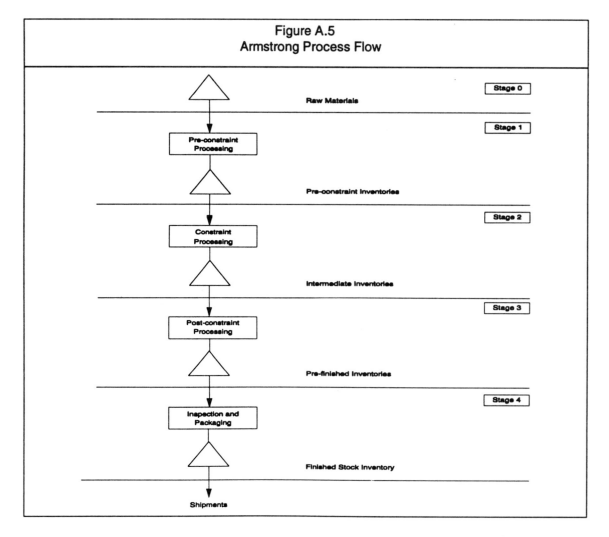

Figure A.5
Armstrong Process Flow

operates at speeds approaching 44 miles per hour. The hot mill reduces the slab thickness by a factor of about 100 and expands the length by a similar amount. The steel strip, which is more than 3,000 feet long, is coiled for ease in handling.

Stage 3 is cold mill processing, where the steel coils are rolled to precision thicknesses, annealed, possibly galvanized and/or aluminized, and generally packaged. Process technology has a major impact on Inland's scheduling. The first stage, steel making, uses a production sequence based on alloy chemistry. In contrast, the second stage processes the steel in a sequence of decreasing widths to prevent rolling grooves into the steel. In the third stage, another resequencing takes place based on cold mill processing requirements.

Figure A.8 is a simplified scheduling flowchart. In the first step, customer orders are checked to deter-

mine if any existing inventories of finished coils or hot band coils can be used (*applied* in the steel industry's lexicon) in filling new orders. Generally, orders cannot be matched to existing finished inventories, and requirements are created for processing steel slabs in the hot mill.

The hot mill is scheduled using finite forward scheduling to create a production sequence (lineup) in decreasing feed slab widths. This hot mill production schedule generates requirements for slabs, which are then checked against existing slab inventories to determine if any inventory may be applied. The resulting net slab requirements are then finite forward scheduled through the steel making operations in a sequence based on alloy chemistry.

Finally, the cold mill processing schedule resequences the orders again. This sequence is based on width and finishing requirements (annealing,

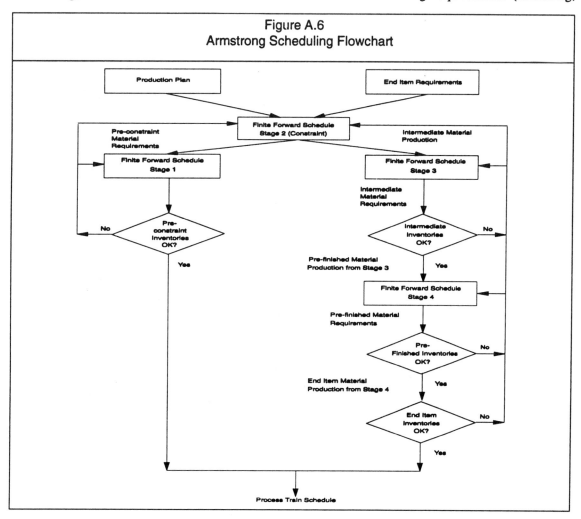

Figure A.6
Armstrong Scheduling Flowchart

galvanizing, aluminizing, or painting). This schedule is driven by both process sequences and customer order due dates.

Inland's scheduling practices have several aspects related to PFS:

- Finite forward scheduling is used to schedule processing units for all stages. This results in efficient use of the equipment and higher quality products because technologically preferred production sequences are used.

- A mixed-flow scheduling procedure is used for scheduling the process train. Thus, scheduling begins with stage 2, the hot mill. The hot mill schedule then pulls slab requirements from slab inventory and steel making and pushes hot band coils to the cold mill for further processing.

- Process stages may have processing units (e.g., furnaces, ladle metallurgy, and continuous casting) that are configured in series and may require separate, but tightly coupled, schedules.

- Customer orders require different amounts of machine time at different stages. The decoupling inventories (queues of orders) between stages also serve as buffers to facilitate high machine utilizations.

- MRP does not fit Inland's environment, where capacity utilization and sequencing are very important scheduling considerations.

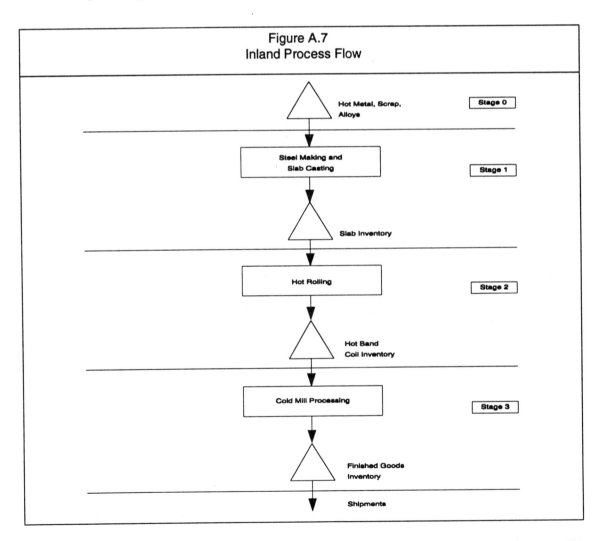

Figure A.7
Inland Process Flow

Sylvania Lighting

his case is based on an article published in *Production and Inventory Management Journal* that we co-authored with Darryl T. Hubbard of Sylvania Lighting (Hubbard, Taylor, and Bolander 1992). The Sylvania Lighting Division—U.S. is part of GTE Corporation's Electrical Products Group. Sylvania Lighting produces a wide range of lighting products, including incandescent, fluorescent, quartz, high-intensity discharge, and various other specialty lamp types. The scope of this case is limited to a representative group of straight fluorescent lamps that are produced on a high-volume line at the Danvers, Massachusetts, lighting plant. The basic concepts described apply at all the lighting plants,

with some variation expected because of the characteristics of each product line's process structure.

The Product

Schematic drawings of a fluorescent lamp are shown in figure A.9, which illustrates how a low-pressure mercury vapor arc is used to generate invisible ultraviolet energy. This energy is absorbed by the phosphor coating on the inside of the glass tube, which transforms the energy into visible light.

The subject production line is dedicated to a specific base configuration. It produces more than 100 end items of varying lengths (ranging from as small as two feet to as long as eight feet), light output, and color. For each length lamp, two light output levels are offered (denoted as options "A" and "B" in this example). The "A" or "B" light output of a certain

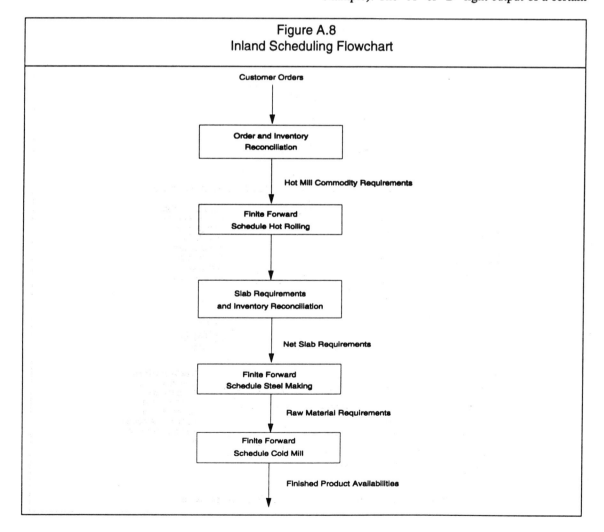

Figure A.8
Inland Scheduling Flowchart

Customer Orders

Order and Inventory Reconciliation

Hot Mill Commodity Requirements

Finite Forward Schedule Hot Rolling

Slab Requirements and Inventory Reconciliation

Net Slab Requirements

Finite Forward Schedule Steel Making

Raw Material Requirements

Finite Forward Schedule Cold Mill

Finished Product Availabilities

length lamp is determined by the mount assembly, which consists of the cathode, lead-in wires, stem press, and exhaust tube, as figure A.9 illustrates. Mount assemblies for option "A," which represents more than 85% of the line's volume, are made on in-line equipment and coded as phantom assemblies. The mounts for option "B" are made off line and inventoried.

This line and its products are a family group in Sylvania's planning systems. The lamps in this family share the same base style and are all 1½ inches in diameter. Using group technology (an engineering and manufacturing philosophy that identifies the sameness of parts, equipment, or process), the family group is divided into 12 manufacturing groups based on the length of the lamp and its rated light output level (option "A" or "B"), which facilitates

effective planning and scheduling. Manufacturing groups may also be separated into subgroups by color (cool white, warm white, daylight, etc.) or by packing quantity to further increase scheduling efficiencies on the line. Individual lamp types are represented at the lowest level of this product planning hierarchy.

Process Description

Sylvania Lighting's high-volume operations are excellent examples of repetitive manufacturing. The *APICS Dictionary* (1987) defines repetitive manufacturing as the "production of discrete units, planned and executed to a schedule, usually at high speeds and volumes. Material tends to move in a continuous flow during production, but different

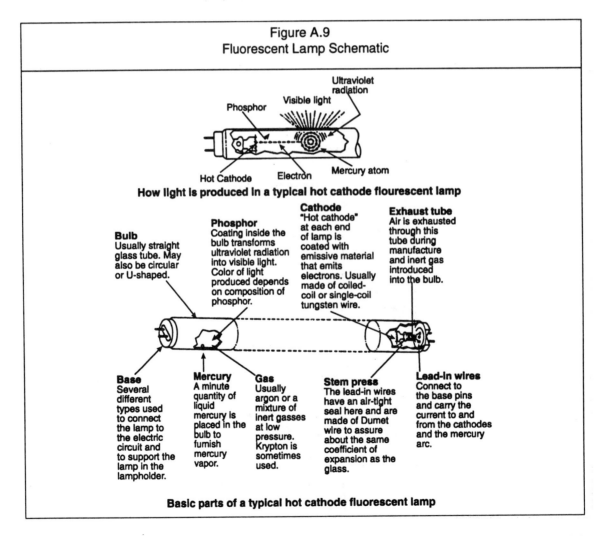

Figure A.9
Fluorescent Lamp Schematic

How light is produced in a typical hot cathode flourescent lamp

Bulb
Usually straight glass tube. May also be circular or U-shaped.

Phosphor
Coating inside the bulb transforms ultraviolet radiation into visible light. Color of light produced depends on composition of phosphor.

Cathode
"Hot cathode" at each end of lamp is coated with emissive material that emits electrons. Usually made of coiled-coil or single-coil tungsten wire.

Exhaust tube
Air is exhausted through this tube during manufacture and inert gas introduced into the bulb.

Base
Several different types used to connect the lamp to the electric circuit and to support the lamp in the lampholder.

Mercury
A minute quantity of liquid mercury is placed in the bulb to furnish mercury vapor.

Gas
Usually argon or a mixture of inert gasses at low pressure. Krypton is sometimes used.

Stem press
The lead-in wires have an air-tight seal here and are made of Dumet wire to assure about the same coefficient of expansion as the glass.

Lead-in wires
Connect to the base pins and carry the current to and from the cathodes and the mercury arc.

Basic parts of a typical hot cathode fluorescent lamp

items may be produced sequentially within that flow."

The production process consists of the dedicated line with in-line mount equipment and several off-line operations. As figure A.10 shows, the line is an integrated operation designed for the high-volume assembly of a specific lamp family. Two or three shifts of production are scheduled per day based on need, with lamps produced at the rate of roughly 40 per minute. The projected replacement cost of this line would be in the millions of dollars.

Sylvania Lighting has used some JIT concepts in the design and operation of its high-volume production lines and is continuing its efforts to achieve the JIT goals of low cost and flexible production. Materials flow through the lines in a JIT manner with no decoupling inventory between operations. This permits the entire line to be scheduled as a single unit

or cell, although it consists of many machines and personnel performing various assembly operations.

A principal difficulty in implementing JIT is setup reduction. Although the benefits of fast product changeovers are well recognized and efforts to reduce setup times have been undertaken, setup times must still be considered in the planning and scheduling process. Changing the lamp length for the entire line may take several hours, while changing the light output level (for mount assembly "A" or "B") within a given length requires a fraction of an hour. Changing colors or packing to produce the individual lamp types takes several minutes. These setups—which can negatively affect capacity, efficiencies, and quality—follow the group technology structure previously described. However, when the timing and sequence of setups are optimized, the line's cost performance is at its best. Following this

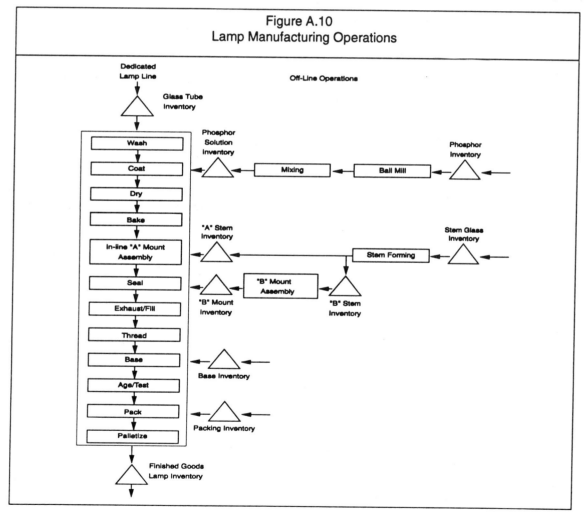

Figure A.10
Lamp Manufacturing Operations

strategy allows manufacturing to produce high-quality lighting products with the lowest possible unit cost.

Planning and Scheduling System Development

Sylvania Lighting's planning and scheduling systems were being developed while the MRP crusade was still largely focused on the discrete-order, job-shop environment where each end item was planned independently of the others. Early job-shop MRP systems were designed primarily to plan and control materials, with capacity (assumed to be infinite and/or highly flexible) considered as an afterthought. Adopting those rules to the group technology environment with its dedicated high-volume production lines would have threatened Sylvania Lighting's product quality and low cost objectives. It was also felt that the volume of transactions needed to plan and control production via work-order-based job-shop methods would require an inordinate amount of clerical support and result in *More Reams of Paper*.

For the above reasons, Sylvania Lighting aggressively pursued the development of proprietary planning and scheduling systems that recognized both the capacity constraints and competitive advantages unique to high-volume repetitive manufacturing. This evolutionary process, which now includes commercial software where advantageous, has resulted in the systems configuration described herein. This configuration also demonstrates the ability of PFS to integrate other concepts into a workable operating system that best matches the environment of each company.

Production Planning Practices

Production and inventory planning, a centralized responsibility of marketing's customer-support function, manages aggregate inventory levels for all product lines by participating in the sales and operations planning process. This group also does planning at the end-item level, with high-volume lamp types planned for weekly production to minimize inventory carrying costs and to maintain a flow through the distribution pipeline. Lower volume types are planned in monthly buckets and cycled to achieve the lowest sum of carrying and setup costs.

Minimum inventory levels for each lamp type are planned by the distribution planning systems, taking critical customer service measures into account.

Run lengths for each manufacturing group are planned based on customer demands, production rates, setup times, and inventory carrying costs. Planned runs for a group may be rounded to full-shift increments to increase operating efficiencies in the plant. Distribution network requirements are used to determine if a lamp type needs to be produced in the given planning period. If so, a production run for the lamp's manufacturing group is planned, though all types in the group may not need to be replenished. The specific quantity of each type to be run in the planned setup is determined based on current and future network requirements, economic minimum runs, and manufacturing group cycles.

Quantities are calculated so that the run-out time for all items being run in the joint setup is equalized. This procedure is similar to that described in an article published in *Production and Inventory Management* (Taylor and Bolander 1986). More importantly, this tactical use of joint replenishment with equal run-out optimizes the total of setup, run, and inventory carrying costs for the group while still meeting the critical business goal of having the right products available to provide customer satisfaction throughout the distribution network.

Because of the high degree of commonality in components, labor, and equipment resources used by the family/manufacturing groups, the production plans may be net changed to respond to the demands of the marketplace. The next step, production scheduling at the plants, is primarily concerned with developing detailed schedules that will meet each item's planning requirements on time and in an efficient manner.

Production Scheduling Practices

Sylvania Lighting's planning and scheduling systems use reverse flow scheduling to backward schedule through the process structure that is shown in figure A.11. All operations in figure A.11 whose schedules are not decoupled by inventories are combined into a single scheduling unit in the process structure. Figure A.12 is a flowchart for Sylvania Lighting's production scheduling procedure.

A commercial, interactive scheduling program, Schedulex by Numetrix Ltd., is used to assist the scheduler. Using known sequencing rules and the weekly/monthly production requirements from production planning, Gantt charts are used to finite forward schedule the lamp line in daily increments. Inventories are projected and displayed with a line graph. When the inventory for any item drops below its planned requirement, problems are highlighted.

Scheduling is an interactive process that uses the scheduler's knowledge of planning priorities and the production process, along with the computer's computational and graphic capabilities. Since the lamp line is the most critical resource, it is scheduled first by finitely loading the available capacity. Setup and run costs are reduced by minimizing changes in lengths and/or light output levels when scheduling the manufacturing groups. This scheduling proce-dure leads to a natural sequence that moves back and forth between long and short groups scheduling adjacent size setups whenever possible, given production planning's priorities. Component inventories are then checked for feasibility. This scheduling procedure illustrates processor-dominated stage scheduling, since the processor (lamp line) is scheduled before materials.

The production planning system has performed a rough-cut capacity analysis for the equipment at all stages to prevent overloading the weekly and monthly plans. The use of dedicated routings, shallow bills of material, and little investment in WIP inventories makes these rough-cut analyses very accurate before the actual MRP explosion is done. In this environment, having capacity planning precede material planning provides significant cost advantages to operations.

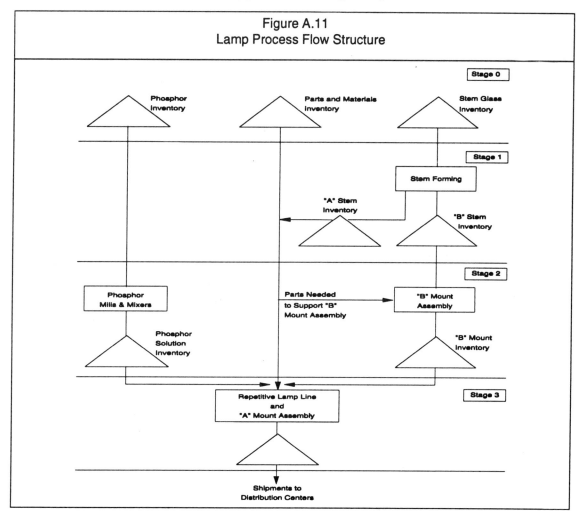

Figure A.11
Lamp Process Flow Structure

After an acceptable schedule for the lamp line (stage 3) is developed, earlier process stages are scheduled. In stage 2, phosphor coatings and "B" mounts are scheduled. Requirements are determined by exploding the lamp schedule (stage 3) into a schedule of material requirements for the stage 2 outputs that feed stage 3.

In contrast to the lamp line, the stage 2 equipment is somewhat more flexible and not generally constrained by capacity. Thus, a material-dominated scheduling approach may be used. Material requirements are calculated and planned based on the lamp line's needs. If conflicts do arise when developing daily schedules, components may be expedited, overtime may be added, safety stocks may be used, or the material requirements may be altered by revising the stage 3 daily lamp schedule. In rare cases,

the weekly/monthly production demands for end items may need revision.

After developing stage 2 schedules, a similar procedure is used to develop stage 1 and 0 schedules for the internally produced stems and the purchased parts and materials, which are managed by the material requirements planning system.

Sylvania Lighting's use of process flow scheduling illustrates several points:

- PFS applies to repetitive manufacturers.
- Reverse flow scheduling is used.
- Processor-dominated and material-dominated scheduling can be used in different stages of the same process train.
- The critical, high-cost process stage uses processor-dominated scheduling.

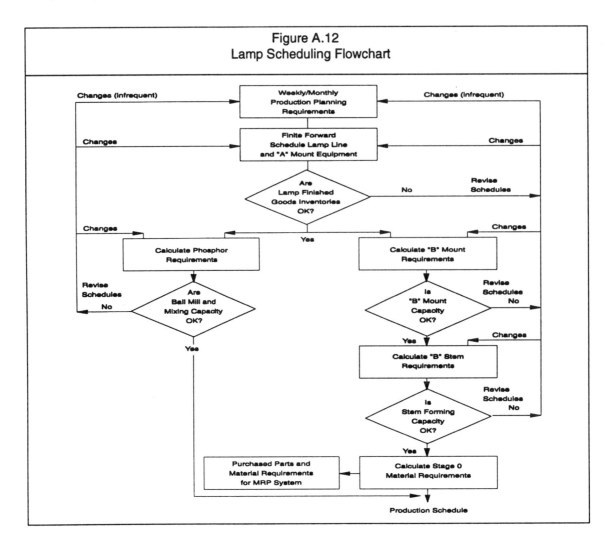

Figure A.12
Lamp Scheduling Flowchart

- Both material and capacity are scheduled and reconciled in a stage before the next stage is scheduled.
- The lamp lines contain process equipment that is not separated by inventories. This equipment is scheduled as a single unit.
- PFS is used for plant scheduling, and MRP is used for material procurement.

The case of Sylvania Lighting illustrates similarities between the scheduling systems of repetitive manufacturers and those of process manufacturers. Another example of the use of PFS in repetitive manufacturing is given in Taylor and Bolander 1990.

References

APICS Dictionary. 6th ed. 1987. Falls Church, Va.: American Production and Inventory Control Society.

Hubbard, D.T., S.G. Taylor, and S.F. Bolander. 1992. Process flow scheduling in a high-volume repetitive manufacturing environment. *Production and Inventory Management Journal* 33 (4): 21–26.

Taylor, S.G., and S.F. Bolander. 1986. Scheduling product families. *Production and Inventory Management* 27 (3): 47–55.

Taylor, S.G., and S.F. Bolander. 1990. Process flow scheduling: Practice and concepts. *American Production and Inventory Control Society 33rd International Conference Proceedings.* 390–392.

Appendix A: Supplemental Cases

Appendix B

Glossary

bill of material (BOM). The product structure used by an MRP system. It shows the quantities of raw materials, parts, components, and subassemblies required to make a finished product.

campaign. A production run of a family of products that share a major setup.

campaign cycle. A production cycle consisting of two or more campaigns. Also known as a rotation schedule or a schedule wheel.

cluster. See process cluster.

complex cluster. A type of stockless process cluster that combines the characteristics of both tightly coupled and loosely coupled process structures into one group of process units.

distribution requirements planning (DRP). A planning/scheduling technique that applies MRP concepts to distribution operations. Like MRP, it uses a material-dominated scheduling approach.

finite forward scheduling. A processor-dominated cluster scheduling technique that builds a schedule by proceeding sequentially from the initial period to the final period while observing capacity limits. A Gantt chart is often used for finite forward scheduling.

flow shop. An equipment layout designed for a family of similar products in which materials follow the same routing for all products.

forward flow scheduling. A strategy used to build process train schedules that starts with the first stage and proceeds sequentially through the process structure until the last stage is scheduled.

Gantt chart. A bar graph where each bar is associated with a process unit. The positioning of bar segments shows the start, stop, and duration of each production run scheduled for the unit. Gantt charts are widely used for finite scheduling. Usually displayed as a horizontal bar graph with time on the horizontal axis; however, vertical Gantt charts also exist. Named after its originator, Henry L. Gantt.

hub-and-spoke scheduling strategy. A type of mixed-flow scheduling strategy that is used for complex process train structures. Two or more master process clusters (the hubs) are master scheduled. Scheduling then proceeds from these master clusters outward until all the support clusters are scheduled.

inside-out scheduling strategy. A type of mixed-flow scheduling that starts by master scheduling an internal cluster and then schedules backward to the first stage and forward to the last stage. This procedure is effective for scheduling internal bottleneck stages.

integer programming. An optimization technique similar to linear programming, but with the addition of integer variables. These variables are used to represent setups and sequencing constraints in integer programming models of scheduling problems.

job shop. An equipment layout organized by manufacturing processes (e.g., drilling, welding, painting). Each product can have a unique routing through the various work centers.

job shop cluster. A group of process units with a job shop layout.

Just-in-Time scheduling (JIT). A real-time scheduling technique where formal schedules are not issued. The authority to produce is a visible signal (card, empty square, etc.) from a downstream unit indicating that material is needed from the upstream feeding unit.

kanban. A visible signal (e.g., a card) that is used to authorize production in a JIT scheduling system.

key unit. A process unit that controls the underlying schedule for a tightly coupled process cluster.

linear programming. An optimization technique that can simultaneously develop mathematically optimal production plans for both material and capacity. Common applications include allocating demand among alternate plants and planning seasonal production.

loosely coupled cluster. A group of isolated process units that perform a similar process step, such as a packaging cluster. The process units' schedules may be linked by use of a common feed or production of a common product. It is one type of stockless cluster.

main-line scheduling strategy. A type of mixed-flow scheduling strategy that first uses forward flow or reverse flow scheduling for the principal sequence of process clusters. Following the scheduling of this main line, feeder lines and by-product/co-product lines are scheduled.

manufacturing resource planning (MRP II). An integrated planning and scheduling system that includes a material requirements planning system. Shows both production volumes and their financial impacts.

master cluster. Process clusters that are scheduled independently during *initial* development of a process train schedule. The first cluster scheduled is always a master cluster. Any cluster that could be scheduled first and not disrupt the initial schedule for any master cluster is also a master cluster.

material-dominated scheduling (MDS). Any scheduling technique that schedules materials before processors (equipment/capacity). MDS initially schedules production based on material need dates (material pull scheduling) or material availability (material push scheduling). This facilitates the development of schedules that minimize inventories.

material pull scheduling. A type of material-dominated scheduling that initially schedules production based on material need dates. This creates a demand "pull." Material pull systems include material requirements planning, distribution requirements planning, order point, and Just-in-Time systems.

material push scheduling. A type of material-dominated scheduling that initially schedules production based on the arrival time and quantities of feed material to a cluster.

material requirements planning (MRP). A manufacturing planning and control framework that uses the product structure (bill of material) to guide scheduling calculations. MRP employs material-dominated scheduling concepts. While MRP can be applied in any manufacturing environment, it fits best in job shops.

mathematical programming. A class of optimization techniques that includes linear and integer programming.

mixed-flow scheduling. A strategy used to build process train schedules that does not schedule stages sequentially from the first to the last (forward flow scheduling) or from the last to the first (reverse flow scheduling). Mixed-flow scheduling is further divided into inside-out, outside-in, main-line, and hub-and-spoke strategies.

outside-in scheduling strategy. A type of mixed-flow scheduling that master schedules the first and last stages in a process train. Scheduling then proceeds from these terminal stages towards an internal reconciliation point where the "pull" from the last stage must be reconciled with the "push" from the first stage.

PFS principle 1. Scheduling calculations are guided by the process structure.

PFS principle 2. Process clusters are scheduled using processor-dominated scheduling (PDS) or material-dominated scheduling (MDS) approaches.

PFS principle 3. Process trains are scheduled using reverse flow scheduling, forward flow scheduling, or mixed-flow scheduling strategies.

process cluster. A collection of process units that is grouped together for scheduling purposes. Process clusters can be single process units, stockless clusters, or job shop clusters.

process flow scheduling (PFS). A scheduling framework that uses the process structure to guide scheduling calculations. Process clusters are scheduled using a material-dominated or a processor-dominated scheduling technique. Cluster schedules are linked using a reverse flow, forward flow, or mixed-flow scheduling strategy. PFS is applied in flow manufacturing environments.

process industries. Manufacturing companies whose production processes involve physical changes (e.g., mixing, grinding, and separation) and/or chemical changes (e.g., cooking, polymerization, and smelting).

process stage. One or more process clusters that are decoupled from preceding and succeeding clusters by inventories. At a minimum, all stages except stage 0 have a single process cluster and an inventory of the cluster's output. Stage 0 is the first stage and has only an inventory of raw materials.

process structure. A representation of the flow of materials through a manufacturing system that shows process units and inventories. Process units are combined into clusters that are grouped into sequential stages. The stages are in turn combined to form process trains. Inventories decouple the scheduling of sequential stages within a process train.

process train. A sequence of process stages.

process unit. Process equipment that shares the same schedule. Every process unit must have a schedule, and every schedule must have a process unit. The equipment in a process unit can be dissimilar as long as it is scheduled as a single entity.

processor-dominated scheduling (PDS). Any scheduling technique that schedules processors (equipment/capacity) before materials. PDS can initially schedule processors in low cost sequences or in economic run lengths. This results in efficient use of processor capacity and in some cases improves quality. Finite forward scheduling is a type of processor-dominated scheduling technique.

product family. A group of intermediate or finished products that share a common major setup on a process unit and ideally are scheduled together.

production activity. Data input for a process flow scheduling system showing all the resource inputs and outputs for a specific operation on a particular process unit. It is often based on one unit of product and shows the amount of input material and the production time required for one unit of output. A production activity may also show other resources, such as labor hours, energy requirements, or waste production.

reverse flow scheduling. A strategy used to build process train schedules that starts with the last stage and proceeds backward (countercurrent to the process flow) through the process structure until the first stage is scheduled.

schedule wheel. A graphical display of the schedule for a campaign cycle.

setup. The work required to change a process unit from one product to the next.

stage. See process stage.

stockless cluster. A group of process units with no inventories. Stockless clusters may be tightly coupled, loosely coupled, or complex clusters.

support cluster. Any cluster that must be scheduled after a master cluster.

support unit. A process unit within a tightly coupled process cluster whose schedule is controlled by the schedule of another unit—the key unit.

tightly coupled cluster. A connected group of process units that have no decoupling inventories. The process units share the same underlying schedule, but the individual process unit schedules are different.

train. See process train.

unit. See process unit.

Appendix B: Glossary

Appendix C

Selected Bibliography

Articles Incorporated in this Book

Chapter 2

Taylor, S.G., S.M. Seward, and S.F. Bolander. 1981. Why the process industries are different. *Production and Inventory Management* 22, no. 4:9–24.

Chapter 3

Taylor, S.G., and S.F. Bolander. 1993. Process flow scheduling calculations. *Production and Inventory Management Journal* 34, no. 1:58–64.

Taylor, S.G., and S.F. Bolander. 1991. Process flow scheduling principles. *Production and Inventory Management Journal* 32, no. 1:67–71.

Chapter 4 and Appendix A

Bolander, S.F., and S.G. Taylor. 1990. Process flow scheduling: Basic cases. *Production and Inventory Management Journal* 31, no. 3:1–4.

Hubbard, D.T., S.G. Taylor, and S.F. Bolander. 1992. Process flow scheduling in a high-volume repetitive manufacturing environment. *Production and Inventory Management Journal* 33, no. 4:21–26.

Taylor, S.F., and S.G. Taylor. 1990. Process flow scheduling: Mixed-flow cases. *Production and Inventory Management Journal* 31, no. 4:1–5.

Chapter 5

Bolander, S.F., and S.G. Taylor. 1993. System framework for process flow industries. *Production and Inventory Management Journal* 34, no. 4:12–17.

Supplemental References

Baker, K.R. 1974. *Introduction to Sequencing and Scheduling*. New York: John Wiley & Sons.

Brown, R.G. 1967. *Decision Rules for Inventory Management*. New York: Holt, Rinehart and Winston.

Blackstone, J. H. 1989. *Capacity Management*. Cincinnati: South-Western.

Bolander, S.F., R.C. Heard, S.M. Seward, and S.G. Taylor. 1981. *Manufacturing Planning and Control in Process Industries*. Falls Church, Va.: American Production and Inventory Control Society.

Bolander, S.F., and S.G. Taylor. 1983. Time-phased forward scheduling: A capacity dominated scheduling technique. *Production and Inventory Management* 24, no. 1:83–97.

Hax, A.C., and D. Candea. 1984. *Production and Inventory Management*. Englewood Cliffs, N.J.: Prentice Hall.

Magee, J.F., and D.M. Boodman. 1967. *Production Planning and Inventory Control*. 2d ed. New York: McGraw-Hill.

Morton, T.E., and D.W. Pentico. 1993. *Heuristic Scheduling Systems*. New York: John Wiley & Sons.

Orlicky, J. 1975. *Material Requirements Planning*. New York: McGraw-Hill.

Sandras, W.A. Jr. 1989. *Just-in-Time: Making It Happen*. Essex Junction, Vt.: Oliver Wight Limited Publications.

Silver, E.A., and R. Peterson. 1985. *Decision Systems for Inventory Management and Production Planning*. 2d ed. New York: John Wiley & Sons.

Taylor, S.G. Focused production systems. 1987. *Production and Inventory Management* 28, no. 1: 28–37.

Taylor, S.G., S.M. Seward, S.G. Bolander, and R.C. Heard. 1981. Process industry production and inventory planning framework: A summary. *Production and Inventory Management* 22, no. 1:15–33.

Taylor, S.G. 1979. Production and inventory management in the process industries: A state of the art survey. *Production and Inventory Management* 20, no. 1:1–16.

Thurwatcher, W.A. 1982. Capacity driven planning. *American Production and Inventory Control Society 25th Annual International Conference Proceedings*, 384–388.

Vollmann, T.E., W.L. Berry, and D.C. Whybark. 1992. *Manufacturing Planning and Control Systems*. 3d ed. Homewood, Ill.: Irwin.